This book should be returned to any branch of the

*Journey to the
End of the Whale*

Journey to the End of the Whale

JOHN DAVID MORLEY

Weidenfeld & Nicolson
LONDON

First published in Great Britain in 2005
by Weidenfeld & Nicolson, a division of
the Orion Publishing Group Ltd
Orion House
5 Upper Saint Martin's Lane
London WC2H 9EA

1 3 5 7 9 10 8 6 4 2

A CIP catalogue record for this book is
available from the British Library

ISBN 0297 84848 8

Typeset at The Spartan Press Ltd,
Lymington, Hants

Printed in Great Britain by
Clays Ltd, St Ives plc

www.orionbooks.co.uk

ONE

The Lost Property Office

The Whale Stone

Of making many books, says the sage in the Upanishads, there is no end. This is one of them, a signature I have written on water. It begins with the whale stone in my grandmother Emily's house, but whether it was a whale stone (whatever that might be) and whether it was my grandmother's house where the stone was kept — whether, come to that, Emily was indeed my grandmother, as she claimed — I would later have reason to doubt. The beginning of the story of my life is really no more than a vague preamble, a makeshift affair, subject to a number of qualifications that were bound, I now realise, to lead it in a quite different direction from the one I had been led to expect as a child.

What my grandmother described as a whale stone certainly looked and felt like a stone. As stones go it seemed quite ordinary, however. Whatever there was about it that made it a *whale* stone, it was not something that could be discerned with the naked eye.

Emily called it a whale stone because it had once been growing inside a whale, where somehow or other it had turned into a stone. I wondered if that was what made it so special. A stone that grew was unusual. A stone that grew in the belly of a whale must be extremely rare. It was probably worth a lot of money, thought Emily. I asked her how much, and she reckoned it might be worth its weight in gold. This evaluation, the phrasing of it rather than the quantity it suggested, made the whale stone seem something magical in my eyes, precious beyond money. One day I would inherit whatever made it so special and its magic properties would be transferred to me. One day the whale stone would be mine.

The sympathetic interest I took in the whale stone from the moment it first lay in my hand may have had something to do with the fact that its genesis was as obscure as my own. I felt, though I could not have put this into words, that we were bonded by the same arbitrariness of fate. Both of us had emerged from the waterlogged interior of floating vessels, not otherwise comparable, in which against all probability we had somehow contrived to grow. Certainly, my birth certificate is in Indonesian, issued shortly after the ferry *Bintang Java* on which I was born during the voyage from Singapore arrived at a destination that was then still posted as Batavia on the timetables of sailing times at Clifford Pier. But whether the *Bintang Java* had already left Malayan and entered Indonesian waters at the time of my *extremely inconvenient birth* (my mother's words) on the bar of the first-class stateroom is a moot point. To resolve the matter on the spot the official in Batavia who signed my birth certificate may simply have taken the point of view that, since I was born on an Indonesian vessel, I was therefore on Indonesian territory, whatever had been the vessel's exact position in the Straits of Malacca at the moment I entered the world.

About the only thing Emily could tell me about my father was that he came from New Zealand. My grandmother, as it remains easier to call her, was to all intents and purposes my mother's mother, which was why she and I had different names. Hers was the Swiss side of the family. I grew up in a house on Lake Geneva, which I was given to understand was grandmother's own house. We lived there alone, though that was not how we regarded it, for we had each other, not to mention a live-in companion by the name of Nervous Complaint. More of her later.

For the first years of my life Emily remained the sole source of knowledge about my world. The only things I knew about my past I knew from her. It became a catechism, which she drummed into me. How my parents had been drowned in a boating accident off the Indonesian island of Flores, where my mother and father had been on a diving expedition, when I was two. How the bodies were never recovered. How she was not informed of their death until a year later by a missionary in the Catholic seminary where I had been taken into care.

Poor baby suffered quite badly from prickly heat during the rainy season, but in the dryer weather we are having now the problem seems to be clearing up. Such a dear little fellow and with such a funny blueish backside, which his father says is quite natural and will pass off in time.

A letter from grandmother in answer to the one from my mother quoted here, still in my possession, which happened to be among the

4

few things belonging to my mother that had remained on shore the day my parents disappeared in the sea off Flores, provided the only contact address. The same young priest at the seminary who had written to my grandmother also brought me to Switzerland when mission business took him back to Europe. Emily could produce all these letters and her prior correspondence with my mother, so what reason could there have been to doubt her word?

I grew up without any memories of these beginnings, although for all I know the unperceived shadow they cast may have been longer than any memories. Even the name on my birth certificate, Daniel Smith, was replaced by Daniel Serraz, the name I took from my grandmother when she adopted me. I reverted to my mother's side, as it were, and there was no doubt that I had inherited her Swiss genes. With one important exception I was an even-tempered, quiet, well-regulated child with a reliable appetite, unbitten fingernails and a digestive system that ran like clockwork. Altogether, my behaviour was irreproachable, giving neither my grandmother nor myself the least trouble. I was an easy child, Emily said.

We lived in somewhat faded magnificence in three rooms at the top of a large lake-front house, most of which remained empty except for two months every summer, when a family from America came to stay. Their visit was preceded by a spring-cleaning that turned the house upside down, entailing the removal of the trans-Alpine railway circuit, complete with the Mont Blanc massif and the tunnel through it, from the snooker table in the hall downstairs. Although I knew from my grandmother that the Appletrees were our guests, they liked to pretend that they owned the house. We agreed that it was charitable to let them believe this was the case, and on no account would I allow myself to be provoked into arguing with the Appletree children about it. American children were insubordinate and contentious, grandmother Emily maintained, whereas we knew better but, being better bred, elected to keep quiet about it.

Being, apparently, so well situated in the house with a large garden on the side of the lake, Emily must have felt it as a cruel irony that she had a phobia about water. *She* managed to handle it, but her companion Nervous Complaint found it intolerable. The phobia was exacerbated by the irresistible attraction that water manifestly exerted on me from the moment my grandmother first set eyes on me. My earliest memories concern scenes of violent struggle between myself wanting to be in the lake and Emily wanting me out of it. Given the

Smith–Serraz family record – a great-grandfather lost at sea, father and mother drowned in a diving accident, not to mention a skating nephew of Emily's who had fallen through the ice – Emily's apprehension was well founded.

For me as an irrepressibly amphibian child, however, with instincts harking back to an early stage in the history of evolution when land mammals were shedding their arms and legs in favour of fins and tails, my grandmother's fear of drowning was nothing more than the hysterical behaviour of a foolish old woman. Fossil discoveries have revealed several of the critical evolutionary steps involved in the transition from land to sea, enabling *Ambulocetus natans*, a whale that walked on land but had a hankering for the sea, to learn to swim by a combination of pelvic paddling and dorso-ventral undulations of the tail. As tractable as I otherwise was, nothing my grandmother could do or say would keep me away from water. She roared, she wept, she smacked me with her hairbrush and locked me in my room without supper, but in the end she capitulated. If a child insisted on getting drowned, she said, *and mark my words, Daniel Serraz*, at least it would do so as a qualified swimmer.

From the age of five and a half I was taken by my grandmother three times a week to the municipal baths, where I was assigned my personal state-certified swimming instructor, a Monsieur Dupont. Already, by some kind of evolutionary imprinting, which for all I knew I may have owed to *Ambulocetus natans*, I flitted jerkily around in water like a newt. But to conciliate Emily, and not to offend M. Dupont, I went through the motions of arm and leg co-ordination on dry land, holding onto the bar at the side of the pool while practising the frog kick, and permitting myself to be supported by a rubber ring, held by M. Dupont who walked beside me. Eel-like, I wriggled rather than swam through the water while Emily looked on in terror.

By the age of five and three-quarters I had been awarded the certificate of Junior Swimming Competence at the elementary, intermediate and advanced level, becoming the youngest child in the history of the Canton of Geneva Swimming Association to achieve this triple distinction. A year later an exemption had to be made for so small a child to enrol in the junior lifeguard force. At the age of seven and a half I won gold medals in all swimming categories for children under ten at the interschool championships. My grandmother wept. She was approached by a talent scout for the Swiss national swimming team and asked if she would consent to my participation in a training

6

programme for young swimmers of future Olympic potential. Emily refused.

It remained a sufficient cause of bitterness to Emily that her phobia happened to revolve around the one thing I was good at. The suggestion that I should make a career of it was monstrous. Not even the heroic occasion when I implemented the junior lifeguard measures I had learned at the municipal baths, saving little Freddy Appletree from drowning in the lake, did anything to mollify my grandmother. It was no source of pride to her that I could easily outswim the oldest Appletree boy, who was almost twice my age. She dreaded the approach of summer, the sound of splashing that came with it, the sight of bathing suits draped over branches, the doggy smell of wetness we brought into the house. It aggravated her nervous condition. Even I, who had grown up in the company of Nervous Complaint and become so used to the manifestations that I found them unremarkable, the scratching and twitching, the whispered self-conversations, the standing rooted to the spot for minutes on end, could not fail to notice how much worse these symptoms became with the official opening of the swimming season when the Appletrees arrived.

What's your grandma doing over there *now*, Freddy Appletree asked one July afternoon, accusingly I thought, as we lay warming our meagre, goose-pimpled bodies on the warm boards of the jetty. I looked up and saw Emily routing with a dust-beater through the rhododendrons, giving them a good thrashing. I told him she was probably chasing away the snake that lived there. Freddy said there weren't any snakes in Switzerland, certainly none worth chasing away, like the kind of venomous serpents to be found crawling all over America, with deadly poison dripping from their fangs that could kill a man in thirty seconds. This was just the sort of remark that Emily had said I was to expect from insubordinate, contentious American boys, and had cautioned me to ignore. But, sensing an attack on Swiss national honour and, in some unspoken way, on Emily, I rose to the defence of our local snakes. A heated argument followed, which I was getting the better of, in fact had just about clinched with the aid of our common adder *Vipera berus*, when Freddy came in with the rejoinder: your grandma's a nut-head, you know. And besides, he added, those bushes she's beating the hell out of aren't even hers.

I had no intention of demeaning myself by asking a puny little boy like Freddy what *nut-head* meant. I'd show him nut-head all right. I got up without a word, dived into the lake and did a fast crawl for fifty yards that would leave him standing if he tried to follow.

An awareness that something was not quite in order with Emily sneaked into my life via the slangy American jargon, words like *nut-head*, which I was absorbing by osmosis from the Appletree boys. These words weren't always in the dictionary that Mr Appletree kept on the shelf in his study. But Mrs Appletree spoke French and could explain to me what nut-head meant. I approached her in the kitchen when no one else was around. *C'est à dire complètement fou*, said Mrs Appletree, who was busy making pancakes. She asked me to pass her the electric egg-beater. I hung around, watching her beat the eggs and waiting for her to say something more, something like, *All right, Danny, I was just kidding*, but that seemed to be it. Although I'd been meaning to follow up with a well-disguised question regarding the ownership of the rhododendron bushes, I was so dumbfounded I left the kitchen without another word. *Complètement fou* was enough for one day.

In Hindustan

The cordial relationship we had enjoyed with our American lodgers never recovered from this blow. My grandmother and I chose not to discuss it. But when, two years later, she sold the house on the lake and we moved into a one-and-a-half-room apartment in the old town, with kitchenette and bathroom down the corridor at the top of six flights of stairs in a converted warehouse, the unspoken feeling was that we had had enough of their annual summer visits, and were much better off in our town residence. Since the lake house seemed to come with the Appletree family, or the Appletree family with the house, and parting with the one entailed parting with the other, then so be it.

It did cross my mind that my grandmother's real reason for selling the house had been to get me away from the lake, but in consideration of her sensitivity on this issue I kept such thoughts to myself. It was not only the lake I forfeited. The apartment was too small to accommodate a railway tour of Switzerland. The trains had to be shunted into what would turn out to be a permanent siding, the tracks dismantled and put in ignominious storage with the Mont Blanc massif in cardboard boxes under Emily's bed. Indirectly my grandmother acknowledged the sacrifices I had made on her behalf by opening a savings account in my name with the Crédit Suisse branch just down the road. Thanks to the proceeds from the sale of the house, the value of my inheritance, which until now had been represented largely if not entirely by the whale stone, would be increased by the sum of one million francs. It's all in there, you know, she said with a flourish of her dust-beater whenever we passed the bank, waiting for you when you come of age.

But my coming of age was very far away, and it seemed to me that even a tiny bit of the inheritance would have come in handy right now. In the meantime I had to get by with pocket money of two francs a week. For a boy of nine going on ten this was a laughable amount. From my peers at school I knew that the going rate for boys my age was three or even five times as much. Money did not enter into my consciousness of the world as long as we lived in the old house, and nor, for that matter, did Emily's dust-beater. I was so accustomed to the sight of my grandmother stalking around the property with her dust-beater, taking the occasional whack at things, that such behaviour seemed perfectly normal to me. Only after our move into town did I begin to realise it was not.

When Emily set off down the street, flourishing her dust-beater, people would stop and stare at her. I felt uncomfortable when I noticed her arm twitching, for this meant she had spotted something she fancied taking a whack at. Objects made of tin, particularly if they were hollow and would make a nice loud noise, such as dustbins, were certain candidates for whacking. The unfortunate *Genève Matin* stand outside the newsagent's on the corner of our street, a box that un-locked when you put a coin into it and allowed you to take out a paper, had to put up with a lot of punishment from Emily. Soon patrons began complaining to the newsagent that, although they had put in their money, they had not got out their newspaper. Shop-keepers on the opposite side of the street pointed their finger at my grandmother as the culprit. She denied all knowledge of the matter and the newsagent threatened her with legal action if she attacked his box again. She had been warned, but it still took a great deal of pleading on my part to get Emily to restrain herself, at least until she was out of the neighbourhood.

The move into town was associated for me with new feelings of embarrassment and frustration. I was embarrassed for my grand-mother and I was frustrated by our lack of money. To do almost anything in town required money. One of the few things that were free in our neighbourhood was looking at the aquarium in the pet-shop window. The best viewing time was around half past five when the pet-shop owner fed the fish in the tank before closing. The moment the surface stirred they darted up and fought over the food. There were fish of all shapes and colours with lots of different markings in the tank: swarms of tiny blue ones that shone like scattered bits of tinsel, red ones with black spots, black ones that were green in the face, and goggle-eyed and grim-lipped swallowtail fish striped yellow and black that looked as if they had been flattened by a steam roller. On my way to and from school every day I stopped to look at the aquarium. The pet-shop owner, M. Garrault, soon got used to the sight of me and invited me in.

M. Garrault kept all kinds of animals in his shop, from the usual pets like rabbits, tortoises and hamsters to less usual ones like bats, bearded locusts and long-tailed macaws, but none of them interested me as much as the fish. These were tropical coral fish from faraway places in the Pacific and the Indian Ocean. I had never seen anything so beautiful. I wanted to possess them. Even the cheapest ones cost two weeks' pocket money, however. Buying a decent-sized aquarium and stocking it with fish would cost me years. Once I had got to know the pet-shop owner better I told him that in the Crédit Suisse just down the road I had a million francs in my saving account. They were not yet mine but they would be. I wondered if, on the strength of this sum, M. Garrault could let me have the model known as *tropical supérieur de luxe*, an aquarium with blue and green fluorescent lighting over a coral floor made of artificial resin, and I would pay him later when I came into my inheritance.

M. Garrault puffed up his cheeks and made a noise like air being let out of a balloon. It was a most enterprising suggestion, he said. Already he discerned the young businessman in me. But why should I choose to pay him rather than to allow him to pay *me*? For sweeping out the shop and feeding the animals every morning and evening, leaving him free to settle his accounts. Why lay out a large sum for the *tropical supérieur de luxe* when I already had an aquarium in the shop that was as good as my own? He would give me a key so that I could let myself into his shop and see the fish as often as I wanted. Wouldn't that be a much better deal?

For the next five or six years I worked as M. Garrault's assistant for half an hour before and after school. I made the acquaintance of fish as marvellous as their names: pompadourfish and angelfish with long swooping tails from the Amazon Basin, red-tuxedo swordtail fish from Central America, three-spot or blue gourami from the Far East. From M. Garrault I learned how to breed fish, beginning with easy ones like the white cloud mountainfish, which would grow in anything from a milk bottle to a lavatory cistern. All that was needed to spawn a pair was to feed them heavily with white worms and place them in a heavily planted aquarium with little light and no snails. White cloud fish had silver scales with a central black line and yellow colouring from head to tail and fan-shaped orange colouring on the fins. It amazed me how such magnificent-looking creatures could emerge from such lowly origins as spawn. I was proud of the part I played in their magical transformation and wondered if life had something similar in store for me too.

I learned how to arrange an aquarium with a profuse growth of sagittaria and cryptocoryne, and – which was more difficult – to roll these long names off my tongue when I had to telephone the aquarium suppliers because we were out of stock. I learned how the water should be half-changed with soft water, how to adjust nutrition, temperature and pH values to accommodate the aquarium's always changing inmates. I learned that when you put together male and female of some species of fish in a tank they just ignored each other, making it impossible to breed them; that others left alone would always fight; that certain species had remarkable powers of recognition for the person who regularly fed them; that in some cases – and such experiences made the deepest impression on me – parents were best removed from the offspring as soon as possible. 'A peaceful species suitable in the community tank' was the highest praise accorded by Garrault. In the absence of a moral authority at home Garrault's judgements on fish served as guidelines for my own life. Whatever I knew about life I had learned from fish in a tank.

Having stirred my practical interest in natural history, my mentor pointed me in the direction of the municipal library, so that I could learn more about the animals I had got to know in his shop. It was in the reading room of the municipal library that I began reading about whales. It was there that I got to know about the whale stone.

Whale stone was a substance more commonly known as ambergris. Legends described submarine springs of ambergris, gushing up out of the ocean floor and discharging it into the ocean. A long time ago it was apparently used in perfumery and cooking. According to al-Masudi, in his history of the world, ambergris was regarded as a great treasure along the coast of East Africa, where clumps of it were sometimes washed ashore. Camels were even trained to kneel down on the sand for the convenience of official ambergris collectors sent out to patrol the shore in search of it. Perhaps the springs on the sea-bed were only invented to explain how ambergris came to be washed up on land. In Malay the substance was called *ambar*. In Java it was believed to be the vomit of the mythical garuda bird. The people of the South East Islands and Timor called it *ikan tahi*, meaning fish excrement. However curious these explanations might seem, they were in fact quite in tune with the modern view that what Emily knew as whale stone was a growth in the intestine of the sperm whale, fragments of which might from time to time be expected to be evacuated into the sea by natural digestive process.

My grandmother Emily was not alone in having no clear idea about what ambergris is. Quite why it forms in the intestine of the sperm whale is still not clearly known today. Ambergris, at any rate, was one of the products derived from sperm whales and one of the reasons why they were so ferociously hunted throughout the nineteenth century. To obtain whale stone would no doubt have been one of the reasons why my great-grandfather Horatio – the father of my grandfather Victor, a native of New Zealand – who was then, by Emily's reckoning, a young man of thirty or so, set out on a whaling expedition near the end of the nineteenth century and never came back. Horatio's ship had 'gone down with all hands', in my grandmother's doom-laden phrase (for years I would see those hands reaching up out of the water), somewhere between his home port of Auckland, New Zealand, and the coast of southern Australia, en route for the whaling grounds off what were then called the Spice Islands and are now known as part of Indonesia.

Mon petit ami, that was what M. Garrault used to call me. And he would put a hand on my shoulder as if to remind himself I was flesh and blood, not something he was dreaming, no, something actually there. No other children lived in our corner of the old town, nor, as far as I could see, did Garrault have any friends in the neighbourhood. Our quarter seemed to be full of old and solitary people like my grandmother and M. Garrault, who at least had me.

He lived on his own in a room over the shop. Photos of the village he came from in Valais hung on the walls. Whenever we went upstairs M. Garrault always pointed them out to me and told me that was where he would be going into retirement as soon as he started drawing his pension just a few years from now. I liked being in M. Garrault's room because I could watch TV there. Emily and I didn't have a television at home, not even black and white. I asked M. Garrault if he would object to my grandmother watching TV with us, and he said certainly not, on the contrary, he would be delighted.

I had begun to realise that I was losing hold of Emily. Emily was slipping away. I hoped that with the help of M. Garrault and his television I might be able to hang onto her.

About a year after we moved into town Emily started her excursions. She suffered from high blood pressure and complained of the heat indoors, the lack of air. At first she just used to accompany Nervous Complaint for a walk around the neighbourhood for an hour or so. Latterly they would take off in the morning and disappear for the whole day. She put supper for me on the table before she left; in case she came back late, she said, although she was nearly always home by the time I finished at Garrault's. We had supper together and she would tell me about her excursions. Even on a train ride to some backwater like Montreux she would have stories to tell of the always violent events – a kidnapping, a robbery, a train derailed, a landslide, some kind of disaster – which she had witnessed en route. Her stories enthralled me, and Emily told them so well that I would be in two minds as to whether they had really happened.

She declined to come and watch television with me and M. Garrault, however. She was too busy with her own life, she said, to have time for other people's. When Emily regularly failed to come home by six I started taking my supper over to Garrault's place, and later, when Emily no longer remembered to prepare my supper before she left, M. Garrault would make it for me. Increasingly, my grand-mother tended to stay out until ten or even later. I watched TV with M. Garrault until nine o'clock, when he sent me home and I would go to bed without having seen my grandmother all day. Sometimes I would still be awake when she put her head round the door. These days Emily had a new smell about her that I didn't like. I pretended to be asleep so that she wouldn't kiss me good night. Deceiving her like this made me sad, and in my sadness I would sometimes lie awake, unable to get to sleep, listening to her rummaging around in the next room.

Her excursions were taking her further afield by now to places I had never heard of, way beyond Montreux. I remember that Hindustan was one of them. The stories she had to tell about her adventures in Hindustan weren't anything like the old ones. They were about her visits to relatives who once lived there but had long since been dead, their weddings, christenings and birthday parties. She rather lost her storytelling touch. At weekends, when I didn't go to school, she always stayed home, *to be there for you*, she said, and we used to go out somewhere, to see a film or an exhibition or something, but these days she just wanted me to keep her company in the kitchen while she told me about people who didn't interest me at all. These days I was there for her.

Along with the unpleasant new smell a terrible other newness came over my relationship with Emily. In the place of my grandmother I now saw just a strange old woman, whose strangeness and oldness repelled me. I found it difficult to be in the same room with her. Weekends became unbearable. If I wanted to get away from her I always had the excuse that M. Garrault needed me. Even on Sundays there were emergencies at the pet shop, new-born animals that might need watching in the incubator, an outbreak of cannibalism among the bearded locusts. That's what I would tell Emily when I could no longer stand being with her in the house. She never tried to stop me. On the contrary, she encouraged me to go out. But I knew that the moment I was through the door I would feel so bad about leaving her that I wanted to come right back.

I remember feeling particularly uncomfortable the evening I sat on M. Garrault's sofa watching *Moby Dick* on TV, knowing Emily would still be sitting in the kitchen where I had left her. It was already past my bedtime and the film went on until half past nine. But a pull even stronger than Emily, the same force that had drawn me into the lake against her wishes, held me irresistibly in place on M. Garrault's sofa. Ishmael's story was not his but mine, Gregory Peck the impersonation not of Captain Ahab but of my own great-grandfather Horatio, who had bequeathed us the whale stone before he was lost at sea. This was the ship, this was the storm, this was the whale Horatio was lashed to when ship, whale and Horatio with it went down, probably at about the same time as my grandmother Emily suffered the stroke that put her in a nursing home for the remaining year of her life.

I was not yet grown up but I had already grasped the significance of the whale stone. Through it spoke the sperm whale, from whose intestines the stone had been taken, of the coil of my sea-borne destiny. I was inescapably tied to it whether I liked it or not. It had shaped my past, it had shrouded my dead, it would form my future, it was memory and prophecy, affirmation and warning alike. An ambition was born in me to allow no one but myself to become the hero of my own life.

Until I turned sixteen I was placed in a boarding school funded by the cantonal orphans' fund. What most children experienced as an unhappy period of their lives I felt as a release from an even more painful confinement. In my mourning of Emily, whom I probably loved more than I would ever love anyone again, no small part of my grief was made up of guilt that when she died my sadness was mixed with feelings of relief.

During these remaining years at school I was allowed to spend my weekends at M. Garrault's place, and after I had left school and was accepted as a trainee by Assurances Helvétiques I went to live with him. For my sake he postponed his retirement by a couple of years, so that when he finally returned to his village in Valais I was well established on my own two feet. At the time, I managed to persuade myself that the period of Emily's decline and death had been no more than a passing turbulence in the otherwise smooth and unexceptional flow of my life.

It was years after Monsieur Garrault had gone that I happened to be in my old neighbourhood again and found myself walking past a branch of the Crédit Suisse. A memory of Emily standing outside the bank with her dust-beater in hand arose in my mind, and on an impulse I went in. Why? I expected nothing. There had been nothing among my grandmother's papers to suggest otherwise. It was more to lay old ghosts to rest that I made inquiries about a savings account, which might have been opened on my behalf ten years ago. The teller established to his regret that no savings account had been opened in either of the names I gave him, and asked if I had any idea as to the nature of the deposit. How about a million francs, I said. In cash. To extricate myself from my embarrassment I tried to make it sound like a joke, but the joke misfired and the teller was not amused. In Switzerland money is no laughing matter. I could see what was passing through his mind as clearly as if it was printed there. *Complètement fou.* The jury had been out a long time, but the verdict on Emily came in just as Freddy Appletree had predicted.

Kozue

When I ran into Kozue I had already spent half my life with Assurances Helvétiques. During those seventeen years, including my three years as a trainee, I had been through all the company's departments. I had done fire, marine, general property and liability insurance, mortgages, underwriting and rate-making, group insurance, health and life insurance, that vast delta into which all other insurance policies flowed like so many tributary rivers.

One conclusion to be drawn from my long experience of the workings of an insurance company was that the general public completely underestimated what a high-risk venture life is. Had such an option been available, we might have felt bound to advise our clients not to embark on it at all. Another was that people's circumstances changed, but their insurance policies failed to change with them. Customers inevitably acquired new possessions and wanted holidays abroad, they had a pay rise, they moved house, started a family, came into an inheritance, watched their children grow up and leave home; they had a tendency to contract terminal or at least incapacitating illness in the later stages of life but they failed to adapt their insurance premiums to reflect the changes to the value of their lives. *Their* lives were somehow exempt.

Perhaps because people who lived in cities had lost touch with a rural world in which there was no end to the toll of natural erosion, to the laborious ratcheting and riveting, the patching, cobbling, mending and general setting to rights of the daily toll of devastation that *force majeure* exacted day in day out, they failed to include in their calculations the dynamic factor in the greater insurance scheme of things. They failed to acknowledge that they and all their possessions remained subject to the same laws of change which governed everything around them, and that because of this universal proneness to entropy what had been new the day before would be in need of replacement or at least repair the day after. This seemed so obvious to us at Assurances Helvétiques that we found it embarrassing to have to point it out. It was necessary nonetheless to jog our customers' memories from time to time with gentle circulars, advising a reassessment of their standing, to remind them that neither they nor their policies were immortal.

After a dozen years with Assurances Helvétiques I was assigned to a department known internally as the Lost Property Office. This was where all policy evaluations landed that did not obviously belong to any of the other departments, the objects insured being neither numerous nor homogeneous enough to allow a reliable estimate of the probable frequency and severity of losses.

My first case, for example, concerned a magician who came to us requesting an insurance policy for his beard. Since this magician's repertoire was built around incendiary objects that appeared and disappeared, and his beard was frequently the place where they did so, the risk of its damage by fire and the resulting impairment of his livelihood was an unusual but by no means unlikely eventuality for which the magician wanted to be insured. There were customers who wanted insurance policies for their hands or feet, their ears, eyes, breasts, genitals, even knees. A professional gourmet working for the Michelin Guide once inquired about an insurance for his liver. We were called in by the manager of an old-established family firm, whose entitlement was subject to a will stipulating that he must produce heirs within a certain time, to advise him on a policy in case his wife remained childless. Insurance is risk management. People came to us presenting their good reasons why they needed particular coverage for scurvy, assassination, death by meteorite impact, bed-wetting, impotence, deafness, drug addiction, whatever, however unorthodox, the bottom line was the all-too-human wish for a policy against unhappiness.

The Lost Property Office dealt with the minority policy holders of the insurance world. Like the magician with the inflammable beard, our clients were one of a kind, and so, went the company joke, were the three agents assigned to their supervision. I was the junior partner in the trio. The small, portly Roche, who so easily perspired, was in his forties, and D'Agostini, our haggard chief, somehow much too tall and desperately thin, was only in his early fifties, though he looked twenty years older. Within Assurances Helvétiques he was generally known as our front man for a famine. It was also generally known that

D'Agostini was the company's best statistician. The reason for his failure to become a vice-president, fetching up in a corporate backwater instead, head of a department of three, lay in a gambling past that had ruined his marriage and his career. What was left of him had been salvaged by the company and given a home in its Lost Property Office.

Although we didn't generate much turnover for the company we did a lot for its name. We gave the insurance business a human touch. For years the company's TV commercials featured minority policy holders whom we had taken into the corporate fold. The message: whatever you do, we have an insurance that covers it. We had long-term prisoners in the canton penitentiary under contract, trapeze artists, midwives, divers, a vulcanologist couple with a professional commitment to conduct their research on the rims of exploding craters. In the days before information could be had with a mouse click on data banks, the feasibility studies on which D'Agostini based his premium calculations meant a lot of legwork for me and Roche. We spent much more time out of the office than in. Roche travelled all over Switzerland, occasionally abroad as well. I covered Geneva and the adjacent cantons, but it was in the faculty libraries of Geneva University that much of my research was done. With patience and application I acquired, over the years, a great knowledge of many useless things.

It was in the little visited institute of Sanskrit studies, where I was researching a life insurance claim on behalf of a member of the Hare Krishna sect who had allegedly willed himself to death, that I made my acquaintance with the Upanishads, or teachings. One of them, in particular, has been buzzing around inside my head ever since. *The walker walks not, nor does the weaver weave*, a paradox that would accompany me, without enlightening me, for years to come. And it was in another library that I made my acquaintance with Kozue, a meeting even more momentous than my encounter with the Upanishads.

Kozue remembers us as having been introduced by her dog Centime in the park, but she is forgetting the scene in the library of the biology faculty the week before that. She was standing in front of me in the queue of people waiting to have their books checked out. Without noticing it she had dropped her library card on the floor. I picked it up and gave it back to her. She smiled and thanked me. End of scene.

Naturally the introduction-by-her-dog story of how our acquaintance began is a much more memorable one. It has elements of poetry and comedy that appeal to the unpredictable streak in Kozue. Nonetheless, I am struck by the persistence of my own memory of the library scene in comparison with the persistence of Kozue in forgetting it. I would later come to the conclusion that actually there had been no record in Kozue's memory of a scene which, for her, had lasted no more than three seconds. For myself, standing behind her in the queue, watching her drop her library card – in fact watching her for quite a while before she did so – the scene had lasted rather longer. The memory of it was embedded in the movie-style gesture of Kozue lifting her hair out of her face when she turned and thanked me with a smile. For her, there can have been no such embedding gesture that helped to make me memorable. I was forgettable.

Had the police held an identification parade the next day for Kozue to pick out with absolute certainty the man who returned to her the card she dropped in the library, and had her life depended on her succeeding, she would not have been able to. For Kozue, the embedding gesture to which I would owe my continued existence in her life was provided a week later by her dog Centime.

A mongrel bitch whose retriever share in her gene pool was the most conspicuous feature about her trotted across my field of vision with a large branch in her jaws. The dog was followed ten seconds later by Kozue pedalling a bicycle, in contravention, incidentally, of the regulations that applied to paths within certain marked sections of the lakeside park. I recognised her immediately as the girl in the library queue last week. Then she had passed out of sight. The next thing I saw was the dog streaking out of a clump of bushes, the six-foot long pole still clamped in its jaws, with Kozue in hot pursuit, this time on foot, the chase through the shrubbery having evidently forced her to discard her bicycle. The dog turned and pranced, waiting until Kozue had almost caught up with her before dashing off again. This game was repeated all the way across the lawn, to the amusement of a number of onlookers like myself who came out to sit on benches during their lunch break. Round and round the park the chase went on. Just as we thought we had seen the last of them the dog would come bounding back with Kozue still in pursuit, and a cheer would go up from the onlookers. They were on the dog's side, wanting the game to go on, because it entertained them during their lunch break. I wanted it to go on too, at least long enough for me to do something memorable that would bring me to the attention of the girl. Clearly that would be to catch her dog.

Equally clear was that the only way to part the dog from its stick would be to offer it another. While I was coming to this conclusion both dog and girl seemed to have disappeared for good. They remained out of sight for so long that the lunch-breakers hoping to see them back gave up and drifted away. Another ten minutes passed. I was about to give up, too, when Kozue came back into view cycling slowly along the path on the far side of the inlet a hundred yards away. She had lost the dog and was looking for it. At the same moment Centime came trotting out of the shrubbery nearby. She stopped with a puzzled air on the lawn just in front of me. I fetched a stick and walked towards the dog, waving the stick as if I were about to throw it. Centime let go of the branch in her mouth, wagged her tail and barked. When I held up the stick in front of her she made a jump for it, and I grabbed her by the collar. There was no sign of her mistress, but that didn't matter. The address on Centime's collar told me where I would find her. Within a quarter of an hour I was there. A month later I moved in. A month after that we got married. According to D'Agostini, in the rather drunken speech he made as best man at the wedding, the chances of this happening if we had set out to achieve it were one in half a billion, significantly smaller than the probability of a comet colliding with the planet Earth.

The Song of the Bereft

At about the time my parents were being drowned off the coast of Flores, Kozue came into the world in Kyoto, the ancient capital of Japan. Her father worked for a food company and was posted to Brazil when Kozue was three. She grew up in São Paulo, spent her teens in New York, where her father was assigned after Brazil, and went to live with a maiden aunt in Paris when both her parents were killed in a plane crash. She returned to Japan to study for three years, majoring in French literature, but finding that she no longer felt at home there she went back to New York. Languages were her obvious asset. She trained as an interpreter in Japanese, Portuguese, English and French, got her first job with the United Nations in New York and later moved to its branch office in Geneva. A threshold situation arose, in which the chances of a collision between comet and planet Earth must have appreciably improved.

I was reminded of D'Agostini's analogy years later when I watched an astronomer on TV guiding us through the countdown stages of the multiple cometary impacts on Jupiter known as S-L 9. Until then, he said, astronomers might have calculated that a comet would impact Jupiter once a century. If at the beginning of 1992 they had been asked the probability of twenty-one cometary impacts occurring on Jupiter within one week the following year, the answer would have been 1 in 10^{70}. By the end of 1992 or the beginning of 1993 the answer would have been that the probability was identical with unity: the impacts were certain, and insurance premiums for anything on Jupiter would no longer have been negotiable. The earlier, entirely different prediction was based, the TV astronomer said, *on the state of our knowledge as it stood then.*

Until hydrophones were first employed underwater for the purpose of tracking enemy submarines, no one knew how much noise there was going on in the sea. People thought of the depths of the ocean as a place of absolute stillness. Naval engineers listened in astonishment to the cacophony of groans, low grunts and growls, creaking, clicking and scraping, squeals and high-pitched whistles that reached them over their earphones. The sounds emitted covered a very wide range of frequencies from 500 to 25000 cycles per second, and they were made not by submarines but by animals in the sea. This discovery seemed to provide an answer to a question that had long preoccupied biologists. Gregarious cetaceans, for example dolphins, remained together in herds, but how did individuals in a non-gregarious species such as some of the baleen whales or the beaked whales of the family of ziphiids, solitary swimmers in vast oceans, find their mates for the reproduction of their kind?

By their calls, it seemed, or what human researchers anthropomorphically termed their songs. The songs of whales varied not only between species but from one individual to another. They might even carry a date and place signature. Typical of the white whale was a liquid trilling, whistling sound. Humpbacks at play produced squeals, whistlings and organ-pipe notes, often with a weird hollow echoing timbre. Below the level of surface noise from storms, oil rigs and shipping, blue and fin whales emitted low-frequency signals that might travel thousands of kilometres along a deep sound channel favouring maximum attenuation and be heard by an animal on the other side of the ocean. Solitary animals were perhaps not solitary after all, but attached to a far-flung herd with which they remained in audible contact even when mutually invisible.

These sensational discoveries were being opened up by marine biologists during the decade I met Kozue. I would often read about them in Geneva's libraries, had in fact been poring over Roger Payne's pioneering work the very day we met, while I was supposed to be researching a minority policy-holder case for Assurances Helvétiques. After our marriage I would find myself involuntarily inside the kind of recurrent daydream I increasingly required, it seemed as mental relaxation, in which I imagined someone, perhaps a cetacean voyeur, who in sea water with a maximum visibility of a hundred feet would naturally be all ears and no eyes, listening on a hydrophone tap placed in the environment my wife and I inhabited. I wondered what sounds he would hear and what conclusions he would draw.

Perhaps I indulged in this daydream for so long because I still found it hard to believe that the extremely able, good-looking and, as it turned out, wealthy woman beside me was my wife. I couldn't believe my luck. The for me more probable course of events that led on from the threshold situation of Kozue's arrival in Geneva was indicated by the episode in the library, when she had looked at me once and then forgotten me, resulting in a minor rearrangement of the course of the universe that would have gone unnoticed by everyone except myself. It has been brought home to me on more than one occasion that I am not a particularly memorable person. When for example I hailed Bénoit, the president of Assurances Helvétiques, as we passed in the corridor, he stopped and scratched his head. Serraz, I said. Although he had been my supervisor for a year and a half when I started as a trainee with the company I had to remind him who I was.

I find it difficult, or perhaps I just don't want to make decisions, to hold an opinion, to have a position on this or that issue. Difficulty in making decisions is a characteristic of me and the life I have led. I have not wanted to commit myself. I have been apprehensive of finality. I have always preferred open-ended situations, ambiguity, the illusion that I am keeping my options open. This is one reason why I have stayed in my job with the insurance company, although I would secretly have preferred to be a marine biologist. I console myself that it might be more rewarding, certainly safer, to *imagine* being a marine biologist than to actually be one. Working for an insurance company remains a better metaphor for my life.

At least on the surface, my reluctance to commit myself makes me an easy person to get on with. I have no resolution, as Kozue remarked at once, no particular feeling that a matter must be like this rather than like that. In inspirational moments I have felt a bit like the walker who does not walk, the weaver who does not weave, but I have not been able to take this line of thought any further. It is undeniable that I do not antagonise people. I can fit in with any situation. A peaceful species, Garrault would have said, suitable in the community tank. What more could one ask? Although I felt myself strongly drawn to Kozue from the moment I saw her, I would not have presumed to ask her to marry me. The closest I could come to that was to bring her back her lost dog. It was she who asked me – and I fitted in with her. I used to wonder at her readiness to take me as I was, until it occurred to me that how I was had been why she had taken me.

If I had known Kozue then as I know her now I would have approached her with more confidence. Her sophistication, or just the manner that went with her international upbringing, covered up for her uncertainty as to who she was. It was her business front, so to speak, something I would come to recognise among Kozue's friends, all of them interpreter colleagues with similarly cosmopolitan back-grounds. In herself she was a shy, self-enclosed person; in fact not all that unlike myself. Once her diffidence thawed I discovered contours that looked familiar. She had a degree of dependency, extravagant needs for reassurance, a greed for love. It was the kind of complete appropriation a child demands of others, the kind of selfishness you came across in adults whose emotional growth has been stunted. Kozue said there was only a Japanese word, *amae*, to describe this condition, as though such needs could be claimed by any particular language or belong to any particular people. I recognised it in her because I saw something similar in myself. One might call it an awareness of one's own incompleteness, which had to do with a sense of being bereft.

The song of the bereft is what the hydrophones placed in our environment would have picked up, but it would have been meaning-ful only to people like ourselves: orphans who had lost an irrecover-able part of themselves before they had time to grow up. Once you suppose that individuals like us are in contact with each other by means hitherto undetected but not unimaginable, perhaps comparable to the 20 Hz long-distance low-attenuation signals of some cetaceans which can be received by others of their kind on the far side of the ocean, then the likelihood of our eventually fetching up in the same place looks much less improbable than might appear from the spoof odds quoted by D'Agostini (an unfathomably sad man who attempted a joke only when he was drunk) – as self-evident, once you know how it's done, as the simultaneous arrival of the male and female of certain species of whales, solitary creatures like the ziphiids, at their mating venue from starting points that may be thousands of miles apart.

It must have been by some such determination that bereft individ-uals like Kozue and I, dimly aware of their incompleteness, were drawn together in their quest to redress it. Complemented by each other, we were fulfilled. So overwhelming was the mutual completion of one another's incompleteness, the embrace so much deeper in the roots of its needs than either of us realised, that we overlooked the person beside the partner who existed in their own right – looked into the light and saw nothing, dazzled by an all-surrounding brightness.

The Boy on the Stairs

Like all great discoveries the Floating Period of my life was something I stumbled across by accident, one humid August afternoon in the Rhône valley.

Kozue, Centime and I were on our way back from visiting friends in Sierre when we stopped for a swim in the river, or rather Kozue stopped while Centime and I took a dip. The Rhône was in spate after a rainy summer, the water muddy, cascades of riverine vegetation in riot along the banks, which for some reason put me in mind of the dank, almost sub-tropical growth of hairs that had luxuriated in the caverns of M. Garrault's ears. After contending in vain with the current I let myself drift, Centime a few yards away. Man and dog, we were borne swiftly downstream. Soon I had lost sight of Kozue. Here and there the river spluttered and seemed to snatch a breath, and we would be drawn into turbulent eddies and roughed up a bit. Something scraped my leg and for a moment I panicked, but already the river flow was smoothing out again, sustaining us on a seemingly endless exhalation. Through the trees along the bank I glimpsed the car keeping pace with us on the road, but there was no turning off to the river, nowhere for Kozue to stop and pick us up. After a while the car accelerated and disappeared. Realising she would be waiting for us somewhere down river, I began to relax and enjoy myself. I had sampled risk and found it to my liking. When I came ashore twenty minutes later I knew how I would be happy to spend the rest of my life.

The year I discovered floating, Kozue sold her apartment in town and we bought a rambling old house in a village on the north bank of the lake. Our vacation that year and most of our weekends were taken up with making the house a more habitable place. The property agent said it had charm, meaning that part of it was a ruin. The front door opened directly onto a busy road without the benefit of so much as a kerbstone. To step outside absent-mindedly for a breath of fresh air meant to risk instant death. For the safety of a new generation of Serraz already on its way, this killer door had to be rendered harmless by blocking it up and moving the front entrance to the back, which in turn meant entering the house via its charming part, i.e. the ruin. We thus became involved in a considerable amount of building. While we were about it we had the rest of the house refurbished from top to bottom, putting a new roof on it and installing new floors. A gate was specially erected to enclose the courtyard where we parked the car, and we always kept it shut in case Centime ran out onto the road. Mornings and evenings I geared up for or wound down from the building labours of the day with a swim in the lake, which was only five minutes' drive from the house. I hadn't swum in seven years. Stepping back into water was like remembering myself.

Floating began in earnest the following summer on the first navigable stretch of river beneath the Rhône glacier. The flow of the river was cold and shallow, but I had come equipped with a well-padded wetsuit. Unfortunately no such protective suit was available for Centime. She had to stay in the car with Kozue, who dropped me off before driving up for some glacier sightseeing and walking through the caves of ice. On her way back Kozue picked me up at a spot thirty kilometres from my starting point. I had reached it intact in just over four hours at an average speed of 7.5 kph. I realised that if I swam while drifting with the current in an unobstructed flow of water I could easily achieve an average of 10 kph and over. More ambitious projects were called for.

On the course of the Alpine Rhine from Chur in eastern Switzerland to Lake Constance in the north I floated a hundred kilometres in four days, traversing Liechtenstein in its entirety almost without noticing it between a late breakfast in Sargans and an early lunch in Buchs. While I was floating, Kozue could take her time doing the kind of sightseeing she so loved and I didn't much care for, poking around the cathedral (twelfth to thirteenth century) in Chur (oldest settlement in Switzerland, Roman fort, records dating back to 3000 BCE) and the castle in Vaduz.

We spent the first week of our holiday that year negotiating the Upper Rhine from the falls in Schaffhausen to Basel. I would have liked to take a shot at the falls (150 metres wide and 20 metres high, the biggest in central Europe) in a rubber dinghy, but Kozue wouldn't hear of it. Instead we put to water just upstream from the border town of Rheinau, Centime in a wraparound thermal suit that had been specially tailored for long-immersion river floating, leaving only the head and tail free, which Centime appeared to use as a rudder. She also had to submit to a muzzle to prevent her from drinking too much polluted water. Crossing the border, we had no need of passports. We just drifted over. Both of us were equipped with an antenna-like rod mounted on a headband and topped with a luminous orange flag, a precaution Kozue had insisted on so that we were clearly visible to other boats on the river. She had got this idea from Japanese tour groups. It was a good idea. River traffic of impressive tonnage was already considerable on the float-in to Basel. Cruise ships the size of floating apartment blocks lay moored at the wharves, and convoys of lashed barges a quarter of a kilometre long set out from here on the journey that would eventually end on the North Sea coast. Big boats like these might have ploughed us under and not even noticed it.

During our second week we picked the scenic bits of the river like the castle-crammed gorge between Bingen and Koblenz (a ruin a minute), stopping overnight in places with particular sightseeing attractions for Kozue (Strasbourg, Speyer, Cologne) or of particular culinary interest to me (Alsace). But the most memorable moments for me and Centime on this float were undoubtedly the water chutes designed for canoes to circumvent portage or passage through locks. What canoes do, I thought, we could do too. By pressing a button on a post in the river I set machinery in motion that would open a sluice and flood a channel. A green light told us when to start. A rush of water carried us down, Centime for safekeeping in my arms. We had thirty seconds to exit the channel, which dried up as soon as the sluice closed. Once we had got down safely I gave myself a swig of rum and Centime a biscuit, provisions I stowed in a waterproof rucksack along with the first-aid kit.

Kozue had miscarried after three months. This was the child we had both seen on the first night we had spent together in her apartment, a fair-haired boy about five years old, standing on the stairs under a tinsel star hanging on a thread from the ceiling. The child came into my mind with no other prompting than the desire to imagine a picture I would try and transmit to Kozue merely by thinking about it. She sat in another room with pencil and paper to jot down whatever occurred to her. She saw the boy standing at the top of the stairs under the tinsel star just as I had imagined him, even producing a drawing of him. For a telepathic transmission it was a highly detailed image. We were less surprised that the experiment worked, however, than disappointed that it only seemed to work one way round. The pictures she saw, or which I as transmitter saw for her, were whole and clear, whereas the images I received of what passed through Kozue's mind were fragmentary and diffuse. When she became pregnant we were convinced it must be with this child that we had already seen and, it must be said, begun to take for granted.

Naturally we were both very upset by her miscarriage, but we consoled ourselves that another child would soon be on the way. There was so much going on at the time, what with the move and the building and the realignment of Kozue's career when she decided to turn freelance, that the miscarriage just sort of slipped away and disappeared in the wake of our busy lives. We were happy. The fourth summer of our marriage was the happiest yet. All we wished was that we had got to know each other five years sooner. All we needed was another five years up front. It wasn't long before Kozue would be forty.

She took up painting and even fishing on the banks of the rivers I floated down, weather permitting, almost every weekend. We collected rivers. I dipped into the Sarine and the Aare, the Inn and the Po. Two summer holidays were spent on the Danube alone. One year took us through Yugoslavia (*rive gauche*) and Bulgaria on the right into the poorhouse of Europe, Romania and the southern fringe of the Soviet Union along the Danube delta. Much of this river landscape was wilderness, populated by wild donkeys, herons, storks and even pelicans. Parts of it looked still unused, moist like the wings of nascent butterflies, places still fresh from the dawn of creation. There were no concrete embankments, no mechanically operated water chutes for canoes, only the signposts marking the dwindling number of kilometres left to the river's destination in the Black Sea. When there was a longer stage to cover I would leave Centime on shore and swim with the current, easily managing fifty or sixty kilometres a day, but I preferred just to let myself be carried along. After I had been floating on my back for an hour or two I felt I was sliding down the sky. I liquidated my human mortality. Weightless, I drifted with the birds through the heavens. Dreams of flight became reality, and at the end of the day I would find Kozue waiting for me and tell her all about it. But when I rolled over to take stock of my surroundings the signposts with the diminishing numbers would remind me that Kozue had miscarried again, again in her third month, and that we were running out of time.

It was as if we had got up too late and missed the early start we needed in order to make it to our destination before dark. The five years we had missed began to matter. For a while we allowed them to matter more than the five we had spent together. We snapped at each other. We reproached and forgave ourselves. We counted our losses. We counted our blessings. We looked out of the window of our refurbished house tucked away in the vines and reminded ourselves of the wonderful view of the lake. We told ourselves how lucky we were. We went through the scenarios of a desolate life in which we might never have met at all. In the night we shrank together in the middle of our prairie-size bed. There was always the consolation that, whatever happened, whatever we might have to face, we would always have each other to share it with.

A Messenger from Lefó

The odds on my meeting Mans Gerardus might have been even longer than the probability D'Agostini had allowed for my finding Kozue. I didn't realise it at the time, but with his arrival in our house the fixed course of my mundane life was impacted by a Near Earth Object that would change its direction for ever.

For an agent of change of such force he was a not particularly large man, even slight, whom one might easily have overlooked had it not been for his remarkable head. It reminded me of one of the high-held marble heads of Roman senators lining a corridor in the library of the philology department at Geneva University, the manner patrician, the close-cropped hair brushed forward, the lips sneering, the eyes wide open but seeming blind or beyond surprise. Neither these features (minus the sneer) nor the skin with its faint copper colouring gave away the fact that Mans was an Indonesian. To me he looked eastern Mediterranean rather than Asiatic. Even less did he look like a fisherman. He would have done for an ambassador. His worldly manner and his impeccable use of English were certainly up to ambassadorial standards. I had taken him for a member of one of the many foreign legations located in Geneva, while the three Japanese legation members he accompanied were unmistakably Japanese, spoke no English and looked like car salesmen.

Since she turned freelance Kozue began to make a habit of inviting clients home for dinner. She saw this as part of the service her job entailed. Outside the simultaneous translator's booth, voices became attached to helpless individuals who needed guidance with every step they took in a strange and perilous environment. They had to be helped with the currency, the telephone, the menu, the plumbing, the toilets. There was the occasional Brazilian or American visitor, but mostly the guests Kozue invited home were Japanese. My role at these dinners was to give them a tour of the house and garden, to name the mountain peaks we could see on the far side of the lake, and to put on a bit of a show with things like sniffing the cork when I decanted the wine. Normally when we had guests I waited at table and carried out dishes, but Kozue didn't allow this with Japanese visitors. It would create the wrong impression, she said. Conversation broke down as soon as she was out of the room, and when she was in it I might as well not have been there for all I could follow of what was being said in Japanese. Something changed with Kozue when she put on her Japanese cloak. I couldn't say quite what it was, but she seemed to become a different person.

The three gentlemen I mistook for salesmen were members of a delegation sent to Switzerland by the Japanese government to present a case that differed from the majority position of the other members of the International Whaling Commission, which had recently passed a vote in favour of a world-wide moratorium on commercial whaling. Although a member state, Japan considered itself to be in a special position. It exercised its right to object and pleaded extenuating circumstances that justified making certain concessions in its own case.

Kozue had accompanied her clients to a conference in Gland. The main point on the agenda had been a ruling which would make exceptions to the moratorium, permitting so-called aboriginal subsistence whaling when the livelihood of small communities was at stake. People such as the Inuit in Alaska depended on the slaughter of whales for survival, or at least could reasonably claim that they did. Demonstrating the existence of such communities somewhat closer to home and establishing their *de facto* right to be doing what they were doing as part of their traditional culture appeared to be part of a Japanese strategy of seeking strength in numbers, even if comparisons of such subsistence whaling communities with Japan's gigantic commercial fishery were wholly specious. Looking around South-East Asia, the Japanese discovered one such community in eastern Indonesia on a remote island off Flores. They sponsored Mans Gerardus's trip to Europe to help present the minority position in the belief that this would help their own. He was their messenger from Lefó.

Marine biology being something of a hobby of mine, I had naturally taken a close interest in the global whaling debate. On first meeting Mans Gerardus, however, I was less curious about him in his capacity as an expert on cetacean fishery than as an Indonesian. Within ten minutes of his arrival I found myself talking to someone who not only knew by name the monastery on Flores where my parents had last been seen alive, but who had actually been there himself. He lived in a town nearby and had spent much of his youth diving on the reefs off the north coast of the island, which he described as being among the richest coral banks in the archipelago. Considering that Mans was in his fifties, it was not inconceivable that he had been there at the same time as my parents. It occurred to me that he might even have seen and spoken with them. I found this extraordinarily moving. I felt tempted to ask him if he had. But the possibility that Mans might have seen and spoken with my parents was extraordinarily moving only so long as it remained a possibility. If he said no, that was the end of the matter. If he said yes, a box would fly open which had been kept firmly shut all my life, and I was not sure I wanted that.

Mans told me his mother was a native of Lefó, but when she met his father she had moved with him to the mainland. Lefó seemed to be an all-encompassing word. It was the name of the island and the adjacent region, the name of the fauna and flora indigenous to the area, of the people who lived there and of the tongue they spoke, an Austronesian language that was quite distinct from Indonesian. Mans understood what his mother said to him in this language but couldn't speak it himself. Having relatives in Lefó he had visited the island many times, and in his capacity as an employee of the Department of Fishery in Flores he had conducted surveys of the whaling that was done off Lefó. He had brought along a few photographs to give people an idea of how this aboriginal whale hunt was carried out, which, he said, had continued unchanged for many hundreds of years.

I still have a clear mental record of the photographs Mans showed me that evening. They were stark black and white images taken with poor exposures that reinforced the contrasts between the brightness of the sky and the darkness of the bodies silhouetted against it. In one of the photos a man was flying across the sky. The whole thrust of his leaping body was brought to bear in the tip of the harpoon in his outstretched arm. No water was to be seen in this picture, only the flying man in the sky. Mans said he had just leapt off a platform extending from the bows of a boat. A split second later he would land on the whale. There was another photo that showed him pulling himself up over the side of a boat with the harpooned whale in the foreground. The force of the rebound when the harpoon struck the whale would check the harpooner's flight and fling him back either into the sea or onto the whale. When hunting a whale, then, the harpooner effectively had to jump onto it, or at least reckon with that as a strong likelihood. With my mind freewheeling around the question of the life insurance premiums that aboriginal whale hunters from Lefó might have to expect to pay, I asked Mans how dangerous their occupation was. He laughed. From time to time men were maimed or killed by whales, he said, but that stood in no comparison to the number of whales that had been killed by men.

If it were the other way round there would be no whale hunt. People would have been unable to make a living on Lefó and have settled somewhere else. This was evolution. The favouring by natural selection of organisms that were able to adapt better, including artefacts which became the extension of their limbs, had determined it that way. But soon it might once again be determined the other way. It was just a question of time before an occupation that was continued as long as it paid was discontinued because it no longer did. Economy was among the priorities of natural selection. The International Whaling Commission banned pelagic catches of sperm whales only after they had ceased to be profitable, leaving a few minor shore-based fisheries in Japan, South America and the North Atlantic. In a few years they would close down, too. The very last sperm whale hunt in the world would probably be undertaken from Lefó.

Before Mans left our house that evening, my curiosity overcame the reluctance I had previously felt about putting the question and, taking him on one side so that the others couldn't hear me, I asked him if he recalled an accident that had taken place about forty years ago near the town where he lived in Flores. Two white visitors, perhaps you would nowadays call them tourists, had been drowned when diving off those reefs Mans had mentioned earlier in the evening. In those days there couldn't have been many tourists who visited such a remote part of Indonesia, so perhaps their death by drowning had caused a bit of a stir. Maybe Mans knew something about it. No sooner had I put the question than I realised I had phrased it rather clumsily. The unspoken implication was that when non-white people drowned, or, for that matter, were maimed or killed by whales, it didn't create a stir, whereas the deaths of white people were memorable and made a headline in the local paper.

But Mans didn't appear to take exception to the question. He sat with his huge head tilted back in his ambassadorial way and thought about it for a while. No, he said at length with a shake of his head, he had no recollection of such an event. Before he and the Japanese left he gave me his business card, offered to make inquiries about the two people who had drowned and asked me their name. Smith, I said, a married couple by the not particularly memorable name of Smith.

On his way out Mans stopped to take another look at my aquarium. I was into *Cyprinidae* at the time – the striped, spotted and brilliant rasbora were my staple, and I was particularly proud of my zebra barbs, exceedingly difficult to breed in captivity. He asked me if I had ever seen them swimming in their natural habitat, and when I said no he told me that many of the fish I had in my aquarium were native to the Indian Ocean around Flores. If I ever visited his part of the world one day he would show them to me. And Lefó, too, before the last sperm whale was caught and the fishery there closed down as well. Oh, I will, I said, I would like nothing better, and I really meant it, even made considerable progress learning Indonesian, taking lessons from a colleague of Kozue's at the UN for several years. But despite my firm intentions I somehow never got round to making the trip.

Among Mohicans

The cetacean mode of swimming by oscillating the tail flukes, known to marine biologists as caudal oscillation, evolved in stages from a mesonychian condylarth ancestor that swam by quadrupedal paddling. Why accumulate useless knowledge unless to show it off occasionally? It is a weakness to which self-educated people in particular are prone. This ancestor appears to have gone through a pelvic paddling and a caudal undulation phase before settling for caudal oscillation as its swimming mode, the mode still preferred by all whales today, some tens of millions of years later.

After the arrival of modern whalers at the beginning of the eighteenth century, you clearly had better chances of survival (from the whale's point of view) if you were a fast swimmer not overly disposed, as some gregarious, rashly trustful species were, to lingering on the surface of the ocean for a moment longer than necessary. The first whale species to be hunted commercially on a large scale were the slow swimmers such as sperm, bowhead, right and gray whales, which could be followed by hunters in rowing boats or under sail and picked off relatively easily with hand harpoons and lances. It was estimated that from the beginning of the nineteenth century, when Yankee whalers started to extend the reach of their killing fields into the Pacific and Indian Oceans, until near the end of it something like a quarter of a million sperm whales had been slaughtered.

In view of the stock depletion of sperm whales, changes in economic trends and other factors, notably the development of steam-powered ships and the invention of the canon-fired explosive-head harpoon, the whaling industry turned its attention from sperm whales to the faster swimming rorquals such as the blue and fin whales, which the hunters had previously ignored because unable to follow them. When blue and fin whales had in turn been depleted to such an extent as to make the hunting of them no longer a creditworthy pursuit, sei whales were selected as the next suitable target. An estimated third of the entire sei whale population in the southern hemisphere was killed in 1965 alone. Sei whales quite soon followed their larger relatives into commercial extinction. They were replaced by smaller minke whales as the target group of the whaling industry until the mass slaughter of sperm and baleen whales known under the semantically more salubrious term 'pelagic harvesting' was banned altogether by the moratorium that came into effect in the 1980s.

A remarkable concomitant of the declining number of whales in the sea was the increasing number of books about them that began to pile up in the libraries, a fairly reliable sign of the subject's imminent extinction. Allen's *Bibliography of the Cetacea and Sirenia*, which appeared in 1882, listed a thousand publications about whales during the foregone three and a half centuries. For the hundred years from the mid-nineteenth to the mid-twentieth century there were estimated to have been between three and four thousand publications. From the 1960s until the closing decades of the twentieth century, according to the *Zoological Record*, some twenty-four thousand papers were published on marine mammals. That was an average of six hundred and fifty a year, eerily corresponding to the peak annual killings of whales, which in 1964 reached an all-time world record of thirty thousand animals.

How you estimated whale populations and their trajectories through past and present into the future was a moot question. For the past two hundred years you relied on the log books of the early whalers, the catch data of modern fisheries, the increasingly sophisticated and more reliable combinations of mark-recapture techniques applied to photographic identifications, acoustic censuses and sightings from ships and aircraft to help you arrive at your estimate. You couldn't catch and count all the whales, but you could catch a sample and calculate the sample mean. I was familiar with related methods of working out probabilities in the insurance business. You estimated the mean, variance and standard deviation. You could calculate how precise a mean value was as the standard deviation divided by the square root of the number of observed values in the data. It was fairly straightforward.

At first sight it might appear to the layman to be something of a paradox, but the more sources of uncertainty you factored into your calculations the more certain your predictions became. If you factored uncertainties regarding the catch record and population biology of whales into your model by the random choice of input parameters you could attain much more precise estimates than if you neglected to do so. In the case of sperm whales, you might then find you had to reduce your earlier estimates of the number of animals alive today, expressed as a fraction of the number of animals that had been alive before modern whaling began, from about two-thirds of the original population to half, to a third, *perhaps even less*. For what the TV astronomer had said regarding predictions about impacts on Jupiter applied equally to impacts on whale populations. All estimates did no more than reflect the state of our knowledge at the time they were made. They told us as much about ourselves as they did about what they were estimating.

What they told me was about a sneaking process of substituting virtual animals for animals in real life. Ghostly whale reconstructions took shape and multiplied in books, statistical averages and mathematical equations in inverse proportion to the dwindling existence of flesh-and-blood mammals in the oceans. This was our modern whale hunt, part of a hypertrophic information food chain into which we were inescapably locked by the consequences of natural selection favouring the development of human brain and hand, harpooning species with a statistic, celebrating them with a status quo morality of conservation that became the more adamant the less there was left to conserve, and celebrating our right to do so in the same way our predecessors had taken for granted their right to do just the opposite.

Mans Gerardus with his images of an antique fleet of sun-bleached outrigger vessels standing off Lefó, the harpooner flying through the air, the sperm whale flensed on the beach, the carcass picked clean as if by an army of foraging ants, figures dark like shadows stripping it down to the skeleton and carrying away on their heads this landfall meat from the ocean – these very definite people and the primary processes of their lives belonged in the Lost Property Office with the minority policy holders, perhaps alongside the fossil remains of the walking whale *Ambulocetus natans*, certainly in the company of other doomed Mohicans such as D'Agostini, Emily and Monsieur Garrault, in the last resort maybe Kozue and myself; one of a kind, for whom there were no mean values and who (as things turned out) had no successors.

Sunday Morning at the rôti *Bakery*

A flock of cream white paper cranes, symbolising longevity and happiness, according to Kozue, arrived in our house and settled on the mantelpieces and window ledges. A pair of them perched on the cistern in the downstairs lavatory. I found several more nesting in our wardrobe. There was one in each of my hiking boots.

The arrival of the cranes was accompanied by a letter from Mans Gerardus with an account of a visit he had made to Lefó, where he had attended a ceremony to keep the mountain from exploding. Recently there had been some quite severe tremors. The lord of the land placed a stone on the ground and stuck bits of iron into the soil all round it to keep the mountain in place. Only two weeks before, at the end of a prolonged rainy season, another ceremony involving the sacrifice of a chicken had been held on the volcano in order to turn the clouds white and stop the rain from falling, so that the lake in the crater would not overflow. Both ceremonies appeared to have achieved their purpose. The earth was quiet, the dry season had come, and with it, usually, came the whales.

Two dozen *prahu* sailed out from Lefó along the coast in search of them every day, although they hadn't caught any yet. Last year they had caught only eight, and the villagers on the island had to fall back on the Hungry Basket, in which each household kept an emergency ration of maize. Prayer alone might not be sufficient to prevent this happening again. More powerful rituals, as practised by the old people before the missionaries brought Christianity to the island, might yet be needed.

Mans added a postscript about the two people I had mentioned who were supposed to have drowned in the Flores Sea. There was no record of any such incident in the files of the local *kantor* where births and deaths were registered, perhaps because their bodies had not been found and therefore they could not well be registered as dead. He would let me know if, as he put it, anything washed up, but he thought that was doubtful.

I was just putting this letter away in a drawer when Kozue came into the room and asked me if I was all right, I looked rumpled, she thought. I told her I had a bit of a headache. Kozue was in any case not all that interested in my answer to her question because she was too excited about the news she had to tell me. For the first time she had felt the child move inside her. Yes, he had moved! We had known for a couple of weeks that it was a boy. She placed my hand on her belly so that I could feel him too, but I couldn't detect anything. I wondered if the child already had his own theme tune, and whether it would be possible to listen to the sounds in an unborn child's environment by putting a hydrophone tap in the mother's womb. I looked at Kozue's expectant face and knew I must tell a lie. Yes, I said, I can feel him, too.

Every night now we lay in bed, touching or listening for the signs of life inside her belly. It was getting to be quite a mound of a belly to stroke, quite a hillock to climb up and down, and in the dark our hands played hide and seek around it, sometimes meeting accidentally and stroking each other instead. When the third fateful month had passed and Kozue had not lost the child a sigh seemed to pass through her body, releasing all the tension that had been bottled up inside her. That was when she began making the paper cranes. She had learned to make paper cranes from the woman who ran the Japanese nursery school in São Paulo, she said, and although she hadn't made one in twenty years, and thought she had forgotten how to, her fingers remembered of their own accord all the creases and pleats and the exact order which they had to follow to get the crane right. That was also when she began singing, songs I had never heard her sing, and which she thought she had forgotten, little ditties about the elephant who had a long trunk like his mother and the dragonfly whose glasses were blue because it flew all day in a blue sky. She made a paper doll and put it in the window. It was like a god of fair weather, she said. If you prayed to it properly the sun would shine. The paper doll on the window sill reminded me of the chicken that had been sacrificed in Lefó to turn the clouds white and bring the rainy season to an end, as Mans had written in his letter.

40

The future of her womb had become the balance of our life, a fragile one, and we went around on tiptoe for fear of disturbing it.

From the fifth month on she stopped working and stayed at home, although she was no less busy on that account. Every other day she would clean the floors in the way that was peculiar to her, ignoring the vacuum cleaner and parquet polishing equipment I had bought for that purpose, as if floors could only be cleaned her way, the way she had learned from her mother, the strenuous, physically uncomfortable way floors had apparently been cleaned in Japan since immemorial times. Bending double, but without her knees touching the floor, she leaned on a folded cloth and propelled herself in a sort of sliding crouch across the floor, her backside up on display in a most un-prepossessing way, pushing the cloth back and forth, lane by lane, not standing upright until she was sweaty and red in the face and had covered every square inch. The satisfaction she derived from this activity had nothing to do with getting the floor clean, because it was clean before she began. Maybe she thought the exercise did her good, though in that doubled-up position I doubted it. There was some-thing else going on here. Kozue seemed to me to be enjoying – I didn't know quite how to put this – a sense of rightness, of approval earned from the invisible audience watching her.

With her pregnancy in working order and a certainty about where she was going, Kozue acquired a heightened awareness of where she had come from and who she was. She discovered, or rediscovered, that she had a Japanese identity. Local books about child care were not good enough, more had to be sent from Japan. Things she had chosen to put out of her mind she now chose to recall. Having spent most of her life as a non-aligned person, a so-called cosmopolitan, who had found a niche in an international organisation but never lived long enough anywhere to be entitled to register as a voter or to sit at the regulars' table in the local café, she now perceived herself to be a link in a chain between what had preceded her and what would come after. Hereditary characteristics began to interest her. What were the strengths and weaknesses, what illnesses ran in the family? She read aloud from a list in her book. Diabetes? Blood pressure? Heart problems? She could vouch for her team but what about mine? Had my father or grandfather lost their hair at an early age as I had? Did other members of my family have poor eyesight and had they been prone to serious overweight in middle age as I was? The book lay in her lap and she was laughing. It began as a game. It was amusing at first.

Then Kozue started wondering why I had never got round to visiting L'Adret, the village where my mother had grown up before she and Emily moved to Geneva. Perhaps I still had relatives living there, or at least people who might have known the family. Wasn't I interested in meeting them? Didn't I have reason to believe that a lot of the things Emily had told me weren't true? Hadn't I told Kozue myself that my grandmother was always making things up? The house on the lake, for instance, which Emily said was hers but which in fact belonged to the American family who had employed her as their summer vacation housekeeper and out of charity allowed her to live there year round. Or the million francs in the savings account she claimed to have opened in my name. Or the biggest question mark of all: Emily herself. Wasn't I interested in finding out the truth?

Not particularly, I said. One couldn't chop and change. True or not, the past I had got was the one Emily had given me. I couldn't just scrap it and put another in its place. For better or worse it was the one I had been rigged out with and I preferred to hang onto it.

Kozue looked at me from her northernmost face. *Anata tsumetai yo.* Whenever my wife accused me of being cold or charged me with my other inadequacies she did so in Japanese. I fetched Mans's letter from the drawer and gave it to her to read. If I thought there were any point in it, I said, I would make the journey to Indonesia to try and shed some light on the circumstances of my parents' death. At least, until very recently I would have. But if Mans had been unable to unearth any record of that event in the one place where one might expect to find it, where else was there to look? As Mans said, if their bodies had not been found they could not very well be registered as dead. That was one possibility. Their bodies had not been found but they were dead. Well, one would never find them now. Another possibility was that their bodies had not been found because they hadn't drowned and perhaps were still alive somewhere.

Who knew what reasons my mother and father might have had for abandoning their child and choosing to do a vanishing trick? And who particularly wanted to know? So far as I was concerned they were as good as dead. It wasn't indifference or coldness, as Kozue said. I felt more comfortable with the truth I had grown up with because, frankly, anything else unsettled me. For the same reason I had chosen not to look for relatives of my mother's who might be living in Switzerland. Couldn't we now close this subject once and for all?

It was rare for me to put anything into words as clearly as I just had. It was rare for me and Kozue to have things out in this way. Although we could communicate to some extent telepathically, or perhaps because of this, neither of us was particularly apt at verbalising our personal feelings. We sent each other signals instead.

Thus, after Kozue had raised a subject she knew I didn't want to talk about, and had made that accusation of coldness, she didn't say she was sorry in so many words but showed me she was by doing things she knew I appreciated and not doing things she knew I didn't, like the way she cleaned the floor. It was entirely unreasonable of me to take objection to her floor-cleaning. I never told her I did, because I knew I was being unreasonable, and I wouldn't have dreamed of asking her to desist. But she knew nonetheless. So when she stopped her floor-cleaning and started coming with me and Centime on our daily swim in the lake I was quite moved, knowing how much she enjoyed the one and how little she cared for the other. I felt grateful, but also a bit guilty for being the cause of her making this sacrifice. Naturally Kozue knew that, too, but on the surface we talked about it being good for her to take exercise in her condition, and what better way than doing so in water, at a fraction of the weight she would feel on land. It was a subject on which I tended to get carried away, partly because on land I weighed ninety-three kilos and was always being reminded of it, whereas in water I forgot about it. In water I was in my element. So were babies.

The theories of Frédéric Leboyer about gentle childbirth were very much in vogue at the time. I first heard of them in garbled form from my colleague Roche, whose wife had recently given birth at a maternity hospital in Lausanne that specialised in the Leboyer method. I had received the impression that the child was actually delivered underwater, just like a whale, but I had somehow got this confused with the warm water bath Leboyer children were given immediately after birth. I found the warm water bath a very appealing idea, a token resumption of foetal life, if you like, a reassurance to the purely instinctual creature ejected from a fluid environment in the womb with eight hundred times the density of air that the strange new world it had entered, although very different, could offer something in common with the one it had just left. The dimmed lights recommended by Leboyer, the muted background noises, the placing of the newborn child on the mother's belly with the pulsating umbilical cord still intact, ready for instant breast-feeding – this rediscovery of a natural process of birth attracted me in the same degree that descriptions of obstetrical practice in modern clinics horrified me.

I bought Leboyer's book and gave it to Kozue. For a long time it sat unread on her bedside table at the bottom of the pile of books she had ordered from Japan. When the book moved to the top of the pile, she was signalling to me that we had achieved *wa*, harmony, again. Kozue professed to despise this word, because it was a cliché, she said, but she still needed what it meant.

Weighing in water a fraction of what we weighed in air, we discovered to our surprise that we could express ourselves most freely and find most harmony not when lying on top of each other in bed but when swimming side by side in the lake. Because the density of mammalian bodies was similar to that of water even a poor swimmer like Kozue was naturally buoyant, as I explained to her while showing her how to tread water with a minimum of effort. Something of that buoyancy carried over into cetacean expressions of their emotional life, feelings of exuberance occasioned by activities such as breaching, lobtailing or riding the waves in the wake of a boat, which appeared to be pure play. Buoyancy favoured size, one reason why at 150,000 kilograms the blue whale was the biggest animal that had ever lived on Earth, knocking even *Tyrannosaurus rex* for six. Perhaps that was also why Kozue, with the additional weight of her pregnancy, could now keep pace with me in the water, to my great surprise. I had noticed that I was a bit short of breath these days and vaguely wondered why. Swimming mammals could maintain their vertical position with little energy cost, I said as we continued treading water, because they did not need to create lift during locomotion as did terrestrial animals and flyers.

For a pregnant woman there could have been no better introduction to Leboyer's childbirth method than a swim in the lake at twilight. Kozue was won over. We agreed on the clinic in Lausanne where Roche's wife had given birth. I undulated in slow circles round her while we talked, shepherding her, drawing a cordon of bubbles around her, which a biologist might characterise as conjugal behaviour, I suppose. It was indeed the sort of occasion, had I been fitted out with tail flukes and able to oscillate them, when I might have flipped over and given them a quick flash. Equipped with a snout, as some beaked whales and dolphins were, I might have felt tempted to nudge her around in the water a bit.

I asked her if she was happy it was a boy. Kozue knew what I was referring to, but all she said was that she would have been happy whatever came along. I submerged and came up. I said I would have been, too, at the same time thinking to myself that I might have felt a lot easier in my mind if we could have parted company with the boy on the landing under the tinsel star, who had so far brought us only bad luck. And taking a breath I went on to say that, although I was very happy it was a boy, I might have been fractionally happier, given the choice, if what came along had been a girl, but in the end it really made no difference to me – none at all.

It was some time before Kozue answered. I wondered if I had ventured in a bit deep. A girl would have been nice, she said eventually, wouldn't it, and we swam quietly back to the shore.

On a Sunday morning in July I drove down to our little local bakery to buy us fresh *rôti* for breakfast. The bakery had opened only that summer. It was run by an Iranian immigrant who was an engineer by training. Being unable to find a job in his own field he had taken up baking instead. His was the only shop for miles to open on a Sunday morning and I became a regular customer. Over the weeks we had struck up something of a friendship. On the Sunday in question I hung around talking, or rather listening to the baker-engineer do the talking, because it turned out that his family came from Hindustan, a place I had last visited with my grandmother Emily in the not-so-good stories from the late period of her life.

Emily's Hindustan turned out to have a surprising amount in common with the Hindustan I was shown by the baker. He sat me down with a cup of coffee on a chair by the counter and took out albums of photographs of his very extensive family, always at weddings or funerals or some kind of family function in tent-like enclosures with wall-to-wall carpeting which required the presence of several dozen veiled or bearded people, all of whom, he assured me, had no greater desire in life than a Swiss residence permit. They looked out of the photographs expectantly at me, as if I would be the instrument by which this was to be arranged. Not wishing to offend the baker by appearing to dissociate myself too quickly from responsibility for the hopes of his family, I sat and looked at their photographs for much longer than I really wanted. What I was seeing was something else.

An image of a child standing under a tinsel star hanging on a string from the ceiling involuntarily came into my mind. It made me feel uncomfortable. A vague sense of unease became a buzzing in my ears.

It got worse the longer I sat there. It was letting me know as clearly as if she had spoken with me, as no doubt she had, by means hitherto undetected but not unimaginable – perhaps comparable to the 20 Hz long-distance low-attenuation signals of some cetaceans which can be received by others of their kind thousands of miles away on the far side of the ocean – that something was wrong with Kozue.

Minutes after I had left the house, neglecting to shut the gate when I drove out of the courtyard, Centime ran across the road and was struck by a passing car. Upstairs in the bathroom Kozue heard a screech of brakes and a crash as the car scraped the wall of the house, swerved back across the road and landed up in the field on the other side. She ran downstairs, got her feet somehow tangled up at the bottom of the stairs and pitched head first onto the floor of the hall. She was still lying there and had commenced labour when she was found by our neighbour ten minutes later.

While I was still looking at photos of the baker's family in Hindustan Kozue was screaming in an ambulance, one foot of the unborn child already protruding from her vagina, on her way to the maternity hospital in Lausanne. In an emergency it would naturally have been much better to drive in the opposite direction to one of the clinics in Geneva, taking half the time it would take to reach Lausanne, but no one seems to have thought of doing that, neither the driver nor the attendant doctor in the ambulance nor Kozue her-self. Everything had conspired to go wrong. Any tiny change would have been enough to divert the course of events, any variant would have been better. We were left with the impossible, impermissible reality of what happened. This was how it turned out to be. The child emerged feet first and strangled itself on its own umbilical cord. By the time I arrived all that remained for me to do was take my leave of a son who had already been dead when he came into the world, to express the inexpressible, to find words to Kozue for things that could not be said, that lay beyond mere human comfort, or remorse, or understanding.

A Thing of no Use

When I was twelve I joined a school skiing party to the Grand St Bernard. We stayed for a few days in a hospice at the top of the mountain, run by monks who organised trekking tours mixed with a little religious instruction. On the last day we were returning from a ski tour when the monk who was our guide called a halt to allow the stragglers to catch up. We were waiting on a gentle slope beside a track cleared by the snow plough between the service lift and the hospice when the whole slope began to slide away beneath us. I was at first too astonished, and then too frightened, to even attempt to get away. I sank in up to my knees. The moving slope carried me slowly down, standing embedded just as I was, until it came to a stop a hundred yards below, bringing down with it loose powder snow that had buried me up to my waist before the avalanche finally came to a rest. No one was hurt, but this sensation of the solid ground giving way beneath my feet, of being buried under the snow and suffocating, stayed with me as a nightmare that recurred for many years. I was carried down and down towards a dreadful abyss, until the fear of what was about to happen to me became so unbearable that I woke up.

The sensation of the ground I was standing on breaking up beneath me came back to haunt me the year that we lost our child. Kozue must have had similar feelings, but it was hard to tell what was going on inside her because she didn't want to talk about it. The subject was too painful, and we fled from it. Outwardly, at least, we resumed our life as it had been before the events of that Sunday in July. We buried our dead and moved quietly on. A few adjustments were made. The paper cranes disappeared from their roosts. The dragonfly with the blue glasses was never heard of again, nor, to my deep regret, the sound of my wife singing around the house. I wouldn't have heard her even if

47

she had, because I was spending more and more time with my aquarium down in the basement these days. The Floating Period came to an end. I still had a swim in the lake occasionally, but the pleasure had gone out of it.

Having kept pretty much to ourselves in the first years of our marriage, we began to go out more often. It turned out to be easier to maintain the appearance of our marriage from the outside than the inside, where we now heard a silence. I was struck by a similarity here, only the other way round, with the tinnitus I developed at this time; since the Sunday morning in the Iranian baker's shop, to be exact. I began to hear a phantom noise caused by jangling nerve ends inside my head. Something like that, at any rate, was the gist of what I was told by the neurologist. The noise could be blocked out by a sufficient level of outside sounds but it became insistently audible as soon as they faded away. It was at its worst when one woke up in the middle of the night.

At Assurances Helvétiques Roche had been transferred to another department. I took over his responsibilities, which involved travelling round Switzerland for a lot of the time, while Kozue's job regularly took her all over Europe. We saw less and less of each other. We failed to pay this insufficiency at the heart of our life the attention it deserved because it took place for professional reasons and was therefore unavoidable. In defiance of the fact that I had ceased to take much interest in my job, I persuaded myself that work was what gave meaning to our increasingly separate lives. We no longer seemed to count for each other. Helpless with a sense of dread, I watched the common ground breaking up beneath our feet and the two of us drifting, though ourselves immobilised, ever further apart, ever further down towards some unforeseeable but imminent doom. I wanted to wake up so that the slide would stop, the dread cease, but this wasn't a bad dream I could snap out of. This had become the base sound, the signature tune in my life, like the chronic whine in my head resembling the sound of a finger rubbing the rim of a glass, to which I woke up shrilly every day.

Throughout the late 1980s and the early 1990s the issue of the moratorium on the killing of whales continued to attract so much publicity hostile to countries acting in disregard of the ban that Kozue was engaged on an almost full-time basis by various agencies representing the position of the Japanese government. All her working life she had attended conferences and served as a mouthpiece for the arguments and opinions of others without becoming personally engaged or even interested in the issues they addressed. A simultaneous interpreter's mind at work was an astonishing machine for reprocessing data. If it was to perform with the speed and accuracy required of it, it needed to remain detached from the function of evaluating or interpreting meaning. When she stepped out of her interpreter's booth she left behind whatever she had said inside it and seldom gave it another thought.

That detached, professional attitude to her job began to change. Intransigence on the whaling issue, coupled with devious vote-buying tactics to shore up its weak position within the IWC, had made Japan something of a pariah. Whaling preferences apart, popular perception of the Japanese was unsympathetic. To me this lack of sympathy seemed to have to do with Japan's success and failure in quite other, apparently unrelated spheres, although both were symptoms of the same insular self-interest: its glittering economic triumph, in some quarters perhaps more cause for envy than admiration, and the dismal moral poverty that became evident in the lack of compassion for those who had been victims of Japan's war. In the popular perception, the carcasses of whales and war victims floated in the same sea.

Kozue had never been interested in what she called politics. Issues like this had been no concern of hers. But giving voice, literally, to the Japanese position in the often heated atmosphere of the conferences to which she travelled year in year out, she found herself also being made answerable for it. There was no emotional charge in a statement given in Japanese. Everyone waited for the translation. It was her choice of words, spoken in French or English, not what her employers had said in Japanese, which the opposition agreed or took objection to, and she tended to become their target. And then there were the technicalities. She wasn't always able to hide in a booth. She sat with her delegates on the other side of the table and was perceived as one of them. Seating arrangements put her in their corner. Delegates responding to a Japanese point of view usually looked at her and addressed her, not her employers. She came home upset by the lack of sympathy she had to face at these conferences and, worse, the ostracism she sometimes experienced as a member of her delegation at the social functions afterwards. For a woman as cosmopolitan as Kozue it was a disturbing experience to find herself isolated at one end of a room in a group nobody seemed to want to talk to, even if the reason for that avoidance could be simply explained by the lack of a common language.

49

In conversations with our friends, conversations that made me feel increasingly uncomfortable, Kozue began by justifying the Japanese point of view, went on to defend it, and finally to share it herself. Whaling activities constituted a tradition that was many centuries old and belonged to the culture. I wasn't sure that Kozue necessarily believed this old chestnut of an argument, or even attached much importance to it, but a principle was at stake, something worth defending, and that was the right to be oneself, including the right to have whale on the menu and a prohibitive dose of mercury poisoning with it, if one so chose. Backstage of the argument it seemed to me she was really justifying and defending herself. As a woman it was her right to have a child, but she had not been able to exercise that right. She had been frustrated and she wanted satisfaction. Her failure, as she perceived it, to have a child undermined her self-confidence and put in question the meaning of her life. This much she admitted to me when we lay in bed at night. Casting around for something to replace what she had lost, she made the painful discovery that beside being a failed mother she was also something of a failed Japanese.

This was the feedback, finely filtered through many layers of courtesy, which she thought she was getting from senior Japanese officials, men over fifty, in the exclusively male environment in which she worked. These were men who had grown up in a society where women knew their place. Kozue wasn't like the women they were accustomed to. She was too independent. Brought up in São Paulo and New York, she had missed out on the patterning that modelled reserved, deferential women for the niche they were to occupy in Japanese society. All the signals she was sending these senior officials she worked for were wrong.

On one occasion, about a year after her third miscarriage, she came home in great distress and told me she had overheard one of them saying that, although Kozue was an excellent interpreter, she would be quite unusable in her own country. It sounded even worse in Japanese. *Tsukaenai mono*, a thing of no use. Not even to give birth to a normal, healthy child. This was the barb she read into the words that so got under her skin. She lay in bed sobbing, delivering herself of a reservoir of tears that had remained locked up inside her at the time she lost her child, and I was grateful for them, because in her need she turned to me and I held her tight and hushed her and we made compassionate love in a way we had not done for a long time, with the tenderness of a shared sorrow. The ground I had felt sliding away beneath us came to a halt and we found ourselves, for a while, secure in each other's arms.

When the Swiss board of trade invited Kozue at short notice to accompany their delegation on a three-month promotional tour of Japan she hesitated, but I encouraged her to go. More than encouraged, I talked her into it. She had not been in Japan since we got married, and the reason she should go now was because she had something to prove, to be usable in her own country, I said, quoting her own words back to her, although she had never said anything quite like that. She cried again at the airport. It was the first time in ten years that we had been separated for more than a couple of weeks. She clung to me. She would miss me. She didn't want to go after all. It didn't feel right to go. I would miss her, too, I said, but I knew how important it was for Kozue to make this trip to a place that despite everything she still thought of as home.

For once I had made up my mind about something. Perhaps because I had a deficit in the department of decision-making, as my wife had mentioned to me often enough, I put on a bit of a show of being firm with her, may even have rather enjoyed this impression of firmness I thought I was making on her as Kozue clung to me, but what she really thought I didn't know, or that she knew better than I did, as I would have known had I been my usual self and receptive to the signals she was sending me after she had gone through the gate, stopping and looking back, stopping and looking back, stopping and looking back three times before she disappeared from sight.

Family Matters

Kozue had been away for six months when I made the trip to L'Adret. This was a trip she had been wanting to make with me for years, but I had always found an excuse for putting it off. That I went there now, immediately after I received her letter from Kyoto, was a belated way of trying to make amends for a number of omissions on my part, the worst of which had been my failure to shut the yard gate the day Kozue lost her child. It was natural that Kozue wanted to prolong her stay in Japan when her assignment for the Swiss board of trade ended; in her native city most of all, where she had been offered a job interpreting at a conference on the world environment. Although the conference for which she had been engaged had ended long ago, Kozue was still there. What she was doing specifically she didn't say, or how long she intended to stay. In her letter she just wrote that she wanted to find out where she belonged. I realised I had let my wife down where it most mattered. I had been unable to provide her with a sense of home. It crossed my mind that this might be because I had an insufficient sense of home myself. There would have been no need for her to return to Japan or for me to be making the trip to L'Adret had we been able to reverse the series of events which had been set in motion by my forgetting to close the yard gate. The home for myself and Kozue that was then destroyed might otherwise – or so I told myself – have been saved. All it required was the closing of a gate. The present had become impassable, and the only way forward seemed to be the way back, both of us embarking on separate journeys into the past to look for that turning we had somehow missed.

I arrived in L'Adret on a wet autumn afternoon. A warm wind blew up the valley where I parked my car. Climbing the steps to the cable car station, I noticed how quickly I was out of breath and wondered if it had to do with the change in altitude. A freak snow fall the previous night had engulfed the village at the top of the mountain, trans-forming everything above the snow line at a thousand metres into a ghostly winter landscape. In the shadow of the mountain below I looked up and saw it glittering in the rays of the setting sun. There was a road that went all the way up, but I didn't have snow tyres, which was why I thought it better to take the cable car. The cable car, after all, was one of the reasons I had come here. To build it was why my grandfather Jean Serraz had been sent to L'Adret as a location engineer in the early 1930s by the Fribourg company for which he worked. The name of the company and various construction details were commemorated on a plaque on the wall above the ticket office. Building the cable car in L'Adret took several years. My grandfather seems to have acquired a liking for the place. He bought a house and continued to live there after the project was finished and his company appointed him inspector of cable cars in the Valais region.

The cable car attendant and myself were the only passengers making the ride that afternoon. We whirled up over slopes of spruce and larch trees, disappeared into a cloud and emerged ten minutes later in a world of startling brilliance above the snow line. The old village of L'Adret was made up of a chapel and a dozen farms perched on a ledge below the summit, elongated on either side by modern chalets and converted farmhouses now catering for tourists. The summer hiking season had ended, the skiing season not yet begun. I seemed to be the only guest in the hotel attached to the cable car station. I told the receptionist I was making inquiries about relatives of mine who had lived in L'Adret before the war, and that I would like to talk to people in the village who might have known them. Yes, she said, perhaps I should look up the schoolmaster who had taught at the village school until it was closed in the 1970s and moved down into the valley. He had kept records of the village for the last fifty years and had even written a history about it. He still lived in retirement in an apartment in the old school building just down the road. The receptionist gave me his phone number. I called him. He asked me to come round that evening after supper.

The old schoolmaster well remembered the Serraz household. Jean had lived in the village for about a dozen years with his wife Amélie, his daughter Louise and an unmarried sister called Emily. People tended to confuse Emily with Amélie, presumably because of the similarity of their names. Besides, Emily was an unfamiliar name in these parts. He once asked Jean Serraz about it, the schoolmaster said, and my grandfather told him that his father had named his two daughters Emily and Charlotte after the Brontë sisters, whose writings he greatly admired. Charlotte was apparently much younger than Emily. The schoolmaster had never met her. So far as he knew she had never visited L'Adret. Perhaps I would be able to trace her in Fribourg, where the Serraz family came from. Regarding Emily, the schoolmaster said, there had been speculation in the village as to why Jean had brought her to live with his family in L'Adret. Perhaps Jean's wife Amélie had a delicate constitution. Perhaps she had been of a somewhat nervous disposition. Who could say? What went on inside families you could never guess from outside. The old man spread his hands and contemplated them for a while. Emily, at any rate, not Amélie, appeared to have been the one who ran the Serraz household, and it was she who by all accounts had been more of a mother to Louise than Amélie, the girl's nominal mother.

When I asked the schoolmaster if he remembered anything of the girl who became my mother a smile flitted across his face. For a couple of years after her arrival in L'Adret Louise had been among his pupils at the village school. She was a lively girl, something of a tomboy and prone to mischief, with a passion for animals, which she was always smuggling into the classroom. He remembered a frog in his drawer and a cricket in his hat, which he only discovered when he got home. It hopped out of his hat and hid under a cupboard, where its chirping drove him crazy for a week. The schoolmaster turned and pointed at the cupboard against the wall behind him, as if it could bear witness to the truth of his story. At any rate, he continued, Jean Serraz wanted a better education for his daughter than what was locally available and sent her off to boarding school in Lausanne, where something must have happened. Happened? What did he mean by that, I wondered. Well now, said the schoolmaster, the sort of thing that happened to girls of seventeen at boarding schools in Lausanne so often one might almost believe they were sent there for that purpose. Louise got a big belly. There was a scandal – pouf! A terrible scandal!

The schoolmaster puffed out his cheeks just as M. Garrault had done. It put him in a time warp. It was something I had only ever seen old men do.

There must have been something beside the pregnancy, the schoolmaster continued, to turn Jean's heart so unrelentingly against his daughter during the remaining year of his life. A child out of wedlock was nothing so unusual in these parts. But Louise was never seen or heard of again in L'Adret. Her father refused to allow her to enter the house. A year later, just after the end of the war, he died of a heart attack. His wife Amélie was French, of course, and remembering her origins when her husband died she sold the house and returned to Annecy, where she apparently still had relatives. As for Emily, the last thing he had heard was that she had found employment as a house-keeper in Geneva. All these things had happened a long time ago, the schoolmaster added, as if he was having second thoughts. The events in question had been rumoured in the village at the time and he couldn't guarantee the truth of everything he had told me.

He had come out of his reverie and looked awkwardly round the room. I sat there dumbfounded by what I had heard from this wholly unexpected, astonishingly loquacious narrator of my unknown past. Perhaps it had slipped his mind quite who I was, not any old listener but the son of the teenage girl who, he had just been telling me, caused a terrible scandal when she got knocked up in Lausanne, and might even have hastened her father's death. Now that he realised the implications of what he was saying he felt embarrassed.

The day I got back from L'Adret I was rummaging in the loft of my house when I dislodged a pile of books balanced on a crate. The book lying face up had fallen open at a page with a rather strange photo-graph of a naked child. I picked up the book and glanced at the cover. It was one of Kozue's books on infant care. She must have dumped the books up here to get them out of the way and prevent them from reminding her.

At first I thought I was looking at a picture of an abused child. There was what appeared to be a blue-green bruise on the child's buttocks, extending to the base of the spine. The caption said this was a kind of birthmark known as Mongolian Spots. It was a normal discoloration which faded and disappeared within the first couple of years of the child's life. It was to be found with over eighty per cent of Asian babies, very rarely among Caucasians. I sat looking at this picture in a trance-like state for a very long time. I could feel a memory growing on me, although I couldn't say of what. The grow-ing memory was a physical sensation, not unlike an oncoming head-ache, a sense of tissue thickening beneath the skull. And then I had it. It was a sentence in one of my mother's letters to Emily.

The last time I had looked through the papers in Emily's chest had been twenty years ago. When Emily died the chest had gone into boarding with M. Garrault. It had lived under the bed in my flat for ten years before moving with me to Kozue's apartment, and now I was sitting on it in the loft as I stared at the picture of the Mongolian Spots. I got up and opened it. The half dozen letters my mother had written to Emily at the Appletrees' house after her departure from Switzerland were still in the original envelopes with rows of Indonesian stamps, tucked into a folder marked 'Louise' in Emily's handwriting. I took out the bottom letter, which Emily told me had been the last sign of life she received from my mother, and spread it out on my knee. Unlike the other letters this one was typed. I had forgotten that. Somebody must have lent Louise a typewriter. The letter was dated 24 April 1947 and had been written from Flores.

My very dearest Emily, the letter began.

A Funny Bluish Backside

With all the travelling we have been doing for the last couple of months I have been very remiss about writing to you since we left Bali, and I send a thousand kisses and ask your forgiveness, but after our departure from Lombok six weeks ago we have never settled down for more than a couple of days in any one place and the baby frets in the heat and often can't sleep at night. We stayed with a Dr Soedjono at his house in the mountains near Mataitu, full of large, luxuriant trees, flowers, waterfalls and the chant of muezzin rising out of the valley at dawn and dusk. The rainy season hadn't ended and we got soaked through during the week-long voyage to Flores on an old bum boat, as Edward called it, with only a leaky awning covering part of the deck, but fortunately the sea was calm and the air is so warm that one's clothes dry on one's body. Swarms of dolphins, literally hundreds, criss-crossed the wake of the boat, and a small group of them stayed with us for the best part of a day, riding the bow waves, and some of them even accompanied us to the quay side in the harbour. There were no ships scheduled to leave for Timor for the next couple of weeks, so we decided to travel overland to the east end of the island and get passage from there, quite a busy port, apparently, with boats departing regularly once or twice a week. The bus broke down and for three days we travelled by cart drawn by water buffalo over non-existent roads until we reached this monastery on the north coast of the island outside a town called Maumere. It is run by monks belonging to an order I have never heard of, Spiritus Dei is its name, I think. There are a few Indonesians among them but the majority are Dutch, German and Portuguese. This has made communication so much easier, as although Edward understands some Malay he can hardly speak it at all. The monks have been extremely kind and provided us with food and lodging and told us we are welcome to stay as long as we like. It has been an exhausting journey in this heat and we want to rest here for a while to give the baby a chance to recover. There is also a post office (!) in Maumere so at last I can send you news of us. As I mentioned in my last letter, poor baby suffered quite badly from prickly heat during the rainy season, but in the dryer weather we are having now the problem seems to be clearing up. Such a dear little fellow and with such a funny bluish backside, which his father says is quite natural and will pass off in time. Edward is still weak from the dysentery he had in Bali, so the rest will do him good, too. Thank God at least I have kept such perfect health so far . . .

Wanda

I still had the old-fashioned idea that New Zealand was a remote place, at a distance of at least fifty years on my personal map of the world, but even then, given the advanced technology available in my office at Assurances Helvétiques in the early 1990s, New Zealand was just a few mouse clicks away. With some help from a Mormon organisation based in Salt Lake City I had located one Arthur James Smith, very probably the younger brother of Edward Smith, who was my father, had written a letter to him at an address in a place called Invercargill, South Island and got an answer back from him, all within a couple of weeks.

Photographs were the first thing to come out of the envelope. There were old black and white snapshots of Edward and Arthur as children, a portrait of Edward playing the violin, a recent photo of my uncle with his wife and children, and a portrait of my grandmother Wanda, a dark-skinned woman in her late fifties or early sixties, sitting beside a man who must have been ten years older. I stood at a table and switched the photos around, putting them in one order and then another, looking for the family resemblance. My uncle Arthur took after Victor, his father and my grandfather. I was more like my uncle than my father. But Edward was unmistakably his mother's son. He reminded me of someone I had met not all that long ago, and with a start I realised it was Mans Gerardus. Looking at the monochrome photos of Edward and Arthur as children, poor quality snapshots which exaggerated the black and white contrasts, I wondered how two such brothers could have come out of the same woman's womb. The reason for the scandal my mother had caused was plain enough. The old schoolmaster in L'Adret had been quite right. It was not his daughter's illegitimate child that had so upset Jean Serraz. It was the fact that Louise had got herself pregnant by a man who wasn't white.

In his letter, my uncle Arthur wrote that most New Zealanders used to take his mother, with her stocky build, dark curly hair and colouring, for a Maori woman. In fact she came from Timor. His father had met her at a port of call regularly visited by the merchant navy ships on which he had served for twenty years from the time of the First World War until he retired from the navy and got a job on land. Wanda herself claimed indigenous Timorese descent with some Portuguese and Malay ancestry grafted in. My uncle said that the marked physical difference between himself and Edward had been a problem for both brothers throughout their childhood. *If*, as he expressed it, *we had been one thing or the other, at least we'd have known where we were.* But they were hybrids, a sibling pair *split cleanly down the genetic middle*, as my uncle Arthur put it, the elder brother belonging to one side, the younger to the other, and the society in which they grew up between the wars in rural New Zealand regarded them as freaks. It was best for them to go separate ways. Perhaps that was why Edward always wanted to get away, which he duly did, winning a scholarship to study at the Royal Academy of Music in London. Edward had written home a few times from Europe, but unfortunately the letters had been lost. Arthur knew he had been in Geneva, where he had met a girl and married her at short notice soon after the end of the war. That was the last thing he heard from his brother. Then he had disappeared. They assumed he was dead. My grandmother Wanda had passed away in 1974, but Victor survived her by sixteen years and had died only recently.

I sat down at the table on which I had spread out the photographs, pulled out the drawer and took out writing paper. *Dear Uncle Arthur*, I wrote. Then I sat there for a quarter of an hour, wondering what to say next. My mind was in such a tumble that I was unable to concentrate on any particular train of thought, and after another fruitless quarter of an hour I gave up. I went into the bedroom and took off my clothes. With the aid of the hand mirror Kozue kept in the bathroom cupboard I inspected myself from all angles in the full-length mirror inside the closet. I hated looking at myself in mirrors, particularly after putting on so much weight during the last few years. In the foreshortened image of the mirror I appeared not just unshapely but stumpy. I held the mirror up over my shoulder and looked at my back. According to Kozue's book, the Mongolian Spots disappeared in early childhood. Naturally one couldn't expect to find any traces of them on the body of an almost fifty-year-old man, naturally I searched for them nonetheless. I inspected the sallow complexion of my skin, what Kozue, far whiter than I, called my natural tan, and wondered if this was something I owed to my grandmother Wanda. In the light of Wanda I re-appraised my lack of body hair, my dark eyes and hair, my little round nose. *My father met her at a port of call regularly visited by the merchant navy ships.* I wondered if Arthur intended any innuendoes in this mention of the circumstances in which Victor and Wanda had met.

As I stood there looking at myself naked in the mirror, a sense of myself as an impostor began to grow on me. I was not what I had hitherto taken myself to be. I was someone else, a person I didn't know.

Unnerved, I shut the closet door and sat down on Kozue's side of the bed. I tried calling her number in Kyoto, but there was no reply. I looked at the bed, her side and mine, and the words my uncle had used to describe himself and his brother, a pair split cleanly down the middle, came to mind. If we had been one thing or the other, at least we'd have known where we were. On your side of the divide or mine, at least we'd have been together. With a shock I suddenly saw the solitude in which each of us had lived during the last few years. I glimpsed the extent of it, a desert plain reaching to the horizon. While I was floating down those rivers Kozue stayed on shore. While I was talking to the *rôti* baker about his relatives in Hindustan my wife fell down the stairs and began labour. We were in different time zones, our rhythms were out of sync. I couldn't reach her. It was getting on for midnight my time, which for Kozue was eight o'clock in the morning. I wondered why she wasn't in. I didn't know what to do, whether to sit or stand, and, if I stood, what for. It was like the onset of paralysis. I moved my fingers to see if they still worked. I stared at the objects in the room around me with a sense of panic. They refused to make sense. For a long time I had been looking at something black sticking out from behind the cupboard, trying to figure out what it was, until I finally realised that it was the leg of my wetsuit. This return of familiarity seemed to hold out some kind of hope.

I decided to go for a swim.

Shades of Emily

Not two hundred metres from our house as the crow flies there is a stretch of public park along the shore from which I always set out for my swims in the lake. There is a particular bench where I leave my things, if possible always at the same end of it, a particular point where I habitually go into the water. It belongs to the routine I have for swimming, one of the routines I have established for almost everything I do in my life. Kozue used to tease me about them and sometimes, when she told me I was so predictable I was boring, they seriously annoyed her, but the fact is that without routines my life would fall apart. As a child I began to cultivate an exaggerated tidiness to ward off the chaos that surrounded Emily and threatened to engulf me with her. As an adult I perfected my orderly habits because they helped me to believe in my continuity. But on this night, perhaps because I was already in my wetsuit and had nothing to carry, I abandoned my routine and walked directly from the car park across the gravel path into the lake.

I could tell how cold it was by the stiffness of the material of my ancient wetsuit, through which I felt the water pressure creeping up my body as I waded in. In warmer water it soon grew supple. For a moment the sight of the lake in the dark made me shiver. It was a long time since I had swum so late in the year. But as soon as I pushed off from the ground and began to float, shedding weight, leaving everything behind me on the shore, I felt free. It was a dark night on the lake. There was no moon. The illuminated buoy a hundred metres or so from the entrance to the marina was still visible, but a bank of fog blacked out the lights on the opposite bank.

I swam out into a darkness on the lake deeper than the darkness on land. Swimming pushed away the unease that was piling up just beyond the threshold of my conscious thoughts. I pushed it away with the strong strokes of my arms. I would soon reach the buoy. I told myself I was at home in water and that I felt comfortable now, because in water I always did. I tried to get into the rhythm of stroking the water and breathing, but for some reason my chest felt strangely tight and I was short of breath. When I reached the buoy I hung onto it and rested for a while, panting. I couldn't understand it. Usually I would think nothing of swimming out a quarter of a mile and back. I looked into the encircling fog and decided it would be better not to go any further tonight. The fog was a hazard, but that wasn't why I curtailed my swim. I didn't feel up to it. After resting on the buoy I was even shorter of breath than I had been before. It was inexplicable. I took gulps of air. I inhaled at ever shorter intervals. The air came into my lungs but didn't seem to be leaving them when I exhaled. My chest grew tighter and tighter with all the unbreathed air in my lungs. Something inconceivable was happening. I still had another fifty or sixty metres to the shore and I realised I might not get there, because I was drowning.

I could see a couple standing under a street lamp at the entrance to the park. I tried to shout, but all I could manage was a gasp. I watched them turn and walk back up to the road. They couldn't have helped me in any case. There wasn't time. No one could help me but myself. I concentrated on breathing in and out as deeply as I could, rhythmically, without panic, however short the intervals became. The diminishing supply of oxygen in my lungs was something I could not just feel but clearly visualise, like a gap which I watched closing, regardless of how much air I breathed in. My lungs were filling up from the bottom. They seemed to be turning solid, as if cement was being poured in. This was what drowning was like. The lungs filled from the bottom up, the gap closed, until you had no air left to breathe. I would drown on the inside from my own body fluids before I had swallowed even a drop of water from the lake.

Twenty or thirty metres from the shore I was breathing very flat and fast, at the uppermost part of my lungs. The air bubbled in my throat and came and went with a little gasp. Then I felt ground underfoot. I stopped swimming and stood with my head tilted back, gulping, expecting the blockage in my lungs to cease, the air to surge in, but it didn't. I took a few steps forward. The water was up to my chest, I was safe, surely, as good as on the shore, but still I went on drowning. I foundered and fell in the shallows. I propped myself up on all fours, panting, panting, panting, while I crawled ashore. There I remained kneeling on the grass for a long time, breathing gradually more easily, until I heard a gurgling in my chest that sounded like water draining out of a bath – and suddenly my lungs were free again. As I got to my feet I heard a familiar voice, announcing as distinctly as if she had been standing there beside me on the bank of the lake: mark my words, Daniel Serraz, if you insist on drowning at least you shall do so as a qualified swimmer. Forty years on, Emily's prophecy of death by water had come home to roost.

In the Hospital

Still in my wetsuit, I got into my car and drove slowly to a hospital in Geneva. I told the doctor on night duty what had happened to me. He asked me if I had suffered from heart pain or had other health problems. None at all, I said, the only thing which had struck me in the last six to twelve months was how quickly I got out of breath. I assumed that was because I was overweight. The doctor listened to my heart and lungs with his stethoscope. I spent the next couple of hours being wheeled around the basement of the hospital, despite my assurance that I could walk perfectly well, and subjected to a series of tests. At two o'clock in the morning the cardiologist who conducted these tests told me what was wrong with me. The aorta valve, which regulated the blood supply between my heart and the body's main artery, was not opening and closing properly, causing emphysema, or what I had experienced as the sensation of drowning.

It might be best for me to stay in the hospital overnight, the cardiologist suggested, and undergo an angiogram examination the following morning. An angiogram was a probe with a tiny camera that could be pushed up inside the artery in just the way the municipality inspected its drains and pipes, he said, right into the heart, to assess if there were any blockages or other damage in need of repair. It was quite painless, and the odds on something going wrong were only one in ten thousand.

A risk factor of 0.01 per cent sounded very reasonable to me and clinched the argument just as I had begun to waver. I agreed to the doctor's suggestion. Although I had been diagnosed as having an acute heart condition, I lacked any subjective awareness of being ill and totally underestimated the seriousness of it. I decided not to call the office as I had taken a week's holiday and wouldn't be missed. I still couldn't reach Kozue. She must have gone on a trip. I told myself I would be home the next day, or the day after that at the latest, and would find a message waiting for me there.

But once I had got myself into hospital I found it much less easy than I had imagined to get myself out of it. On the day following my admission I waited in bed all morning and didn't even leave the ward until a very poor lunch without wine was served at three in the afternoon. On the day after that my bed was wheeled down into the basement and parked in a line of beds reaching all the way down the corridor. The queue was repeatedly held up by emergency cases – two or three heart attack patients brought in on stretchers in as many hours – and by the end of the day I had still only moved up to fourth place in the queue. On the third day I was the last patient to be wheeled into the examination room at the end of the afternoon. Since I had to remain in bed for six hours afterwards, with a bag of sand on my groin to close the wound in the artery that had been made to insert the probe, there was no question of my being discharged that night.

By this time my morale was at a low ebb. I had never been inside a hospital, not as a patient. After three days on the ward I could imagine what life must be like for an animal caught in the wilds and transported to a zoo. I discovered that to lose one's freedom meant to be deprived of one's privacy. Captive animals ate, defecated, copulated, mourned and slept in view of the public. I had been put naked into a draughty night gown open at the back and tied at the neck like a giant bib. On the ward there was no one my own age or younger. I found myself in the company of people who were at least twenty years older, all heart patients like myself, people who dragged their feet and talked to themselves in the corridor, many of them with terrific scars from navel to throat and stories to match of the gruelling surgery they had undergone.

Overnight I seemed to have become old, sick and dependent. My life had passed out of my control and now lay in other people's hands. That it lay anywhere at all, hadn't been extinguished in the lake, was no consolation to me. I was a bad patient. I took my illness as if it had been a punishment meted out to me, a judgement passed down from someone who disapproved of what I had done with my life. In the night I heard voices inside me whispering: if you had closed the gate that Sunday morning none of this would have happened.

A cardiologist and a heart surgeon came to visit me on the fourth day. What they had to say was shocking. I was in no fit state to be walking around, they told me, let alone going for swims in the middle of the night. An operation would be unavoidable, the sooner the better. They advised me to stay in hospital under observation in case an emergency arose before surgery, which could be performed before the end of the week. The defective aorta valve would be replaced with an artificial one. This was a routine operation nowadays. Nothing else was wrong with my heart. I asked if there were any alternatives to an operation and I was told there were none. In two weeks I could leave hospital. After rehabilitation I could go home and get back to normal life within three months. Having stated the situation, the doctors left me to come to terms with it.

Almost in passing the surgeon had mentioned that when it came to replacing a defective valve you had a choice between a mechanical valve, constructed with man-made materials, or a biological valve made of animal tissue. Both options had merits and drawbacks. A mechanical valve practically never wore out, but because it was accompanied by the risk of thrombosis it required the patient to monitor his blood regularly and take anti-coagulants every day for the rest of his life. No medication or controls were needed with bio-valves. However, after ten or twelve, perhaps as many as fifteen years – fluctuations that probably reflected not so much the product as the way the patient lived, the surgeon said – bio-valves wore out and had to be replaced. Why submit voluntarily to the ordeal and, it had to be said, the increasing risk of repeated heart surgery if it was avoidable?

Even before I was made acquainted with all the arguments, I had instinctively preferred the biological alternative. Given my line of interests, perhaps that was no wonder. But if I had been confronted with an evaluation like this in the course of my work for Assurances Helvétiques I would have spent weeks researching and weighing the pros and cons before coming to such a far-reaching decision. In my private life I managed to steer clear of such decisions altogether. It disturbed me that my instinctive choice was probably not the sensible one. I fretted. Time was running out. The surgeon had given me forty-eight hours to make up my mind.

I had been in hospital for several days when Roche appeared without warning at my bedside and told me a strange and wonderful thing.

Kozue had called him in the middle of the night to find out why I wasn't at home. She had been trying to reach me there for the past two days. She knew I wasn't away on a business trip because if I had been I would have left a message. Roche said Kozue had asked him to go to the house immediately and, if I wasn't there, to find me and give me a message. She had seen in a dream the boy on the landing at the top of the stairs, which was how she knew that something must be wrong. That was the whole message. Kozue said I would understand. Roche had no idea what was going on. He hadn't missed me at the office because I had taken a week's holiday. But then I wasn't at home either. Roche checked the house again the next morning. He noticed my car was gone. One of the neighbours thought he had seen someone in a wet suit in the car park a couple of nights before. Roche knew that could only have been me. He went to the police in case they had reports of drowned or missing persons or anything like that. Tracking down legacies and legatees, people or property gone missing, was an everyday part of Roche's job. Soon he began calling the hospitals in the area. It hadn't taken him long to find me.

Why hadn't I let him know where I was, Roche asked, a little angry, a little hurt, why hadn't I told him what had happened? I had been expecting this question and knew I wouldn't be able to give it an honest answer. A truthful answer to Roche's question would have entailed telling him about my visit to L'Adret and the letter my father's brother had written me and the reflection of someone I didn't know in the mirror, which I had found deeply disturbing, and although this had nothing to do with why I had gone for a swim in the middle of the night it would be difficult to explain it to his satisfaction. I wasn't sure, besides, that it was any business of his or even mine to be telling him this, or who would be telling him about whom, these images that didn't square, of myself and of someone purporting to be me, whom I didn't know. For the moment I wasn't sure where I stood. So I told Roche I had been in shock and left it at that, and he went away puzzled and upset by my behaviour.

The surgeon showed up again on the ward late in the afternoon, wearing a dark blue smock and looking ten years older than when I had last seen him a couple of days before, tanned and with a spring in his step, as if he had just got back from holiday. An ashy colour showed whitely through the tan, there were rings under his eyes and his forehead was damp with sweat. He must have come directly from the operating theatre. The exhaustion of whatever he had been through there had left a devastation on his face from which it had not yet recovered. I felt sorry for him that he had to make another call on my behalf at the end of such a strenuous day, and I was glad that all further discussion of what kind of valve I wanted could be settled by his answer to one question. Suppose, I said, that after this operation I were to go to Indonesia – just suppose – and live for perhaps months in out-of-the-way places, islands without electricity or sterile water, a day's journey from the nearest medical assistance, which would in any case be rudimentary. What type of hardware would he think it best to install in that case?

To my surprise his face lit up. Indonesia, he said. Funny I should mention that. He had been there on a hiking and diving tour just a couple of years ago. A place full of surprises, with medical facilities to match. The drawback with a mechanical valve was not so much the maintenance, he said. The problem was the thinness of your blood, its reluctance to coagulate. Suppose you cut yourself nastily, for example in the sea. Plenty of sharp things lying around on a coral reef, likelihood of infection with possibly serious consequences such as endocarditis, and in the worst case, if you were out on your own somewhere and failed to staunch the wound, the risk of bleeding to death. In view of these considerations, he concluded, a bio-valve might be one's best bet. The body took valves made of animal tissue better on board and required no anti-coagulants at all. Just an aspirin a day. His recommendation would be a Perimount bio-prothesis of the HK series, which had never yet let any of his patients down. I thanked him for his advice. I always appreciated a professional approach, I said, nowhere more so than in the present case. The matter was settled then.

The matter was settled then. I walked up and down the corridors, wondering if I had done the right thing in rejecting the mechanical, the more prudent option. I concluded that I had. For the first time in my life I had chosen the present rather than the future, to live as I wanted to now, and to hell with the consequences. Now I was committed. Within forty-eight hours the deed of commitment would be sewn into my heart.

Preparing a patient for his operation is not unlike preparing a condemned man for his execution. The subject experiences everything in the third person and the present tense. He is woken at dawn while everyone else is still asleep. The nurse accompanies him to the bathroom. They shut themselves in and collaborate in silence. When necessary, they talk in whispers, as if the operation has made conspirators of them. The nurse rubs disinfectant all over the patient's body and gives him an enema, squirted into the rectum. He washes the patient's feet and puts plastic covers on them so that they will not come into contact with bacteria on the floor. After the patient has opened his bowels the nurse cleans him and he gets back into bed.

His pulse rate has risen to a hundred and twenty. The nurse gives him an injection to calm him down. He has an hour to prepare himself mentally for the operation. Until this moment it has been far away from him, but now he can feel it approaching and he is afraid. To the patient looking down a narrowing tunnel at his now imminent operation it feels just as he imagines it would feel if he were going to his execution. Being in the third person, he may even experience a flush of cruel satisfaction that it is happening to someone else. He dozes off nonetheless. This is his saving grace.

Suddenly his bed is in motion. As it is wheeled down the corridor he can feel a breeze, suddenly there is this great hurry and everything is in motion. Hurry, hurry. He hears a voice calling to the nurse that the operating theatre has just phoned the ward again because they want the patient right away. He is grateful for the tranquilliser. It numbs the panic that would otherwise be bubbling inside him. The bed reaches the lock in the corridor dividing the operating theatres from the rest of the hospital. The lock opens automatically and they pass through. He feels a sudden climate change. They have arrived in a cold zone. He is wheeled into a windowless steel chamber. Inside the steel chamber the polished surfaces gleam, sterile, functional, offering no hold. Waiting there is a man with a mask in a dark blue smock, who helps the nurse to lift the patient from his bed onto the operating stretcher.

The nurse leaves with my bed. Wait, I say, for this is happening to me. He is up and gone with my life, to which I shall never return. The man in the dark blue smock who attends to me in the chamber is the anaesthetist who visited me last night to clarify a few details before the operation. He chats with two technicians doing something to a machine on the other side of the room, and I lie between them as if I didn't exist. They talk about the weather, what was on TV last night, their plans for the weekend. Then he turns and addresses a few brief, reassuring words to me. This waiting will be over for me before he even gets to the end of his sentence, he says, and I am grateful, because everything I have been listening to him and the technicians discussing at what seems to me a critical moment in my life is utterly banal, and without being consulted I have been made a part of it. Soon I will feel a prick in my foot, he says, but he has forgotten I already know that, he told me himself the previous evening. Then I will feel nothing more. I wonder if this is end of his sentence. A sliding wall at the back of the steel chamber opens and I get a glimpse of the operating theatre. This is a view of the landscape of the last things I shall know with certainty. Nothing in it is memorable. I feel the prick in my foot

when I awoke I asked the time and wondered how it was possible that thirteen hours could have passed since I felt the prick in my foot. I had a train to catch. I was the keeper of time, the hand on the clock that was supposed to stick to the timetable, but I had fallen asleep and neglected my duties, perhaps missing my connection. The toil of the hand of the clock tracking time through all its flickering moments was indescribable. Yet I must not miss a single one of them. I compared my count with the hand of the large clock on the wall as it passed through the seconds, minutes and hours of the night. First it was midnight, but not until a long time after that was it one o'clock. Hours more dragged by unbearably before it reached two, an eternity before it was three, then ten past three, a quarter past, and so on, until it began to get light.

All night long the illuminated displays of the control units above the drip-feed dispensers flashed on and off. Alarms beeped incessantly. There was always someone coming or going to make an adjustment to them. I was in a bed parked under the traffic lights at the busiest intersection in town. Wide awake, I watched the neon lights, compulsively I ticked with the digital advertisements flashing CONNECT around me. I had pain in my chest, which was why I must not turn over. But I couldn't sleep on my back. Sleeplessness, the situation of being *unable* to sleep owing to physical circumstances, had a curious parallel in the psychological persuasion I had of being *forbidden* to sleep. In the intensive care unit a patient had no business to be falling asleep. On the contrary, it was his duty to be wide awake. I had to learn to connect. The red neon displays of the drip-feed dispensers kept flashing this word to remind me. CONNECT.

Unless I learned to connect, my life would slip by. I must watch and wake in case it tried to sneak past. I must seize and arrest it. This thought was the fever that fretted in me. Until I had undertaken something to this end, such as helping to further the cause of world peace, or to bring Kozue back, I would feel no better and get no rest. Cautiously I moved along the bed, trailing cables that stretched just far enough to let me squeeze round the end of it, and achieved a sitting position on the other side. I stayed put like that, realising I was marginally better off sitting than lying. After a while I had to concede that I would be unable to contribute to the furtherance of world peace, at least not for the time being. I lay down again, completely exhausted. But lying was even less bearable. I levered myself into a sitting position with the intention of getting up again.

A nurse came over to my bed. What on earth do you think you're doing, she asked. I have to leave, I said. She hurried off and returned with reinforcements, a burly male nurse who advanced down the aisle with a menacing appearance that showed he meant business. I offered no resistance. I said I wouldn't give them any trouble. They put me back into bed. From then on they kept me under close surveillance. There was always someone looking in to see what I was up to. I would have to be on my guard, to wake and watch, but my task had become no easier.

One might suppose that the intensive care unit in a hospital, being a kind of library for the critically ill, or rather its bookbinding department, where tattered, comatose folios are stitched together, would be among the quietest places on earth. But in my hospital one area led on into the next without doors or any partitions except glass screens, and the staff were constantly milling in the communal space between, talking at the tops of their voices, laughing and clattering coffee cups. No one thought of lowering their voices, nor did it occur to me to protest. I accepted this noise as if it was some extraneous burden they had dumped on my bed, just as one accepted everything here. Perhaps I even derived comfort from the proximity of such a circus of triviality to the deepening gravity of my own situation. For while all this background noise went on night and day, I continued to monitor the closer happenings within myself, and there came, as I had always known there would come, a moment when I felt frightened to death. There was something terminally wrong with me. I was failing to connect. I felt the life force draining out of me. A vapour, an essence, whatever it was, you could feel it leaking out of you. After its departure it left an emptiness. This was how you knew you were dying.

To no one in particular I said out loud: 'I'm afraid.' The patient lying opposite me, whom I never saw because he was behind a screen, evidently heard what I said. He passed it on to the male nurse who was setting up a multi-display drip-feed unit in the communal area where there was a coffee machine. 'He needs a doctor, he says he's frightened,' I could hear the invisible patient telling the male nurse, and already he was hurrying off down the passage.

Soon afterwards the nurse returned, accompanied by a doctor with a familiar face, a small man with a thin face and fine movements, like so many of the doctors assembled here for a light-fingered, pick-pocket-surgeon kind of work, groping in hearts without the patients noticing, which seemed to require a generally finer configuration of man. Kowalski. I could even remember his name. I told Dr Kowalski that I was afraid. One's condition could give a body cause for concern, I said as neutrally as possible, verging towards the third person, as if I were discussing the case of the other patient lying beside me in my bed, whom I sometimes still confused with myself. I asked if anything could be done for him. Dr Kowalski was concerned that I was concerned. I saw the astonished expression in his face. It irritated me that a doctor should look astonished when a patient said he was afraid. But before he hurried off again he arranged for me to be given medication that would make me feel better.

Later he came back in the greyness of light that made it hard to tell whether day had broken or night was falling. He said something about my heart no longer being able to transmit the electric current that regulated the rhythm of the heartbeat, due to the conduits in the tissue that transmitted the current having been inadvertently severed during surgery, something to that effect. This didn't often happen, he said, but now it had. In fact right now things didn't look in particularly good shape. He compared the condition of my heart to an accumulator or storage battery with not more than about twenty per cent power left in it. Unless provided with a back-up system, this reserve would run out too. For this reason it had become necessary to implant a pacemaker, he said, soon.

They came to fetch me at three or four o'clock in the morning, by all reports the established dying hour before dawn, and naturally I was expecting them, this was why I kept watch at night and learned to connect. The team was led by a ginger-bearded doctor I hadn't seen before. His manner was calm and deliberate, masking a sense of urgency, I suspected, because during the hours that had elapsed since the conversation with Dr Kowalski my situation had become, as the new doctor put it, less stable, and when a doctor communicated a sense of urgency beneath a façade of calmness the patient easily misunderstood it as panic.

My bed was wheeled down the centre aisle into a room that was empty, as far as I could tell, but by the time my bed and pieces of mobile equipment had been brought in it seemed full. An operating theatre would be improvised here, I was told, and I wondered why it was necessary to do this in a large modern hospital in which, presumably, there was no lack of facilities, especially at this hour of the night. I was given a local anaesthetic and a provisional burial beneath layers of a coarse-fibre blue operation sheet rather like paper. Here I lay without moving for several hours.

My supply of oxygen underneath these layers began to run out. I repeatedly had to ask one of the operators to make me an air hole so that I could breathe. Implanting the pacemaker seemed to be causing more problems than anticipated, and time was pressing. Up there, above the sheets, I supposed it must be quite bright, otherwise they couldn't have done their work. But I couldn't tell down in my lair in the dark, where I was having no less a hard time of it than they were above. The scraping, searing, pressing and probing sensations around my chest had already gone on without let-up for a couple of hours. 'How were things looking with that reserve battery,' I asked. Not too good. After all this labour and nothing to show for it the operator sounded less calm. They would have to improvise something, he said. So one of the assistants went away and came back with electrodes, which he taped to my chest, connecting the cables to an external pacemaker mounted on a stand behind my bed. As soon as I was wired up the operator flipped open a laptop and put his fingers to the keys, but of course I was his interface with the living world, it was I who was the screen on his machine, the moving hand on his clock, and the instant he touched the keys the screen went blank, the clock stopped

TWO

When the Eye of the Day Opened on Lefó

Waiting-for-the-rain-to-pass

The wedding party had been caught by the downpour just like I had. In ten seconds we were wet through. We ran into the long house by the river and took refuge while the downpour lasted. That had been two hours ago, when I got off the bus that ended in Mataitu. All that time it came straight down like a beaded curtain unfurled from the sky, solid-state rain that seemed to fall without motion.

The men kicked off their sandals and sprawled on a dais in the half-light of the long house, smoking and drinking tea; very much on their dignity for all that. I suppose I call it a long house because it was a long airy wooden structure, once a godown, perhaps, for cargo travelling by river. Now it was doing service as a tea house. I counted six of them, six young men on their way to a wedding, composing a tableau both refined and tigerish. All but one wore gaudy sashes folded into a kind of turban; embroidered silk jackets left open to reveal shadowy chests with glints of light on moist bare skin; skirts of sarong in sombre colours bunched between their knees. The sixth wore a buttoned tunic, dark glasses and a black hat in the Sukarno style. Their women sat separately in bright sarong, stripping and weaving palm leaves into plates with upturned edges on the floor. Neither group paid any attention to the other. But for the children who ran back and forth between them it might have seemed they had nothing to do with each other.

The man at the centre of the group held a cock under his arm. He never left off stroking over the cock's comb and the back of its neck with the two extremely long fingernails on his index and middle finger, rhythmically, calming the bird, almost inducing in it a state of hypnosis. From time to time he extended his arm, offering the cock a perch, where it could be seen and admired in all its finery – a magnificent fighting breed with burnt orange and black plumage flecked white. The cock must have been used to being admired, and it didn't care. It settled frostily on the offered perch with no regard for anything around it, only the aloof unseeing stare of a fighting cock inflated with the all-possessing sense of its own superiority. Its owner held up the cock to show it off better. Glints of light betrayed the razor spurs taped to its claws. I was struck by the proximity of razors, claws and fingernails. There would be a cockfight at the wedding, the waiter said, or rather shouted, to make himself heard over the din, when he brought me my tea. They would bet sums up to a million rupees. A hundred dollars – a fortune.

From my vantage point on the river side of the long house I watched a bulldozer moving earth along the shrinking margin of solid shore between river and sea. Probably a channel was being opened to divert the flood water. The level had risen a metre in the couple of hours I had been sitting there. I could feel the swirling motion of the river through the floor. The rats rose with it. Flood debris came drifting by, islands of matted vegetation in which animal cadavers lay entangled, a grove of palm trees, one end of a wood-frame house. With the swirling motion of the river there sometimes came cool exhalations, moist gusts of air that passed quickly through the long house and died out. The never ending barrage of rain on the tin roof drummed itself into my brain until I ceased to hear it. Happenings around me were detached from their sounds. I watched the rain silently pit the surface of the river with a fine-meshed net. The rain splashed inaudibly through the roof, cascaded from the gutters without a sound. Noiseless cars with their headlights on groped through the curtain of rain in the street as if they were blind.

It was like this every day during the rainy season, stupefied afternoons – usually afternoons – given over to waiting in whatever shelter one could find. This seemed to be one of the chief occupations of the population, at least in rural Indonesia, for as long as the monsoon lasted. Whoever we were, wherever we happened to be, the rain threw us together under such shelter as was available. In a shop entrance, under an awning or the nearest hospitable tree, I made the best of an enforced acquaintance with strangers on the common ground, really the common state of mind, which we shared for the duration of waiting-for-the-rain-to-pass. Every day I became close to people I would never see again.

Under the Ficus Tree

When the rain stopped, a silent-movie world went audible again. Outboard motors blasted off down the river. The traffic rolled on cue onto the soundtrack of the street. Emerging a little regretfully from the tea house, I stepped back into it. My waiting-for-the-rain-to-pass companions soon scattered, the wedding party by barge down river.

During the brief twilight, life swarmed back into Mataitu. Night descended. Very quickly it was dark. The darkness enclosed me like warm water, something to trail one's fingers through, the aftermath of the heat of the day washing softly around one. The rain had filtered the air and cleaned the street, but still the shopkeepers came out with bundles of bound feathers to dust off the wares at the front of stores exposed all day to clouds of sand trailed by vehicles passing down the road. This appeared to be the ritual wherever stores were closing. In Mataitu it was not a road that ran past the stores, just a dirt track, ending in a trench at the town's main intersection. The public works department had dug up the street for some project which had been abandoned. The deep trench had been left as it was. A woman stood motionless with a tray of shopping on her head, as if undecided whether to risk a jump over it or to turn back the way she had come.

Flickering points of light sprang up everywhere in the dark. They were little oil lamps, sometimes just rags spitted on a stick and soaked in oil. They provided light for the owners of the food stalls that had appeared on the street as soon as it grew dark, offering noodles, vegetables and rice to labourers on their way home. This was the hour of the motorbikes, the corso of small shiny machines parked in the middle of the road, surrounded by admiring boys oblivious of the traffic. I walked past a brightly lit entrance from which Indonesian pop music was blaring. DISCO read the sign over the door. I went in to ask the way. Cassette tapes were sold at DISCO. There was no dancing inside the tiny shop, but young girls pretending to shop arched their backs and pushed out their breasts, watched by the boys who sat smoking on their motorbikes outside. They paid no attention to the group of shawled and gowned girls, carrying oil lamps to light them home.

The storekeeper in DISCO didn't know where the Soedjono guest house was, so I asked one of the motorcycle kids. Up there, he said, pointing back over his shoulder. I looked at the dark mountain and decided it would be a long walk with an uncertain conclusion. The motorcyclist must have thought the same thing. He offered to take me up there for ten thousand rupees. Five thousand, I said. He nodded and flicked his cigarette into the road. I paid him the money and got up behind him.

The motorbike drove out of the village and followed a track that led up through a dark forest without any sign of human habitation. The air became cooler the higher we climbed. As the track levelled out a light became visible in the dark, revealing a vaguely Dutch-looking house with curving gables, standing on its own in a clearing dominated by an enormous ficus tree. It was no longer a private residence, the guide book said, but had been converted into a guest house still under the family name. The motorcyclist dropped me off at a dimly lit entrance with a sign outside reading 'Registration'.

The place seemed to be deserted. *Selamat malam*, I said into the emptiness, and when there was no reply repeated it several times. It was like saying a prayer, words spoken in solitude on my own behalf. But after a minute the prayer was answered. I heard a noise and a man came out of a dark niche in the wall behind the counter where the keys were hanging, rubbing his eyes. Apparently I had woken him. He had on a sarong and was naked from the waist up. He could let me have a room for forty thousand rupees, he said. I signed the register. He handed me the key to Room 1 and pointed to an outhouse just visible through the door. The keys to all the other rooms were still hanging on their hooks. Apparently I was the only guest.

It was a clean room with white sheets on the bed, a fan that I wouldn't need and a blanket I reckoned I might. I had come up only a few hundred metres on the motorbike but already it was much cooler in the hills than on the coast. I was grateful there were no mosquitoes. I would have been too tired to unpack and hang up my mosquito net. Changing my shirt, I caught a glimpse of my chest with its long white scar in the mirror over the bed and looked away, disturbed by what I

80

saw. I lay down to rest for five minutes before going to the reception to ask about something to eat. Instantly I fell asleep.

I was half-woken by something nagging and battering in the night. It might have been rain. It might have been a dream. It might have been a doctor trying to bring me back from the dead. It tried to tug me up. I struggled with it briefly before keeling back over into sleep. I awoke again later to a feeling so distinct, so completely formed, that it must have carried over from something I had dreamed, something which had welled up during sleep. It was a feeling of deep sorrow, for which I knew no cause. 'I grow out of this sorrow like a tree growing out of its shade.' I repeated this sentence several times to myself, like a mantra, before I fell back asleep.

Later I woke to what I thought was the familiar ringing sound caused by the tinnitus in my head. I lay and listened. It was something else. In the night outside I could hear voices keening. I got up and opened the door. It led onto a veranda. I slipped into my sandals and walked along a path. The path ended on a rocky outcrop, where I stood and listened to the sounds around me. As the darkness thinned into threadbare light, the sound of more and still more of those harsh strangled cries rose up from the valley below. All around me on the mountain were the invisible dwellings from which the chorus of voices came, praising the greatness of Allah. I had left Buddhists and Hindus behind me in Bali and had arrived in a Muslim enclave on a Christian island.

At daybreak the chorus ceased. In the grizzled light of dawn I could make out figures moving in the landscape, women carrying bundles. Along the terraced slopes beneath me they came to wash or do their washing in pools that formed where spouts came gushing out of the bamboo pipes channelling spring water into the paddies. In the distance I saw a horde of small brown naked bodies jump into one of these pools with a hardly audible splash. Just beneath me stood an old man, staring into the tree above him at a large green fruit. On the soft green mountain it felt to me like a magic place, full of mysterious comings and goings, sounds and smells that harboured memories or the illusions of memories.

Hearing voices, I turned round. Labourers had appeared at the end of the drive carrying boxes of plants, which they set down on the lawn bordering the veranda of the outhouse where I had slept. A woman stood on the veranda and gave them directions. A man of about seventy, whose leg had been amputated above the knee, leaned

81

forward in a wheelchair at her side, smoking while he listened to what the woman said. She was a distinguished-looking lady, a few years younger than the man I took to be her husband, with the patrician manner of a person who had been giving instructions to servants all her life. I followed the path around the ficus tree and along the tennis court until I was walking back towards the couple on the veranda. I wished them good morning. They returned the greeting, perhaps mildly surprised to hear Indonesian coming out of my mouth. While they continued to discuss the bedding-out of plants I strolled on, taking another turn past the tennis court. Clusters of bougainvillaea had taken over the wire fence, largely concealing the court from view. The posts were still there but the net in the middle had gone and weeds had sprung up all over the place. It was a long time since anyone had played tennis here.

The branches of the ficus were so spreading, its foliage so dense, that it was noticeably darker, cooler, in the shade underneath it than when one emerged into the morning sunlight. Many other large trees with an almost extravagant leafage like the great ficus at the centre of the drive dotted the extensive property. I guessed they had all been planted at the same time. Maybe they went back a hundred years. They were already 'large, luxuriant trees', according to my mother, when she described them at the time of her visit here half a century ago. Maybe they had been planted by a predecessor of the man in the wheelchair with the amputated leg. In those days, when the Soedjono guest house was a private residence, he might still have had his leg. The court would have had its net. In the cool of the mornings he and his wife might have played tennis with their guests, young people like themselves. Looking up into the boughs of the ficus tree, I closed my eyes. If I listened into the stillness long enough I might still be able to hear it, the *plip-plop* of a tennis ball striking the strings of a racket.

The Coral Builder's Island

I flew into eastern Flores in the afternoon. It grew close and sticky in the aircraft cabin as we taxied in to the terminal. The air-conditioning wasn't working properly. The plane jolted over cracks clearly visible in the paving on the runway. Through the portholes of the old Junkers propeller machine I could see the wreckage of a hangar on one side of the airstrip. The roof had twisted and collapsed in the middle. It hung impaled on two bent pylons that had remained standing at either end, as if tossed and gored by the horned eaves of some futuristic Buddhist temple designed in torn steel and broken glass.

Mans Gerardus was waiting for me at the bottom of the gangway. With age he seemed to have shrunk. He was much slighter than the imposing figure I remembered from his visit to Geneva ten years earlier, and more like my father Edward Smith than the similarity in the photograph sent to me by my uncle Arthur had led me to expect. My father had already put in an unexpected guest appearance, thanks, well, to his violin, I suppose. That must be why. It was the first time they had ever seen or heard a violin in this place, said Mr Soedjono in the conversation we had before I left the house his grandfather had built. That must be why he could still remember the *orang asing* so well, the fair-haired woman from Europe who gave him a peppermint, if I got his meaning correctly, and her husband, described in more detail than my understanding of the language was able to absorb, the small-built, dark-skinned violinist – this bit was certain – who might almost have been Indonesian.

From the airport we took a taxi into town. Several years had passed since it had been at the epicentre of an earthquake that had killed thousands of people and destroyed their homes. To me it looked as if the disaster had struck only a week ago. Whole streets still stood in ruins. Some buildings had slumped on their foundations and leaned to one side. Others had folded up entirely. That had happened to his own house, said Mans as we left the town and headed out into the country. At the time of the earthquake he was a hundred kilometres away at the eastern tip of the island. He felt the earth shake under his feet. A chasm opened across the road down which he had just come in a bus. It was the last to get through. No other vehicles reached eastern Flores for days. As for the earthquake relief, Mans added wryly, the victims were still waiting for that to reach Flores, too. The international aid remitted to banks in Jakarta had yet to come through to the recipients for whom it was destined.

In a quarter of an hour we reached a straggling village by the sea. Mans had invited me to stay at his house. Having just learned that it had been destroyed by an earthquake, I wondered where we would be living. I noticed as we passed it that the harbour wall had collapsed, leaving only a pile of rubble sticking up out of the sea. I wondered if the earthquake had done that, too. The taxi pulled up under a palm tree where an itinerant food vendor had parked his cart. Goats nibbled at the refuse in the road. Three men squatted on the sidewalk in the shade. They greeted Mans like an old friend. I thought we might have stopped to have a chat with them, but it turned out this was as far as the taxi was going. For the last two kilometres we would need a boat, said Mans, pointing to an island in the bay. That was where he lived.

As Mans and I were putting my luggage into the boat and climbing in after it the sky darkened. The fisherman who owned the boat pushed off and jumped in. After a few tries he started the outboard motor. Mans shoved my bags under the awning because it would begin raining, he said, before we reached the island. Halfway out there the rain came down and shut us in. We couldn't see either shore. The bay disappeared. Mans and I sheltered under the awning in the middle of the outrigger. Soon we were sitting ankle-deep in water. The boatman crouched at the tiller out in the rain with his knees under his chin and a pointed straw hat on his head. The rain engulfed him. Waterspouts stood off from his shoulders like epaulettes. Rivulets coursed round his neck and poured down his legs.

A dark green line of shore loomed and disappeared again as the fisherman put the boat into reverse. Mans jumped off the stern and stood up to his knees in the water. I passed him my two bags and splashed after him up the beach. By the time I reached the shelter under the trees the double outrigger had become no more than a spidery grey shape teetering on the rain-swept plain of the sea. It was only another hundred metres to the house, yelled Mans over the percussion of the rain on the corrugated iron roof. We made a dash for it. Half a dozen dwellings stood in a line under the crashing trees. Beyond them there was a brick cottage fronting onto the rocky beach.

For the next ten days it rained with almost no let-up; a biblical rain, a deluge to wash out the world. During this long waiting-for-the-rain-to-pass under the cramped circumstances of a one-room cottage I could have had no better companion or more painstaking teacher than Mans. Everything exchanged between us was said twice. First he spoke in English, then repeated what he had said in Indonesian. Later he spoke only in Indonesian and I paraphrased in English what he had said. My Indonesian improved, but it was Mans making progress for me. It continued to astonish me that the cultivated English spoken and the refined ideas expressed by this dock labourer's son who had left school at the age of twelve was completely self-taught. The thought that it might be no less remarkable for an orphan who had spent his life as an insurance company employee in Switzerland to have taught himself Indonesian for no more pressing reason than curiosity didn't cross my mind. This wasn't modesty. Such were the assumptions of ingrained European condescension.

Mans had retired from his job with the department of fishery a few years previously, just before the great earthquake destroyed his house and killed his wife, who happened to be asleep inside it. His son worked in Malaysia. His daughter had married and moved to Java. He could have gone to live with either of them, he said. But when it was discovered that the earthquake had also destroyed a popular tourist attraction, just that coral reef in the Flores Sea where my parents were said to have been diving when they drowned, the Nusa Tenggara board of the environment found something else for Mans to do. He was appointed a builder of the ruined reef. He monitored pollution. He bred marine fauna and flora and grafted them onto the bed of the largely still barren sea. His task was to build the broken coral back to health.

They gave him a house on a whale-shaped island you could walk around in half an hour. There was a narrow rocky shore along one side of the whale and a sandy one on the way back to the tail. It was a bristly kind of whale. Trees grew all over the island to within thirty metres of the sea. In the mornings, when there was a break in the rain, I took off my clothes and waded into the shallows. I sat down and enclosed myself in the sea. I immersed the scar all the way up to the collarbone. I drifted through the shallows with a snorkel mask, lazing with coral fish so tame that they nipped at my fingertips, but I didn't swim. Mans said that the best snorkelling was along the shore of another island a hundred metres away, but I was shy of the water and stuck to our island. There were groves of a kind of pine that grew around the Mediterranean, papaya and banana trees and a thorny scrub so dense it was impossible to pass through it. There were birds, butterflies, cockroaches, snakes and lizards. There was no water, however. The developer who bought the island installed tanks and had fresh water ferried over from the mainland. He built a long house, a kitchen and staff quarters with electricity in the middle of the island and holiday huts on the shore. Lots of tourists came to the island resort in the first two seasons it did business. Then the earthquake destroyed the coral that had been its main attraction. Few tourists visited the island now.

During the rainy season Mans was the only inhabitant of the island. There was a fixed phone line to the mainland in case he needed anything, a freezer in case he ran out of food. He put me up in one of the palm-thatched tourist huts and cooked for us in the resort kitchen. We had entirely to ourselves a dining-room in the long house the size of a tennis court. Behind the kitchen Mans kept the salt water tanks stocked with the coral fish he was breeding, many of which I knew. He had other tanks in which he experimented with the marine flora he hoped to transplant to the reef. Close to the shore he had also dug out a knee-deep trench, fitted it with plastic which he filled with sea water, and built a shelter over it. It became home to hundreds of turtles, not much longer than my thumb at the time of my visit. As they grew larger and became able to fend for themselves Mans introduced them to the sea. He paddled round the islands in the bay and released them in warm shallow waters where they would have the best chances of survival.

In a week or two, when the rainy season ended, he would be busy again. For the time being there was little to do. We sat on the covered veranda of his cottage and played canasta as we drank chilled vodka and watched the rain fall. In two languages we put together a scrapbook of the episodes in Mans's life from the big island of Flores on which he was born to the small one where he now lived and hoped to die, so small that it had been given that as its name, *Pulau Kecil*, Small Island. His life became the island, washed round by a mythical sea, fables of the animals he had taken out of it as a young man and put back into it when he was old, what he called the tidal movement of his life, flow in, flow out. His life had achieved a balance, he thought, which in the end outweighed the losses he had to bear.

Mans showed me his scars but I never showed him mine. I knew that so long as I kept them hidden I was far from achieving any kind of balance. I said nothing about Kozue. I still felt sore and ashamed.

When another week passed and still the rain showed no signs of letting up Mans called the mainland and asked for the ferry to come and pick me up. I was given detailed instructions on what to do. Once I reached the mainland I should catch a bus to a place called Lapang Buhan. There I was to make my way to the *rumah sakit*, a mission hospital run by the Catholic order Spiritus Dei, and when I got there to inquire for a Belgian priest named 't Maart. Pastor 't Maart had been living in Indonesia for fifty-five years. Although now in retirement, he was still active at the hospital in Lapang Buhan, where Mans had met him a few months before and brought up the matter I had first asked him a decade ago. The Belgian priest knew all about me, said Mans. It was this priest who had taken care of me after the death of my parents, and who had made the journey with me to Switzerland when I was two years old.

Waiting-waiting

I caught a taxi to the bus terminal, but as the taxi turned onto the main road the driver saw the bus coming, got out and stopped it so that I could board it without delay. I congratulated myself on having made it just in time. The bus was empty. I had my pick among a dozen of the disembowelled seats from which dirty yellow styrofoam poured. After ten minutes we reached a terminal, presumably not the one the bus had just come from. Lapang Buhan, yelled the conductor a couple of times through the open door of the bus as it took a couple of turns round the terminal, and then more urgently: Lapang Buhan! But no one was interested.

Soon we were on our way again. We passed a turning that looked familiar. This was where the taxi driver had stopped the bus for me to get on it half an hour ago. I checked with the conductor if it was headed for Lapang Buhan. *Wah!* Headed, he seemed to agree. But first looking customer-customer. That sounded reasonable. The bus was empty. This time we made a left at the main road instead of a right and pulled up at another terminal. A young couple got on. There were now three of us on board, assisted by three bus company employees. They took no fares but shared the driving and the shouting. 'Lapang Buhan! Anyone for Lapang Buhan?'

We circled the town perhaps a dozen times on as many routes. I had been patient first, then indignant, then annoyed, before I was finally resigned. None of the other passengers showed the least sign of impatience. I realised I was making my acquaintance with *jam karet*, an Indonesian version of flexitime, rubber-band time so expandable that you quickly lost sight of both ends. The bus had no fixed departure time, let alone one of arrival. It would depart, in due course, but only when there was agreement that it would be of advantage to do so. Passengers could help with this process of consensus finding. They could suggest where other passengers might be located. The sooner the seats filled up, the sooner the bus could leave. Roaring and shaking, it wallowed off over dirt tracks in search of possible candidates, a sick woman with a baby and a grandmother living in the middle of a plantation. They would probably have been unable to get to the bus and had counted on the bus getting to them. Other passengers apparently had to be persuaded, more than that, to be actively pursued to make the journey. Lapang Buhan? *Ibu-ibu bagaimana?* Perhaps they did have a vague idea of travelling to Lapang Buhan some time. But with this bus? Bus would leave them to think it over and come back for them in half an hour. Anyone for Lapang Buhan? Some now agreed to come aboard. Others had meanwhile thought better of it.

Wherever the bus went it provided people with an opportunity to receive or pass on news. It delivered packages, groceries, a live goat missing half a leg, free lifts to schoolchildren. It took four hours to get started on the road to Lapang Buhan. During that time the bus company had shown itself to be a remarkably versatile and public-spirited institution, providing transport, delivery, postal and welfare services to the community without bureaucracy and by maximising the one resource there was no shortage of – time.

Between waiting-for-the-rain-to-pass and waiting-for-the-bus-to-depart much of the time I had so far spent in Indonesia had been taken up with waiting for this or that; not exactly wasted time but not optimised either. I waited, in a state of quite unfounded expectancy, between one event and another. After one thing had happened I waited for the next to take place. My waiting, even when I occupied myself with a book, was a gap. In their own language I heard that the local people waited-waited, apparently in the same kind of way they walked-walked. It didn't seem to be a waiting *for* anything or a walking *to* anywhere in particular. Waiting-waiting had no object, or none that couldn't be deferred, walking-walking no unalterable destination. However quotidian it might appear to be, it was a state of being, entire and self-fulfilled – not-waiting, in fact. This was the quotidian sublime.

The walker walked not, neither did the weaver weave. Nor, come to that, did the waiter wait. Once I was ready for the text I didn't have to go to it, not by an act of my own memory, it came to me of its own accord. This was the subjectless state at the root of the paradox from the Upanishads. Briefly, dimly, it illuminated my mind and warmed my heart. The other passengers in the bus talked, munched banana fritters, looked out of the window and slept as I did. But while I was always aware of being in transit between one place and another, they were nowhere other than on the bus. They were not inwardly straining, as far as I could tell, to already be in a place at which they had not yet arrived. I decided to stop inwardly straining. Step One. I put away my book and tried to be like them, just sitting-sitting on the bus. Step Two . . . but the quotidian sublime wasn't as easy as it looked.

The Man with the Conch

Why the inward straining? What, after all, happened when the waiting ended? A conclusion worth waiting for? A real insight? A new departure? When the bus dropped me off at a clearing in a forest the waiting would begin – began – again, albeit in expectation of a for me potentially momentous meeting, at the isolated mission hospital on the outskirts of Lapang Buhan. A tall emaciated nun in a dark blue tasselled gown with a pannier of white cloth piled up like a picnic hamper on her head left me to my own devices for half an hour while she went off in search of Father 't Maart. Birds shrieked in the surrounding trees. I watched goats straying over a dusty compound, copulating with a casual interest that was easily distracted by the sight of something edible. It was not the backdrop for the momentous meeting I had imagined. If the birds continued shrieking and I watched the goats copulating for ten minutes more I knew I would begin to get depressed.

But the tall nun managed even better. She returned with news that disappointed me – disappointed wasn't the word: hurled me into deep confusion, a dungeon of dismay. Father 't Maart had left for Jakarta only the day before and was not expected back for a couple of months. Could she be of assistance in any other way?

She could be of assistance by taking responsibility. What do I do now, I wanted to ask her. What happened to the long journey I had made, not to mention the heart surgery I had undergone to have a maintenance-free bio-valve implanted, if Father 't Maart wasn't here? Please what, in the absence of the Belgian priest, was I now supposed to do with a life that had been restored to me largely for the purpose of finding him? Instead I chattered away, playing my Indonesian shadow play. *Tidak apa-apa.* It didn't matter. In the meantime, perhaps, just waiting-waiting. Ha ha! I made light of it. The tall nun appraised me warily. I would go to the harbour, I said, where I hoped I would be able to catch a boat to Timor. And slinging a bag over each shoulder I set off down the road.

It took me an hour to reach the harbour. By the time I got there it was dark. I was exhausted. In the distance of the night a brawling-babbling ululation was audible, emanating from I couldn't imagine what source. It was punctuated at intervals by blasts on a horn, perhaps signalling the departure of a ship. I entered an alley guarded by someone in a uniform who was asleep in his box at the entrance. I found myself on the edge of a large concrete area, skirted by illumin-ated tent-like stalls and heavy with the rotten smell of the tropics, a heat-stirred compound of sweetness and pungency that arose from the refuse of fruit and vegetables, old tyres, oil and excrement piled up on the wharves. In the background I discerned a low building resembling a bus terminal. When in doubt about what to build in Indonesia, construct a terminal and it would answer to whatever purpose the building might later be used for. In this country all buildings served as waiting-rooms and their archetype was the bus terminal. The brawling-babbling cacophony issued from this building with increas-ing volume the nearer I came to it, and through its doorless concrete frames I was given a view of the pen of people and animals responsible for the hubbub inside.

A sign identified the building as the Nusa Tenggara shipping company terminal. A crowd of several hundred people seethed in the dimly lit arena inside – men, women and children for the most part asleep on the floor between crated doves, hobbled goats, pigs and trussed fowls, motorcycles, petroleum canisters, fish, vegetables, tiers of groceries sometimes balanced on the women's heads, and sur-rounded by the profuse array of odours and noises that went with all these belongings. An undertow of murmuring washed over the crowd, dissolving into muffled slapping echoes under the high ceiling, chas-ing each preceding one bat-like through the gloom. I stood on the edge of this mass that contracted and distended like an amoeba, and tried to breach it. On the far wall I could see what appeared to be a timetable of shipping departures posted over a row of ticket counters under a clock inset in a cross, but I seemed to get no nearer to it. Feeling dizzy, I went back outside.

Someone blew a horn close by. I had heard the sound before and thought it came from a ship, but it came from a man standing on the harbour wall blowing a conch. I had never seen anyone blowing a conch. I approached the man to get a closer look. He was a gang-ling lean-to sort of man dressed in a makeshift turban, shirt and shorts with a sarong draped over them, all much the worse for wear, nonetheless with a manner that contradicted the shabbiness of his appearance and even managed to suggest elegance. Facing the sea, he held a purse-shaped shell with inwardly curling rims and blew into it, his inflated cheeks reminding me of my childhood mentor, the pet-shop owner M. Garrault. He blew three blasts, waited for a while, then blew again. The clear strident tones must have carried a long way out to sea, wherever the sea was. It was low tide, and the sea had gone out so far on this moonless night that from the shore there was no sign of it.

The conch man went down into a squat, placing the shell on the ground beside him. He shook his head and clicked his tongue. Then he made a succession of crooning sounds – words, for all I knew, in an unintelligible language – gentle rocking sounds that curled upwards at the end and faded, as if he lost the melody when it reached a higher pitch. That Bapak Cor was scolding his fellow villagers, in the wryly bemused manner characteristic of the man, was something I would learn later on the not infrequent occasions when he drifted into the sing-song mode to express his bafflement at the behaviour of people around him. He pushed the turban up his forehead, scratched his bald pate with its fringe of curls and frowned, but seemed to be smiling through the frown.

Barangkali, he began all at once in Indonesian, apparently still talking to himself, although with a sideways glance in my direction that seemed to invite me to listen, there might perhaps be better ways of spending a night than crossing the sea in the dark to fetch an old fellow with pain teeth, waiting at the harbour in Lapang Buhan. Even if there were *beberapa urusan yang harus selesai untuk penduduk di desa* – various affairs to be undertaken on behalf of the village people, like buying diesel for the Yamaha engines, batteries for Pak Ani's radio, cough medicine for Nasu's wife – why cross the sea on a dark night when you could sit comfortably at home with a jug of *tuak*? Who would reproach that serene man who preferred jug of *tuak* to job of fetching pain-teeth *bapak* home? He spoke slowly and distinctly, not, it turned out, for my benefit, because I was a foreigner, but because this was how Bapak Cor habitually spoke, wry speech that went with the wry manner. Although I didn't follow everything he said there was no missing the ironic flavour of it.

He stood up again and blew another three blasts on his conch. This time a shout answered him out of the dark. He shouted back. There followed a long, it seemed angry, exchange between the mutually invisible parties. Bapak Cor shook his head and went into his bewailing sing-song mode, of which I understood not a word. Alternately clicking his tongue and bewailing, he walked over to a pile of five- and ten-gallon plastic canisters stacked on the edge of the harbour wall, reluctantly picked one of them up and clambered down the rickety ladder onto the beach. It would be a laborious way of moving fifty canisters, so I stepped in and started passing them down to him.

Preoccupied with his running commentary deploring the situation, Bapak Cor took my offer of help for granted. When we had got all the canisters down from the wharf, and he started carrying them two at a time to a point some way down the beach, I felt bound to continue a job I had voluntarily begun and helped him carry them the rest of the way. It took us a total of twenty trips or more to move all the canisters. Worn out, I flopped down on the beach. Bapak Cor produced a tin from a fold in his sarong and rolled himself a cigarette.

Where was I from, he asked. From Swis, I said. And going to Lefó? I said I had no definite plans. I might wait around for a boat to Timor. But we are going to Lefó, said Bapak Cor: Alo and Stanis, who at the moment were still sitting out there on a sandbank, waiting for the tide to float them off, and *saya sendiri*, Cor himself. Why plans? Boat was now. I could go with them. Arriving on the south side of the island, Lefó Selamat, when the eye of the day opened over the village where they pricked whales, *tikam paus*. It was the first time I had heard this phrase. Meaning you are hunters of whales, I ventured. Meaning, said Bapak Cor.

The tide rose in the channel beside which we were sitting, floating the refuse strewn over the beach, and a double-outrigger skiff came sliding silently into the shore. We loaded the diesel canisters onto the middle of the boat, then tied an awning over them. One of the men stood in the bows and pushed off with a pole. The other started the outboard motor. Wind came up as we gathered speed. The harbour lights disappeared in the darkness behind us.

Animal-around-the-Mountain

More lights came up as we rounded the mountainous tip of Monkey Island and followed the curve of the bay on our starboard side. Long-tailed monkeys used to roam over all of the island, Cor said, giving the island its name. A Muslim people lived here who also pricked whales, but only small whales, baleen whales too, because they did not respect taboo, and only from motor-driven *prahu*. They were not true hunters of the sea like the people of Lefó. He had visited the island once and not found it to his liking. Why not, I asked. *Kotor*, said Cor unhesitatingly. A dirty place. I was surprised by the contempt with which he spoke.

Emerging from the lee of the island into the open sea, the bows of the boat began to plunge. Spray broke over us in bursts. Cor told me to move up to the front of the boat. He and the old man called Stanis sat opposite each other on cross-ties in the middle of the boat and began to bail. I thought they were bailing out water that came in over the side, but when we had crossed the open stretch of sea and the boat was riding smoothly in the lee of the next island they still continued bailing. After an hour I replaced Stanis, who took his turn at the tiller while Alo bailed and Cor rested. So it went on with hardly a break, two men bailing, one steering, throughout the six hours we spent at sea. From time to time Stanis would crawl under the cross-ties, smearing something he took out of a tin into the cracks through which the water seeped. I wondered how he could see. Couldn't see, said Stanis in a rare, bitter utterance, didn't need to see, boat always leaking, same with wives, married two and buried both, lived in close proximity to leaking places all his life and knew them inside out. For much of the journey Alo and Cor conducted a conversation in Lefó to which Stanis contributed hardly a word.

Since leaving Monkey Island behind us I had seen not a single light on land or sea. The land was solid darkness, of mountains mostly, silhouetted against a lighter texture of sky or floating like vast black icebergs on a still lighter texture of sea. There was no moon but I could see the stars. I wondered if the relative lightness of the sea was a reflection of starlight. Sometimes something broke its surface. Once we steered through a squall of flashes that came like lightning flails over us before they vanished back into the sea. *Kemanu,* said Bapak Cor. This was a Lefó word. Apparently it meant flying fish. And once we saw curved wing-tips knifing through the water across our bows.

Already on the eastern horizon ahead of us the sea began to glimmer. When the eye of the day opened on it the sea seemed to body out, an ever rising expanse that overflowed towards us as the dark rolled back and the so solid-seeming mountains, paling into the background of the sky, receded with it, reversing the impressions of the night. In the dawn light I saw the first settlements on the southern coast of the island, sticks and tufts of thatch, like things that had been thrown away and gone unnoticed by the forest in which they had landed. Lefó proper, the village of Alo, Stanis and Cor, had many forerunners, many practice attempts on the run-in under the volcano which in the Lefó language was called Sack of Snakes; clusters of three or four houses with sampans hauled up a narrow strip of shore; habitations so makeshift they didn't even merit a name.

Places that could be identified began with a string of houses along a white scar of road, the first outlying community of Lefó, high up on a cliff, bearing a name translated by Bapak Cor as Animal-around-the-Mountain. Even higher up the mountain, barely visible in the surrounding forest, was a collection of dwellings called Does-not-have-Loincloth. It was so well concealed in the surrounding forest that I could only find it by taking a bearing with my finger on the steeple of a massive stone church with a tin roof, standing on the promontory overlooking the sea, and following it up in a straight line. But not until we rounded the promontory and passed within a stone's throw of the houses above that made up the community of Sitting-in-Palm-Tree, where Bapak Cor said that he and Alo lived, did we come within sight of a sandy beach tucked away in a cove and lined with a row of sun-bleached sheds where the whalers kept their boats. Without prompting from Bapak Cor I knew that I had arrived in Lefó.

It was not just excitement I felt during this stolen journey by night across the sea to Lefó. It was exhilaration. I had been planning to go in search of Wanda's relatives in Timor, but I had changed my mind on the spur of the moment and gone to Lefó instead. I was free to do just as I pleased. All those securities and support systems on which I had come to depend during my thirty-four years with Assurances Helvétiques were just so many encumbrances. I would jettison all that ballast. Living in Animal-around-the-Mountain, I would learn to make do with less. I had been given a second lease of life, with six months' leave from my job almost a mandate to do so. The wheel had come full circle. After fifty years I was returning to the point from which I had set out, to make a new beginning, I now knew, as a free man.

Lords of the Land

According to the lore of Lefó as related to me by Bapak Ani, a retired teacher and something of an ancient mariner, who administered the village's Hoard of Stories from his vantage point in Sitting-in-Palm-Tree, the ancestry of the present-day people of Lefó could be traced back through three different descent groups. He represented the score of households or roughly a hundred and fifty people who inhabited Sitting-in-Palm-Tree as the indigenous population with the oldest claim. Of the three they were the sole possessors of true tenure, theirs the lineage that provided what in other cultures were called chieftains and here were known as lords of the land. Sitting-in-Palm-Tree did not acquire its name, however, until the arrival of the second descent group on the back of a whale.

That they had travelled to Lefó on the back of a whale was the only uncontested truth among the many versions describing the arrival of this second group. Less certain was when and from where they had come. Pak Ani took the view that they came from islands far to the north-west, perhaps from Sulawesi, perhaps even from Borneo, but he thought that didn't particularly matter. What mattered was the great flood from which they had been fleeing when their boats capsized and they took refuge on the back of a baleen whale that happened to come swimming by. Baleen was the name for the family of whales that had comb-like plates instead of teeth hanging from the upper jaw. Why it should have been a baleen rather than a toothed whale that had done the ancestors this great service Pak Ani could not explain. It set them down on the beach at Lefó where the indigenous inhabitants, sitting in the tree tops tapping palm wine, *tuak*, as it was called, did their best to deter the new arrivals.

No room here, we're full up, they called down, hurling a few coconuts at them for good measure. Since immemorial times this had been a sufficient show of force to discourage visitors from staying. But the *orang paus* or whale people, to use a neologism of Pak Ani's, were not so easily put off. Since the palm tree people were protected by the natural stronghold of the promontory on which they had settled – not completely inaccessible but very difficult to reach by climbing up from the shore – and the whale people seemed content to make do with the beach, the two communities that came to define themselves by a process of mutual exclusion left each other in peace. But they were now no longer in a state of innocence. To cover their bare existence they needed names. From this time on they became known as Sitting-in-Palm-Tree and Back-of-the-Whale.

Floating log people, as the casual seafarers were called who made a chance landing in Lefó, might have been dissuaded from staying because of the arduous climb up to the promontory where papaya and banana trees grew. Nothing grew on the narrow strip of rocky shore. All that a castaway could expect by way of nourishment would have to come out of the sea. Worse, there was no fresh water. But by a stroke of good fortune the Back-of-the-Whale people found a spring in the seabed close to the shore which was uncovered at low tide. Thus, where many before them had failed and gone away, the flood immigrants who arrived on the whale succeeded and stayed.

According to Pak Ani, the third descent group was made up of individuals or groups of individuals who had reached the south coast after wandering through the mountainous and densely forested interior of the island. Pak Ani referred to these as *orang hutan*, literally forest people. An intriguing ambiguity arose with this Indonesian word. As a loan word orang-utan had passed into English with a specific zoological meaning. In the absence of a time scale, however, it was not clear to me whether the term as used by Pak Ani designated an anthropoidal ape of arboreal habits or humanoid forest-dwellers who had come to succeed them during hundreds of thousands of years of evolution.

The forest-dwellers, at any rate, traced their ancestry to Peni-Bamboo-Leaves, a girl child who was discovered inside a bamboo. They owed this discovery to two dogs. They barked so long at a stand of bamboo that the forest people stirred themselves and came to investigate. One of them split a bamboo open and found Peni-Bamboo-Leaves inside. With the splitting of the bamboo the forest people divided into two groups and founded separate communities. These they named after the two dogs who had sniffed out their ancestress, Animal-around-the-Mountain and Does-not-have-Loincloth.

I rented a room from Pak Ani and his wife in a hut that they normally let to visiting anthropologists, most of them American. There was no running water, no electricity, an abundance of mosquitoes, and a bucket of water to pour over yourself in place of a shower. Pak was thin and about sixty, the only person in Lefó who wore spectacles, which gave him a suitably bookish manner. I called his wife *ema*, the generic name for married women in the local language. Ema was plump, also most unusual in Lefó, perhaps evidence of having her husband's pension as a standby in times when other people in the village went hungry. She was a poor cook, or so I thought after I had eaten nothing but dried fish and maize for a week, sometimes with a bit of greenery thrown in, plucked from the bushes around the house. Later I discovered that unless fresh fish had been caught that was indeed about all there was to eat. Pak Ani and Ema had children who had long since left the village, which was why they welcomed guests, for company, as Pak confided when he had got to know me better.

The Americans were booked in again this year but so far had failed to show up. In the meantime I moved in as resident listener to Pak Ani's tales. After years of cheek-by-jowl association with anthropologists Pak did a fair impersonation of one himself. I got the impression that much of what he told me was no longer pristine testimony from Lefó but had been subject to an order more characteristic of a Western intellect than of the local cast of mind.

One wall of the anthropologists' hut was papered with complicated charts and graphs illustrating aspects of social organisation in Lefó. Red arrows conducted social interchanges in one direction and blue ones back in the other. They reminded me a bit of a diagram of the hot and cold flows in the manual of my central heating system at home. The most intriguing chart was the one showing cycles of marriage alliance in Lefó. Basically, this alliance was forged between clans that were wife-giving and clans that were wife-taking. Sisters had to be given to wife-taking clans and wives taken from wife-giving clans. Sitting-in-Palm-Tree and Back-of-the-Whale belonged to the latter, Animal-around-the-Mountain and Does-not-have-Loincloth to the former. Thus Pak had given sisters away in marriage to Animal-around-the-Mountain and had himself taken for wife a daughter of the Back-of-the-Whale clan. This far it was not too difficult to follow. But when I learned of all the sub-clans within the main descent groups the arrows on Ani's chart began to flow thick and fast. In the course of generations, with wife-givers by dint of necessity or perhaps just by oversight doubling up as wife-takers, the hot and cold flows sometimes got mixed up. In the many-branched family tree of Lefó a measure of monkey business was not to be ruled out.

What still lingered on was a sense of caste. Wife-givers were perceived as superior to wife-takers, a perception not confined to Lefó or even to Indonesia. To me it seemed self-evident that in the universal struggle for status members of descent groups like Animal-around-the-Mountain and Does-not-have-Loincloth were already put at a disadvantage by their names. More self-assurance was naturally to be expected of a man claiming kinship with Sitting-in-Palm-Tree than of a man who derived his pedigree from Does-not-have-Loincloth. Given the lack of consumer choice in Lefó, all the inhabitants were to some extent shabby but very few of them also managed to be genteel.

Bapak Cor was one of these, the scion of a long line of lords of the land whose prerogatives had gradually fallen into neglect, whose magic resources had gone rusty with lack of use. When I asked him about the ancient ceremonies that used to be held to end the rainy season or to keep the mountain from exploding, described to me, it seemed not all that long ago, in letters from Mans, he said it was years since such ceremonies had taken place. He was doubtful if people still believed in them today, and they wouldn't work unless people did.

Cor was a natural aristocrat, a gent with something of a disposition to melancholy and a taste for expensive living. It sounded preposterous for a man born into a society of scarcity that required everyone to work from morning to night simply in order to put food on the table, but what a man with Cor's temperament really needed was a conservative investment fund yielding five per cent per annum. This was the conclusion I reached when I had got to know him better. In Cor's society, based on a barter economy that still functioned largely without money, Lefó's visiting anthropologists would have felt bound to rule out the role model of decadent capitalist as an impossibility. In my view, however, Cor was there to prove them wrong.

His name, I learned, was an abbreviation of Cornelius. Distributed around the tin-roofed huts among smooth grey rocks that breached the ground like whales surfacing between the papaya shrubs of Sitting-in-Palm-Tree lived enough people with names like Cornelius to have filled a calendar of Catholic feast days. Beginning with Petrus and Paulus, all of them were *nelayan*, fishermen. If asked for a job description most of them would have preferred the term *matros*, meaning that they crewed on a boat. Among them there was a Gregorius, a Dominikus, a Benediktus, a Bartolomeus and a Matias. Some of them, such as Aloysius, had a particular expertise like weaving palm leaves into sails or mats. Cor, or rather Cor's entire family, played the conch with varying degrees of mastery. Cor played the Jew's harp in addition, extemporised with a variety of percussive instruments, usually to be found on the ground wherever he happened to be sitting, and described himself as a musician.

I never heard of anyone else in Lefó who blew a conch. It was hard to say why not. In a place without electricity, let alone telephones, a conch provided a means of sending messages over quite long distances. In Cor's family it was used to summon absent members for a meal, a meeting, a job of work that needed to be done or to bring something from wherever they happened to be. On occasion two conches might be used to conduct a conversation. The meaning of these signals was allegedly understood by other residents of Sitting-in-Palm-Tree as well. Neighbours listened in. According to Pak Ani, Cor and his wife had been known to have quarrels by conch. If the wind was blowing from the right direction, signals could be transmitted by conch when the signalee was several kilometres out at sea.

Cor himself could coax quite other sounds out of a conch. He could play it softly like a trumpet with a mute. These were moaning, under-the-lid sounds that escaped furtively from a suppressed blast. Cor liked to sit on a rock in some shady spot overlooking the sea and conch to himself or twang his harp. Between setting out for work in the morning and coming home in the afternoon he might pass a day doing nothing else. He was happy to be disturbed by someone coming by with a can of *tuak* and offering him a swig, quite content to be drawn by a conversational gambit or detain others with a subject he broached himself. Like the rest of Sitting-in-Palm-Tree he couldn't help but listen to the news on Pak Ani's transistor whenever it was working. The names of politicians, terrorists and the bombings they had perpetrated flitted through the trees around Pak's house. Cor tried to work out how they all fitted together, imagining a kind of United Nations building with interconnecting passages, secret doors through which the politicians and the terrorists made their entrances and exits, allowing them to meet when this was desirable and to avoid each other when it was not. He wanted my help with this undertaking, but I didn't have much to offer.

Instead we sat on a rock and considered the prospect of the sea below us. To my eyes it was a magnificent prospect we had from Sitting-in-Palm-Tree: the dark golden curve of the beach, the shallow waters blue-green beyond the surf before darkening as the sea deepened. To the east the bay was closed in by Standing Person, a ridge of mountains that fell sheer into the sea as if they had been sliced off. To the south lay thousands of kilometres of ocean. But Cor dismissed it all with a wave of his hand and a single word – *kosong*, empty.

At the beginning of the dry season in a week or two from now the whales would start coming up through the Straits of Timor. I gathered Cor wasn't much looking forward to their coming. He thought whaling was a job like any other, like working for an insurance company, for instance – he had not forgotten our conversation at the harbour – only not so nice. Most *bagus* of all would be a job playing in a jazz club. Bapak Cor shook his head and relapsed into his bewailing sing-song mode. Even at the best of times, when many whales came and the people of Lefó made a good living, it was hard long work all day in the heat, there were injuries, boats would capsize and the crew be left to swim. *Tena terbalik, matros berenang!* When the whales didn't come and the sea remained empty it was even worse, he said. The insufferable boredom, and at the end of the season the insufferable heat. For the last two or three years this was how it had been. He favoured the wet time of year from November to March, Cor said, when the whale boats were laid up and the whaler rested with them, savouring the damp smells that overlaid his snoozes on the bamboo couch, the percussive scoring of rain on the roof, the seasonal jugs of rain-cool *tuak* and the scampering of mice around the house of a Does-not-have-Loincloth kinsman high up on the mountain, where Cor went into retirement during the rainy season.

In the Garden of Skulls

I called on Cor's cousin, the boat master and harpooner Nasu, at his house in Back-of-the-Whale, with the cough mixture which Cor had bought for Nasu's wife Tika and forgotten to leave with her. At Pak Ani's suggestion I also carried with me a five-gallon canister of palm wine, purchased for two thousand rupees from Pak's neighbour, the mat- and sail-maker Alo. The family seemed to have something of a local monopoly on palm products. From the promontory it was a steep climb down to Back-of-the-Whale but no longer a hazardous one. Steps had been cut into the slope and stones cemented into the steps to keep them in place. Soon, it was said, a cut would be made for a road leading round the promontory so that four-wheel vehicles, if they ever came to Lefó, could drive all the way up to Sitting-in-Palm-Tree.

Probably not all that much had changed in Back-of-the-Whale since the flood refugees had climbed off the baleen and carried their chattels ashore. On the washing lines around their houses the inhabitants still hung out strips of whale meat to dry in the sun, presumably just as they had done when Portuguese ships first arrived in Lefó four hundred years ago. Along a slightly curving beach about a hundred metres long stood boathouses for some two dozen double-outrigger sailing vessels, or *tena* as they were called in the language of Lefó. The boathouses had roofs made of palm-leaf thatch. On all other buildings palm had been replaced by corrugated iron. It wasn't as cool or as pretty as palm leaf but cheaper. Behind the boathouses stood a row of brick huts backing onto the village street and another row fronting onto it. It led down the steep hill from Sitting-in-Palm-Tree through the village square and up another hill to the outskirts of Lefó, a football field, a church community hall and an ever lengthening cluster of newly built houses along the cliff. In Lefó and its outlying hamlets – Animal-around-the-Mountain, House-of-Three-Families and Does-not-have-Loincloth – lived a total of some two thousand people.

Nasu's house stood on the village square, still called Clearing-under-the-Banyan generations after the banyan after which it was named had been felled and replaced by a *budi* tree. According to Pak Ani, the banyan had been there before the village that grew up around it. When the air roots of the banyan began to turn a single tree into a forest, so Pak explained, and the village street became impassable, the banyan had to be cut down.

From Nasu I heard a different story.

The banyan tree was cut down on the orders of the Catholic mission that came to Lefó to Christianise the inhabitants. It was not the air roots hanging down from the banyan that troubled the mission – why should a mission feel itself troubled by air roots, Nasu asked – but the sacred stones set up as seats for the heads of the clans when they held their meetings under the banyan. These stones were ancient relics of the cults practised by his ancestors, Nasu said. They believed in *pung alep*, spirits which could not be seen but inhabited all the things around them. The Christian missionaries wanted to banish these spirits, to root out all traces of what they vilified as *guna-guna*, black magic. So when they cut down the banyan tree whose air roots, they said, were turning the street into an impassable forest, they also took away the sacred objects where the *pung alep* were believed to reside, such as the ancestral seat-stones under the banyan, and buried them in the foundations of a church they were building on the hill behind Sitting-in-Palm-Tree. Many people, said Nasu, his own grandfather among them, believed that cutting down the banyan was just an excuse for getting rid of the stones. A group of villagers abducted one of the spirit stones and hid it in a secret place. No one alive today could say where it was, for the events he was relating had taken place a long time ago.

I first saw Nasu in the yard beside his house where he was building a boat. A bright orange awning tied to the surrounding trees and a corner of the house provided shade for the boatbuilder and his assistant. They worked in the coloured light it filtered, an orange-tinted haze, which surrounded them like a tent. The keel was already laid, some of the ribs and the bottom strakes. Now he squatted and chipped away with an adze at the planks for the sides of the boat. His assistant held the plank, turning it as needed for Nasu to shape. *Reo*, he called when I came into the yard. This was a Lefó greeting to a friend, as I later learned to my surprise.

It transpired that Nasu already knew all about me from the old man who was helping him, Stanis, whom I in turn had got to know during the boat trip from Lapang Buhan to Lefó. Stanis must have told him how I had helped Bapak Cor to carry the diesel cans to the pick-up point along the beach. Probably it was this gesture of good will that had met with approval and earned me the *reo* greeting. Nasu would know that I was staying with Pak Ani in the anthropologists' house. He would know that I came from Switzerland and worked for an insurance company. Everyone in Lefó would know what anyone else knew. From the moment I set foot in the village I forfeited my claim to privacy and became public domain.

I found it difficult to tell how old the men of Lefó were. Probably they were younger than they looked. Hard labour and exposure to the sun had dried them up. This was probably exacerbated by the very little they drank when they were out in the boats, as I found out when I later accompanied them. Desiccated and shrivelled, the juices of his body dried up, Stanis looked seventy. He could have been sixty. Nasu might have been my age or even a few years younger, but he looked ten years older. When I asked him his age he hesitated, as if having to work it out first. He reached the conclusion that he was fifty-one. There was the same hesitation when I asked him how old his children were. He couldn't say for sure. Thus began a process of discovery for me which I would be reminded of almost every day I spent with the people of Lefó: how natural a mental habit it was of mine to quantify, to attach numbers to the things around me – perhaps to control them, to own them, to make them safe, to make them profitable, an insurance agent could think of many reasons why – and how alien it was to them. After I had lived for some time in Lefó, it became alien to me too.

During the months I knew Nasu I never saw him in anything but a pair of khaki-green army camouflage shorts. They were joined by a shirt and a hat when he went to sea, a concession to the toll the sun had taken of the Lefó whalers until quite recently. Long after the missionaries had put blouses on the women of Lefó the men had still gone out in their boats without a stitch of clothing on. I had seen photos of them in Pak Ani's records, charred figures like the remnants picked out of a furnace, vomiting and sometimes delirious, Pak said, from overexposure to the sun.

Nasu's shorts, shirt and hat were as scuffed as his body was, bore the same scarring and appearance of general fraying. He spent most of his working life either squatting in his boat-builder's yard or crouching on the harpooner's platform at the bows of a boat. Even when standing he retained a hunched appearance. I recalled the photos Mans had shown me of a harpooner flying through the air and landing on the back of the huge animal he was trying to kill. Into that image of the harpooner I had projected an ageless figure, which had remained in my mind ever since. My impressions of that idealised harpooner, the speed, strength and agility such a leap must demand of him, were still very much with me at the time I met Nasu – unlike the changing things they imaged, the images themselves didn't change. It came as something of a shock when I first set eyes on Nasu. I found it hard to believe that this buckled individual could transform himself back into a flying harpooner, capable of feats requiring the tautness of a young man's body and spirit – Nasu as he had been twenty-five years ago, perhaps, but not the balding, wrinkled, battered man who squatted in front of me in his ragged shorts.

Ini obat untuk batuk ema, I said, holding out the bottle containing the cough mixture for Nasu's wife. Ah, grunted Nasu. And *tuak*, I added. As he made no motion to take bottle or canister from me I put them down on the front door step. I glanced into a room with a concrete floor, a curtain, a votive picture of the Virgin Mary and not a single piece of furniture.

Nasu bawled out something. A woman's high-pitched, harsh voice shouted something back. Nasu laid down the adze and straightened up. *Mari*, he said, let us go. Stepping out of the orange shade of the awning into ordinary daylight he lost a certain warmth of tone and appeared paler. I followed him round to the front of the house. We passed under an arch supporting cascades of some yellow blossoming shrub and entered a miniature sandy cove, almost a replica of the beach it overlooked, bound by what at first sight I took to be some kind of stockade. It was made of irregularly sized club-shaped slats, the thin end rammed into the ground, the thick end sticking up, light grey in colour, like weathered boards. Some of them were not more than thirty or forty centimetres high. They were topped by a trellis with a vaguely bone-like appearance, entangling cylindrical objects I couldn't identify. I wondered what purpose such a stockade could serve.

The back seat of a car was placed on the ground in the middle of the sandy area, facing the sea. Nasu invited me to sit down and fetched another chair for himself. The car seat could have comfortably accommodated three, but as it was the seat of honour Nasu expected me to occupy it alone. For a few minutes we sat without talking, taking in the view from Nasu's front yard. House and yard perched on the edge of a kind of rampart, or sea wall, several metres high, built with dirt and stones. Some of it had collapsed, pitching rubble into the back end of a boathouse just below. The car seat was so aligned that I was able to look through a gap between the boathouse roofs at the sea. The tide was out, exposing part of a reef that appeared to extend to the mouth of the inlet. An ever-present smell of fish seemed to bear down on the village the further the tide receded. When the wind dropped and the heat came up off the sand during the middle hours of the day called *siang*, the stench enslaved one's sense of smell and made one a sufferer without recourse to any relief but to walk away up the mountain.

The canister of *tuak* I had left at the back door of Nasu's house now reappeared via the front. It was carried, with considerable difficulty, by a ragged, unkempt little girl about five years old. She had straggling hair and was wearing the remains of what might once have been a white frock. Frock and face, both were smeared with the same dirt from the puddle in which I had noticed her sailing a leaf when I passed down the street, clear winner of the contest for grubbiest child in the neighbourhood. Behind her came her mother in a printed cotton dress beneath which I could make out her ribs. I had never seen such a thin woman. Her face was grey and she looked feverish. Her mouth twisted into a smile on behalf of the guest, genuinely welcoming, I thought, though thereby making only more evident the expression of pain in her eyes. She set two tin mugs and a plate of what seemed to be sweet potato down on a stool beside me. She coughed and tapped her chest. *Batuk*, she said, less by way of explanation than as an appeal for interest in her condition. I knew that she must be Nasu's wife Tika, for whom Cor had purchased the cough mixture in Lapang Buhan.

Having furnished the necessary instruments, mother and daughter retired to a little bamboo cot by the house wall to watch the five-gallon *tuak* challenge faced by the two contestants inside the arena of the stockade.

Sorga! Nasu raised his mug and I followed suit.

We alternated as givers and receivers of *tuak*, plentifully. Perhaps there were analogies here – Pak Ani would know – with the equilibrium guaranteed by the observance of wife-giving and wife-taking rules, the observance of a principle of reciprocity in all things. Palm wine looked like lemon barley water. It didn't taste like an alcoholic drink. Palm squash might be the better name. Dispensed in pint-size mugs it quenched the thirst. When *siang* gave way to *sóre*, and the cool of the early evening relieved the burden of the afternoon heat, you could quaff four or five Nasu-sized mugs in a row and feel no effects beyond a refreshing return of liquidity to the parched cells of your body. On this, my first encounter with *tuak*, I was fortunate in the quality of the palm wine I had bought from my neighbour. It was fresh and smooth, uncontaminated by the generous helping of insects and flies usually washed up out of a canister, the acidic side taste that brewed up after a day or two in the heat. Alo had the *tuak* brought down that morning by a kinsman who tapped his trees high up on the slopes above Does-not-have-Loincloth. Palm trees, fruit, vegetables, hens and hogs, even Bapak Cor in his rainy-season retreat, all manner of life seemed to thrive better at higher altitudes.

At sea level, meanwhile, thanks in part to the *tuak*, of which Nasu and I had drunk getting on for a gallon, my position in the car seat in the fisherman's bower had improved. The wind had turned around, dispersing the worst of the landlocked smells of whale meat on washing lines and driving them back out to sea where they belonged. The light of *sóre* was softer on some of the more ugly sights around me, while the incoming tide made pleasant sloshing sounds as it unrolled waves against the beach, not unlike the growing murmur of voices from the cot behind me. Six children had now gathered there. I asked Nasu if they were all his. The number question gave him the usual pause for thought. Not, he exclaimed with force, and his wife concurred, no less vigorously, from the rear, where she set an ambush for which I was wholly unprepared. How old were my children, Tika wanted to know. Not if or how many but how old my children were.

Nineteen and twenty-two, I said without hesitation, the daughter being the older child, the son the younger. Two children seemed to be the minimum. Invention danced on the spume of *tuak*. The son had just finished school and was considering what to study, probably marine biology. The daughter worked in a bank.

Woh! called Nasu, giving me a nasty fright. For a moment I thought he had caught me out. But it was only a greeting to his boat-building assistant Stanis, who now entered the stockade via the yellow-flowered arch, followed by Bapak Cor. Stanis squatted. Cor joined me on the back seat of the car. We seemed to have run out of mugs – two were already in service – and the little girl improvised other receptacles as beakers for the newcomers to the *tuak* arena. Stanis made do with a coconut shell. Cor got the cap off a ten-gallon drum. Nasu poured. *Sorga!* I was still wondering how I had acquired two children, if it was a secret wish that had carelessly surfaced, or whether I had already begun to succumb to the expectations the village had of me. In Lefó a man of my age clearly had no business not having children. But fortunately Nasu changed the subject. He got up, walked over to the arch through which Stanis and Cor had just passed, pulled aside the hanging tendrils of yellow flowers and asked me what the arch underneath was made of. I took a closer look at it. It seemed to be bone, and it was, the skull of a whale.

The stockade around Nasu's front yard, all of it, was made of the skulls of animals harpooned by his father Aro, by Nasu himself or his son Ioh. The objects I had taken for weathered slats were the skulls of giant manta and smaller rays, killer whales, pilot whales and sharks, rammed into the ground and topped with a kind of fence, a wicker-work of bones taken from these animals' bodies. The arch by which I had entered this garden of skulls had been contributed by a male sperm whale, killed by Aro when Nasu was a boy just beginning to learn his trade. It was the biggest creature he had ever seen in the ocean. It may also have been one of the oldest. When flensing the whale they found embedded in its blubber an old-style Yankee harpoon that had gone out of use a hundred and fifty years ago. A visiting whale expert had once calibrated the size of the living animal on the basis of its skull measurements and told him that the whale must have been twenty metres long. Surprisingly, this enormous creature had not put up much of a fight. It had gone to its death meekly, Nasu said. Perhaps it was ill. Perhaps it was old. It lay down quietly in the sea and died. When the whale had ceased to thrash and could do no harm the boy was allowed to swim out, like all the other *matros* whose stabs had already given the animal its mortal wounds, and plunge his long knife into it before its life passed away. He climbed back into his father's boat, the blood of the whale pouring off his own body. Such were the rites of passage for a boy who would become *lama fa*, the making of the harpooner Nasu.

An Ill Omen

It rained that night for the last time. The roof of the anthropologists' hut leaked torrentially. I stepped into a large puddle when I got out of bed in the morning. The prevailing winds gradually came round from the south-west. With the advent of the south-east monsoon from the great landmass of Australia the dry season began in Lefó.

When Nasu was a boy, this was the time for his father and the other leaders of the clans to go to the mountain to call the whales. At a spot on the open hillside near Does-not-have-Loincloth stood a lone rock known as Nose-of-Whale. Nasu showed me the rock. It was the same kind of smooth dark rock as the ones that came up through the ground around my house. Nose-of-Whale was long and blunt. It stuck up at an angle and did indeed have an unmistakable similarity to the head, or, as some biologists preferred to call it, the nose of a sperm whale. It had become stranded on the mountain in the middle of the night. The whale was on its way back to the sea when it had been harpooned by daylight and turned to stone. At the tip of the projecting head one could still see the blowhole. To call the whales to come with the south-east monsoon the leaders of the clans inserted a blade of grass into the blowhole and tugged, to help the stranded whale get back to the sea. Then the other whales would come. But if the grass broke or you pulled it in the wrong direction, back up the mountain instead of down, no whales would visit Lefó.

In the old days all the clans had whale spirit houses. Now only one was left. It belonged to the lord of the land of Does-not-have-Loincloth. The whale spirit house looked to me just like any of the huts with a palm thatch and a raised floor that dotted the landscape all over rural Indonesia, providing people with a place to rest in the shade. The whale spirit house was a place for the souls of whales to rest. Certain relics of the whales also lodged there. There were none in the spirit house I saw. It had fallen into disrepair.

In the old days all the clans preserved the skulls of their ancestors in the boathouses on the beach, just as they preserved the relics of whales in the spirit houses. Nasu had handled them as a boy. At the start of the south-east monsoon the skulls were rubbed against the sides of the boat. This ceremony was an ancestral blessing that would bring the boats luck. There had been many such ceremonies, Nasu said. He indicated that a few of them had been kept, such as the occasional feeding of sacred stones, but the majority had fallen into disuse. The missionaries had removed the skulls from the boathouses and buried them in the church graveyard. Now a mass was held on the beach and the missionary blessed the boats before they put out to sea at the start of the season of deep-sea fishing. I was more intrigued by the old ceremonies Nasu mentioned. He seemed reluctant to disclose further details, however. I had to make do with the mass.

By seven in the morning hundreds of people had gathered on the beach. Women, children and visiting dignitaries, a number of them foreigners, sat in the shade of the boathouses. The Lefó missionary, assisted by another local priest, stood in cassock and surplice on the steps of the shrine leading down from Clearing-under-the-Banyan to the beach. In the early morning sun the two frocked men were already looking uncomfortably hot. A few tourists had arrived by truck the day before, among them two Italians who had found refuge with Pak Ani in the room next to me in the anthropologists' hut. A TV crew from Hong Kong was there to videotape the ceremony, and had moved into Lefó's only *losmen*. The Italians had spent a night there, too, a place on the waterfront where the air was so heavy with the smell of unseasoned whale meat hanging on the surrounding washing lines, the Italians said, that they had been unable to get a wink of sleep.

The men of Lefó distanced themselves from this rabble. With great dignity they sat out in the sunlight along the sea edge of the beach, a couple of hundred of them divided into two groups respectively facing east and west, dressed in their best sarong and shirts. Perhaps by chance the seating arrangements of facing ranks that mirrored each other resembled a pair of outspread wings. Seeing them for the first time in such numbers, I was struck by the ethnic variety of these men. Some of them had Malay physiognomies, like old Stanis. Others were aboriginal Austronesian types, like my neighbour Alo, with curly black hair and midnight skin. And some had the Mediterranean appearance and ambassadorial bearing of my friend Mans Gerardus, the kind of faces one might expect to meet on an Etruscan urn or a Roman coin.

A long, convoluted speech in a formal Indonesian I found difficult to follow preceded the celebration of mass. The priest asked God to send fish and whales to feed His children in Lefó. He asked Bapak to keep them from harm, to prevent wives from becoming widows, children from becoming orphans. Making reference to the Sea of Galilee and how Tuan had taught His disciples to become fishers of men, he appealed to them, as fishermen and the disciples' spiritual kin, to observe the rightness of ways befitting a Christian. To me this address sounded more like a sermon than the kind of emotional appeal that would summon *pung alep* to step out of the sacred rocks in which they slept, disposing them to deal kindly with the people of Lefó, filling their nets with the fish of the coastal waters, their shrines with the souls of the whales from the deeps of the sea.

When the address was over the men queued up at the steps to receive the sacrament. Then the priest walked the length of the beach, whisk in hand, and sprinkled holy water in summary fashion over the boats, almost hurled it, I thought, as if he was quite cross. The act had more of a dismissal than a blessing. He had now been standing in the sun for a couple of hours in full regalia and was perspiring visibly. Clearly he was impatient to retire with his colleague into the shade of Clearing-under-the-Banyan to do justice to the snacks the village had prepared there. I wondered if Nasu was as satisfied with these proceedings as with the rock-feeding, whale-tugging rites of his fathers, and rather doubted that he was. His attention, everyone's attention, must in any case have been distracted by the antics of the old woman who had been wandering around the beach throughout the ceremony.

I knew her by sight from her occasional visits to Sitting-in-Palm-Tree. She was the mother of Fina, the girl who did household chores for Pak Ani and his guests in the anthropologists' hut. If in the isolation of Lefó that had lasted hundreds of years wife-givers and wife-takers sometimes got mixed up, leading to taboo infringements of an incestuous nature, then that was not altogether surprising. The offspring that resulted were a burden to be shared by all the community. This was done not by segregating retarded children but by appointing them full-time members of the community's struggle for its daily existence. They were not expected to go fishing, to light fires or to cook meals, nor even to attend church, but they could fetch and carry, sweep, clean, wash and make their gargling sounds without restriction. But they had to pitch in. There was no suggestion of making allowances for such children. They were accepted and integrated just as they were, and I was surprised to find how normal for much of the time they then turned out to be.

Fina's peals of laughter belonged to the acoustic backdrop of Sitting-in-Palm-Tree. At first they startled me, but soon I found them blending in well with the barrage of squealing pigs, crowing cocks and barking dogs that laid siege to the house all day and night. Her mother, by contrast, was aloof and totally silent. She seemed always to be nursing some unspeakable sorrow. But when she showed up on the beach that morning she was in a cheerful mood for once. It was plain that something tickled her fancy. She carried a stick, which she used to poke around in the refuse on the beach. She seemed to have taken a particular liking to a plastic bag that blew around and eluded capture. Perhaps it was the bag's obstinacy to be captured that amused the old woman. But her laugh didn't have that sort of sound to it. It was more of a snigger. The plastic bag flapped around in the breeze. The old woman stalked it and sniggered. Sometimes she waved an arm in a dismissive gesture and could distinctly be heard to cackle. At some point I had the feeling that it was us she was laughing at, or, even worse, our ceremony.

Normally the villagers left their strange people to the strangeness of their ways without interfering. But more and more the men on the beach began to mutter at the old woman. They were so busy muttering their discontent that they ceased to pay attention to what the priest was saying. For the first time I understood what it meant to be a pariah. During the ceremony the weak-headed woman was the one dissenter on the beach; the rest of the community was against her. Everyone looked at her, wishing her good riddance. Even the Hong Kong TV crew had found the scene worthy of recording on video. Eventually a couple of able-bodied men bundled her off and put an end to the embarrassment. Later, people would say that the troubles which beset the village that season, culminating in the catastrophe caused by a *makhluk istimewa*, an extraordinary creature, had their origin in this unfortunate incident with the mad old woman.

Spirit of Yamaha

The old woman's performance on the beach may have provided an inauspicious start to the fishing season and left an unpleasant aftertaste. The business of the Yamahas, however, posed a much more serious threat to the whaling prospects of Lefó.

A couple of years previously a sampan fisherman by the name of Ino had acquired, imported and put to use an outboard motor for the first time in the fishing history of Lefó. With phenomenal success. Almost every day Ino's motor-powered boat returned with a catch while the crews of the traditional sailing vessels came home empty-handed. Returning empty-handed was nothing unusual to them. *Nasib*, said Stanis with a shrug. Such was fate. In Lefó the crews of the *tena* had always lived by this stoic philosophy without ever questioning it. The acceptance of *nasib* became something of a problem, however, when it became clear that the *nasib* applying to sailing vessels was not the same as the one applying to Ino's motor boat. With good reason. The *tena* were slow and cumbersome to bring round. Unless prey passed within a few metres of his platform on the bows the harpooner had no chance of a shot at them. But with a motor boat you could hunt down and kill even fast-moving animals such as dolphins.

The success of Ino's first fishing season with Yamaha backing must have caused serious doubts, not to mention envy, to take root in the minds of *tena* sailors. It was no contest, quite unfair. The consequences for Lefó's traditional fishing industry, which centred on sperm whales, were unthinkable. What had worked for five hundred recorded years might become obsolete within a single season.

But Ino was the victim of Yamaha hubris. Not content with the smaller stuff, the staple of dolphins, rays and sharks, he took on a medium-sized sperm whale. It was still quite a bit bigger than his boat. The whale dived, and on his way down demolished the stern of Ino's boat with a flick of his tail. The boat that had been baptised *Spirit of Yamaha*, breaking all boat naming traditions in Lefó, was damaged but could be repaired. The outboard motor, however, had sunk in a thousand fathoms of water and would never be seen again, a loss of ten million rupees.

I went to visit Ino at his secluded house high up on the mountain overlooking Back-of-the-Whale. Ino's wife had died. His three children had left the island. He lived by himself and appeared to be something of a recluse. Maybe it took a loner to initiate a course of action which, had it worked, would have pushed Lefó with one shove out of a world in which shadows of the Stone Age still lingered straight into the twentieth century. Ino's son worked in a factory in Jakarta. He had invested his savings in the joint Yamaha venture with his father, putting up half the capital and getting a loan from the bank for the rest. It was his son's idea, said Ino. Now the loan had to be paid back with interest. After the loss of his Yamaha Ino was back to old-style sampan fishing with nets. His daily catch provided enough food but no cash. Ino's son had a job and earned money. In seven years he would pay back the money they owed to the bank. Such were the costs of living in Jakarta that he would have to postpone starting a family until his debts had been paid.

This twist to the *nasib* of Ino and his son was pondered by all the fishermen in Lefó. There was agreement that the nose of Ino might have been held a bit high. Perhaps it only went to show that *nasib* was indeed even-handed after all, applying equally to everyone. From this time on Yamaha became established in the Lefó language as a noun meaning a motor-powered deep-sea fishing boat. It was something to be tolerated but not liked. The word went on to acquire connotations of a necessary evil, pride coming before the fall, and it came to be applied to cynical actions in any circumstances. I wondered what anthropologists a hundred years from now would make of the term. The traditionalists, older men like Nasu, had always known that Ino's Yamaha venture was doomed. They commented on the outcome without malice but not without satisfaction, because they had wanted it to fail, had indeed believed it must. Someone had deserved and duly got his comeuppance. Younger men, however, who perhaps lacked their fathers' long-sufferance with incurable poverty and had wanted the venture to succeed, sat around Clearing-under-the-Banyan discussing Ino's Yamaha and why it had gone wrong.

They came to the conclusion that it would have succeeded if Ino and his son had not made two mistakes. The first mistake was to have burdened the fabulous sum of ten million rupees on the head of a single person. The *tena* had always been run as co-operative ventures involving many families, who all shared its fortunes and misfortunes. The same must apply to Yamahas. The second mistake was to use a Yamaha to hunt sperm whales. A destroyed or damaged *tena* could be replaced or repaired at no other cost than labour. A Yamaha could only be replaced by cash, and nobody had cash in Lefó. At best they had reserves, heirlooms, such as the nugget of ambergris Bapak Cor had traded in Lapang Buhan to pay the dentist's bill. For as long as Lefó existed they had lived by barter, exchanging fish for the fruit and vegetables grown by the mountain tribes. They had not needed money. Whatever the people of Lefó required they either obtained by barter or manufactured themselves.

People outside Lefó did have cash, however. These were the sons and grandsons of villagers who had left the island in search of work as teachers, electricians, carpenters, mechanics, even the occasional professor or deputy to the UN. They could put up the cash or arrange the bank loans, sums wholly unimaginable for the villagers, to finance Yamahas that would pull anything from turtles to killer whales out of the water. Only sperm whales should be left well alone. Something like a collective sigh of relief must have rippled through the crews of the *tena*, perhaps a hundred and fifty men, all told. They would not become redundant after all. Their traditional role as whalers, a role that really defined Lefó and gave the village its soul, setting it off from any other fishing village in Indonesia, in South-East Asia, perhaps anywhere in the world, would not be threatened after all.

A year after Ino's abortive venture there were three Yamahas operating out of Lefó. They did well. Yamahas could easily take their catch to Lapang Buhan and sell it directly at the fish market for cash, where manta gills fetched a hundred thousand rupees. It wouldn't be long before the investors paid off their loans and began to turn a profit.

By the time I arrived in Lefó there were already seven Yamahas in operation. An eighth was currently under construction in a builder's yard in Back-of-the-Whale. This was the boat being built by Nasu. It was quite a bit shorter, narrower and lighter than the *tena* Nasu had traditionally built. Still, he seemed to underestimate the task, perhaps because he wanted to get it over with. It would be ready in four weeks, he said. He had been saying this for the month I had already stayed in Lefó. Building the boat was the reason why he had no time to go out whaling in the *tena* of which he was boat master. None of the other boat masters had time to go out whaling either. They all had one pretext or another for not putting out to sea.

Tena were individual beings, more than just boats. They were called by names commemorating ancestors or events a hundred years ago. It seemed to me a sign of the changing times that the Yamahas were known only by a generic term, not by the individual names they had been given. But unlike the *tena*, the Yamahas puttered off every morning and returned every afternoon with something to show for the day spent at sea. They had been doing so before the official start of the deep-sea fishing season and would presumably continue after it ended. Seasons no longer mattered to them. They were not hunting sperm whales, after all, and baleen whales were protected by taboo. I could see how independent they were, not only of winds and currents but of all the resources the village traditionally placed at the disposal of its arduous common enterprise, from the men who scoured distant forests for suitable timber to build boats that would withstand ramming by whales to the carpenters, harpoon-manufacturers and rope- and sail-makers – not to mention the skill and experience of whalers working under sail, their rituals and beliefs, and the collaboration of the *pung alep*, sometimes moody spirits that must be persuaded to endorse their enterprise. The sight of the Yamahas that could be started with a pull on a piece of string, jetting in a straight line out to sea without prayers or preliminaries of the kind that were indispensable for the launching of a *tena*, still took his breath away, Pak Ani confided to me. That a substitute for the joining-of-many-hands in the great struggle with the sea could so easily have been found seemed a kind of blasphemy to him.

Coming from a devout Catholic and self-confessed nationalist, who believed that Indonesia's greatness must lie along the path of modernisation, that was quite something. Although he never said so in as many words, Pak would probably have given the Yamahas his blessing in exchange for electricity. Throw in running water with sanitary facilities for every household and he might have agreed to the closing down of the spirits in Lefó. As a former teacher living in salaried retirement, he was one of the very few people in the village who had any cash. I later found out that Pak was a partner in an investment group operating two of the Yamahas while he continued to officiate as keeper of the Hoard of Stories enshrining the souls of the *tena*. Such were the contradictions a man had to live with in Lefó today.

Baléo!

Writing a letter to Kozue, I was dozing off one afternoon when the singing of the neighbour's girl kept pulling me back from the edge of sleep. I heard her now from one side of Sitting-in-Palm-Tree, now from another, flitting around and chirruping like a bird.

Baléo baléo baléo!

What a strange bird call, I thought. Perhaps it meant something. Then I heard others making the same call. A babble of voices could be heard approaching along the path from Animal-around-the-Mountain. Soon it seemed that I could hear *Baléo!* singing out all over the mountain. I got up from the bamboo cot where I took my afternoon nap, grabbed my rucksack, put on my sun hat and clambered down the hill to the path. Men and women from Animal-around-the-Mountain, with a flock of goats they were herding down to the lower village, stood on the edge of the promontory, looking out to sea. I couldn't understand what they were saying in the language of Lefó. What can you see, I asked. One of them turned to me and pointed an arm.

Paus! Lihat bagaimana semburan air! Besar? Tidak!

Somewhere out at sea a whale was spouting, but I couldn't make out anything. I asked if it was a big one and the man seemed confident it wasn't. I decided to go down to the beach to find out what was going on.

On my way through the village I stopped at Nasu's house. There was no sign of him or Stanis in the boat yard. I went round to the front of the house. Tika lay on the bamboo cot with her head in her little daughter's lap. *Baléo!* sang out Tika and her daughter too by way of greeting. They pointed in the direction of the beach. I scrambled down one of the broken places in the sea wall, threaded my way through the bits of spar, hanging nets, outriggers crammed into the narrow spaces between the boathouses, and came out onto the beach. Clusters of men stood there talking excitedly, looking out to sea.

I walked along the beach until I came to where Nasu's boat, the *Aro Tena*, lived. Half a dozen men were standing or sitting on the sand in front of the boathouse. Most of them I knew at least by sight. There was Stanis, sitting beside an even more shrivelled old fellow whom I had never met. Bapak Cor was there, a man wearing a felt hat with a Marlboro logo, a neighbour of Nasu's with a terrific scarred chest and a turban, whose name was Petrus but whom I immediately dubbed the Pirate. In addition there were a couple of young men inside the boathouse, who were checking the gear. Nasu was nowhere to be seen.

Can you row, Cor asked me. I said I could. And swim? I said I was something of a swimmer, too. A man came running along the beach towards us. I started to ask Cor about *baléo*, and what was going on. *Mari*, he interrupted me, pulling me to my feet, we need another rower in the boat. He told me to say nothing about whales. It might be better if I said nothing at all until we were back on land. He would explain later, said Cor.

The running man was Nasu's eldest son, Ioh, a very dark, handsome young fellow in a scowling sort of way. The moment he came to the boat he took a woven palm cover off the prow of the boat, picked up a couple of heavy round logs and tossed them onto the sand in front of it. The crew already stood inside the boathouse along either side of the two outriggers. They bared their heads. Cor nudged me to do the same. Stanis hurriedly muttered a prayer, of which I caught only the end. May the Virgin Mary always stand by us in our need. Amen, said the men, kicked away the supports propping up the boat and put their shoulders to the outriggers. All of ten metres long and made of massive teak-like planks, the boat didn't budge. I thought one might as well have tried to move a stone that size. *Satu, dua . . .* called Ioh rousingly from the bows, *satu dua tíga!* We all bent and strained. I felt a tug at my heart. I wondered if it was a good idea for me to be doing this. But now the boat just seemed to glide away as if we had given it wings. Bystanders ran back and forth, picking up the rollers uncovered by the hull as it passed over and laying them on the sand in front of the *Aro Tena* so that it could slide on rollers all the way down across the fifty metres of sand that separated the boathouse from the sea.

The *Aro Tena* went smack into the surf with a *woosh!* – and we all jumped helter-skelter into the boat any way we could as it went pitching out. I sat at the back on the left just in front of the helmsman, where Cor said I could do least damage and, hopefully, have the least damage done to me. I pulled out a short paddle jammed between a rib and side plank of the boat, took a stroke, missed and almost fell out. I was glad I had no rower behind me, fouling up his stroke. Old man Stanis was bawling out a rhythm for the rowers to keep time. *Wailabe, wailabe, wailabe!* I needed to get my balance before I could paddle, needed to lean forward more, to put my foot somewhere to give me leverage. But first I had to sit, on a portion of cross-tie, or thwart, about as thick as my wrist and offering half the space of an airline seat. The sail, the boom, various ropes and poles lay lengthways down the middle of the boat, taking up all the room. I managed a sort of crouch, one foot tucked under my backside, and belatedly hit my stride.

Wailabe, wailabe, wailabe!

Most of the men bawled out the chant every time they pulled on the oar. I heard one voice occasionally peppering our shouts with an explosive high-pitched *po po!* sound, another doing long teetering calls that sounded like the neighing of a horse. Only the helmsman behind me sat still and silent. The grim-browed Pirate and the man with the Marlboro hat sat facing us on a raised thwart, pulling awkwardly at short steep-angled oars in rowlocks fixed to the gunwale just in front of the harpooner Ioh. The latter was standing – perhaps hovering was the word, more bird than man he seemed poised for imminent flight – on a platform reaching out over the bows. The Pirate shouted at us with a thunderous face as if bringing down terrible curses on all our heads. Cor and Stanis bawled back. Soon everyone was yelling at the tops of their voices. The noise was deafening, the pace frantic. Ioh stood with wing-like arms stretched out behind, wrists striking his thighs, flapping his hand rhythmically, as if spurring us on to even greater efforts. Faster, faster!

To the left another boat pulled level with us. I saw one lidless wide-open eye, the name painted along the bows: *Horo Sapa*. Eyes were painted on the bows of all the boats, to spy out the whales, said Nasu, in the depths of the sea. But where *was* the whale? I still saw nothing, my view of everything in front blocked out by piles of tackle, heads, flailing arms, an about-to-soar harpooner on his platform. I watched the *Horo Sapa* now pulling ahead, a floating menagerie of howls, rowers writhing in effort, and thought: is this what we look like? To my right another prow nosed into view, fell back, nudged forward again. Another prow, and eye, and name: *Mata Tena*. I glanced over my shoulder. I was astonished how far we had already come from the shore. A mountain had sprung up behind us which you never saw on land. We were three in a race, three boats fleeing the Sack of Snakes out onto the Endless Water. One had already overtaken us, another was catching up. Ioh flapped his hands, beseeching more speed. The Pirate roared. I was so drained I could hardly ply the paddle, let alone delve more strongly into the sea to drive the boat on still faster. A mixture of groan and gasp passed through the ranks of rowers. All of us saw the blow at the same moment, a leaning tower of spume, surprisingly high, not the low bushy blow of a sperm whale, falling and slowly breaking apart about two hundred metres ahead on the starboard side.

Woh!

Shouts passed down the boat, it seemed bodily, made furious room between the rowers. Pieces of heavy iron were pulled out from the bottom of the boat and handed back in response – harpoons. Marlboro Man held them over the gunwale and dipped them in the sea. Ioh whetted them on a whetstone while his assistant laid coils of gradually thickening rope between the thwarts on the floor of the boat, section by section, in each of which two rowers sat, pulling frantically on their oars. From the lead section no thicker than a finger to the middle section as broad as an arm, the rope resembled a giant snake asleep in coils the length of the boat. Ioh took the largest of the harpoons, attached the lead rope and rammed the shaft of the harpoon into a long bamboo pole which his assistant had already taken from the rack on the outrigger and held ready for him. These two went calmly about their business while the rowers flailed and roared – I couldn't say what, but perhaps by way of whetting their own harpoons, applauding the protagonists, as if roaring down the whale and building their courage up. Ioh crouched on the bucking platform, toes squirming, seeking balance or strength to spring, his harpoon arm raised above his shoulder. Beyond this silhouette I could see the *Horo Sapa* pulling alongside of the whale. The harpooner flew and in the same moment was already thrown back, flung away by the recoil like a broken toy.

Seconds later we entered the whale's water, a dark, roiling patch of sea.

An animal, or the outline or the shape of something vast, could be seen broadside beneath the surface. It was about as long as the shadow of our passing boat, eleven metres, perhaps twelve metres long. The harpooner seemed to trace contours with the tip of his lance. He wavered. The sperm whale rose and rolled away, giving us a glimpse of its flipper, an ear-like, fragile-seeming protrusion on its massive head. How small, how unexpectedly vulnerable that flipper looked in comparison!

As the boat passed the head of the whale on the starboard side the harpooner leaped, bringing to bear on the thrust of his lance the full weight of his body, reinforced by the momentum of its flight. The harpoon penetrated above the flipper close to the eye. The harpooner landed on the whale's head, skidding down the animal's flank as it rolled sideways and sank out of sight. The bamboo shaft self-ejected from the head of the harpoon. It floated on the surface where the whale had gone down. Stanis made a grab at it and missed. Ioh caught hold of the curved stern piece of the *Aro Tena* as it came past. He shot up out of the water and pulled himself aboard in a single motion. He sprang between the rowers, pouring water, half leaning on us for support, half cuffing us out of the way as he hurdled over the thwarts and bounded back to his platform at the bows. The Pirate took another pole from the rack on the starboard outrigger. He inserted a second, smaller harpoon and handed it to Ioh as he passed.

To our starboard the *Mata Tena* intervened. It stood between us and the whale. The whale must have surfaced on the far side. We could see nothing. All I saw was a third harpooner, legs and arms spread spider-like, leaping into the sun. A jet of spray, another blow, lower this time, rose where he had gone down. We saw him come up under the boat and haul himself over the gunwale. The bows of the *Mata Tena* came rocking round slowly to the west, facing into the setting sun, an empty sea. I saw water the plunging whale had ploughed, the furrowed surface it had left behind. Of the whale itself there was no sign.

Rope snaked out in slow coils on the port side of the *Mata Tena*, following the direction taken by the whale. It had gone down and round to the port side. Three harpoons stuck fast in it. Three ropes it trailed from the bows of the boats bound it to us and us to it. The positions of the *tena* formed a triangle, twenty-five to thirty metres apart, with the submerged whale somewhere down there in the middle. Its hunters waited for him to come up.

I was surprised by the sudden noise of motors. Two Yamahas came from either side in long flanking arcs. They stood off from the *tena* a hundred metres further out to sea. A man incongruously wearing a white dress shirt and long pants was among the passengers on one of the boats. The Hong Kong TV crew were on board the other. The old sailors around me screwed up their eyes and muttered, making signs to them to stay away.

The crew of the *Horo Sapa* began yelling and scrambling to either end of the boat. A second later it was rammed by the whale.

The sperm whale took the *Horo Sapa* on its huge snub nose and tried to lift the boat out of the sea. The boat tilted sharply to starboard, exposing the bottom plank along its flat keel. The whale strained and shoved, pushing it almost clear of the water. The whale's violence seen at such close quarters, its unmistakable determination to destroy the *tena* and the methodical way in which it proceeded to do so, were terrifying to watch. In this narrow space we shared with the whale we would surely be overwhelmed by its size and power. I had no doubt the *Horo Sapa* was doomed. It moved up and down with the whale in a direction that seemed extraordinarily contrary to the usual sideways motions of boats at sea – had the whale thrust a little bit more we might have seen the *Horo Sapa* tumble through the air and land upside down in the ocean.

For a few moments the *tena* and its crew stood appreciably higher above the water line than the onlookers in the other boats. But far from being intimidated, the crew used this proximity to the whale afforded by the extreme position of the boat to lean far over the port gunwale and plunge gaffes into the side of its head. Streams of blood were now pouring down its flank. Frustrated, spent, badly wounded, the whale withdrew. It shrugged the burden of torment off its back and went under, pitching the *tena* broadside into the sea. The crew cheered and jeered. The dorsal humps of the animal showed again briefly as it arched its back and prepared to dive. Its flukes came up with a sucking sound, making a hole in the surface where it scooped water, pouring it in a solid-seeming curtain back into the sea. For a moment they hung vertically in the sky. The crew crowded into the stern, ducking their heads as the whale went down and with a flick of its tail dealt the bows of the *Horo Sapa* a passing blow that sounded like a thunder crack.

The boat's heavy timbers were smashed as if they were parts of a matchstick toy. The bows had been demolished – just gone. In disbelief I watched the harpooner's platform spinning through the sky and splashing down thirty metres away. Planks had been ripped out fore to aft as far back as the mast. All that was left of the front section of the boat was a jagged hole that went down to within an arm's length of the water line.

A furious exchange of shouts followed. Apart from cuts caused by flying splinters, none of the crew appeared to have been hurt. Within moments of the shock they had already regained their presence of mind. Someone severed the rope dangling through the hole in the bows, presumably still attached to the harpoon embedded in the whale. Others rowed the boat in reverse, backing out of the whale's immediate water. The helmsman behind me thought that in a calm sea the *tena* could stay afloat. If the wind came up and brought waves it would sink, but under present conditions there seemed no likelihood of that.

Disabled, the *Horo Sapa* pulled out of the pursuit, standing off at a distance of fifty metres. The crews exchanged shouts. We came alongside the *Mata Tena*. Cor and Stanis told me to climb aboard. It was for my own safety, he said, and no less for the crew's. They would be better off if I were out of the way. With the exception of the harpooner and the helmsman, who now joined the *Aro Tena* to complement its strength, the sailors on the *Mata Tena* were all older men. It remained for the younger *matros* on board Nasu's boat to carry through the killing of the whale.

In its brave attempt to destroy the *Horo Sapa*, exposing itself to the deep thrusts of gaffes at close range, the sperm whale must have sustained mortal wounds. Soon after the animal had dived it surfaced again, its mottled grey back emerging in the dark red stain that was already spreading out, colouring the sea. It was blowing water mixed with blood. I could feel an aftermath of the blow, a fine pinkish spume, which I watched drifting slowly through the still air before prickling warmly on my face and arms. The whale lay on the surface alongside the *Aro Tena* and breathed and bled, spraying crimson hot exhalations over the men who stood watching it from the gunwale. The *tena*'s white-painted planks streamed rivulets of blood. Blood ran down the bare chests and arms of the whale's tormentors. They poked at it with their gaffes and lances, but the animal was out of reach. Ioh dived in. With a few strokes he reached the whale. He pulled himself onto it and began hacking at it with his long-handled thin-bladed *duri*, the whaler's knife. It thrashed its tail and shook him off. Then it rammed the boat, bringing its head under it and trying to lift it out of the water as it had done before with the *Horo Sapa*. But it no longer had the strength. As the whale sank back the men hooted and jeered. Ioh bobbed up on the far side of the boat. He hauled himself in, his body streaked with the blood of the whale that lay on the surrounding sea in a sluggish film. I was reminded of the scene his father had described to me, the initiation of Nasu as a boy.

Man after man swam out to the whale, their knives deepening the cut Ioh had made anterior to the dorsal fin. They swarmed over the recumbent leviathan like malevolent gnats, stinging and fleeing the moment it stirred. From sortie to sortie, as the whale did less and less to hinder them, the raiders became bolder. They boarded the object of their butchery to hack and saw at it the better. They had blood in their hair, blood-streaked faces, contorted by the violence of the emotions that took possession of them in their killing frenzy. Perhaps it was only in such a frenzy that a man could overcome his fear of joining in mortal combat with such a formidable animal. By the time they finished they had carved a trench across the back of the whale wide enough for a man to lie down in. They severed the muscles along the spinal column that wielded the terrible power of its flukes. They crippled the whale. They bled it to death.

Throughout these final scenes of slaughter the Yamaha with the Hong Kong TV crew on board cruised round the three whaling boats to provide the cameraman with a variety of angles from which to videotape the killing. The man in the dress shirt watched the events through his binoculars.

A third Yamaha came out with Nasu and his grandsons on board. They brought food and water with them for the *tena* crews, whose families on shore had been following the action four or five kilometres out to sea. The food parcels were delivered in banana leaves tied up with fibre and accompanied by the name of the recipient on a slip of paper. Bartolomeus, Gorys, Mans, Yohanis. The parcels were handed round. But no one ventured to eat, drink, or even to smoke. They would wait until the whale was dead.

For an hour it lay within the triangle formed by the three *tena* in a protracted agony of death. The three Yamahas had cut their motors and drifted on the light evening swell. Their passengers and the onlookers on board the *Horo Sapa* and the *Mata Tena* followed the dying of the whale in silence. Only the crew of the *Aro Tena* still occasionally raised their voices in a muted cheer when the whale showed some sign of its ebbing life. Its dying was their survival. The setting sun highlighted men who had shed hats and shirts and were

126

clad in their ragged shorts only. They were caked with blood that had dried in fantastic costumes on their bodies. Whalers become harlequins, unrecognisable as the individuals I had got to know on land. They stood in tight-fitting waders that were leggings of dried blood. They had striped backs, smeared faces, necks encrusted with collars of blood. United by the dangers faced in the mortal combat they had fought with the whale, they remained apart from us in a darkness of blood instincts from which they had not yet been released.

At last even these celebrants grew weary and fell silent. With the going down of the sun the whale died, three and a half hours after it had first been harpooned by the *Horo Sapa*.

Enter Professor Ponce

Only a couple of years ago, before there were any motor boats in Lefó, the *tena* would have had to take the carcass of the whale in tow and sailed or, if there was no wind, been rowed back to land. That might have lasted all night. If they had to wait for the tide to bring the whale up the beach it might have taken them much of the following day, too. Now, with a Yamaha as tugboat, the convoy of *tena* with the whale in tow made it back to land in just over an hour. I was moved from the *Mata Tena* onto the Yamaha from which Nasu and his grandsons had watched the killing of the whale. These were the five- and six-year-old sons of Ioh, who had placed the second harpoon in the whale. One day they would follow in their father's footsteps. Or so Nasu assumed. That was why he had brought them out to make them acquainted with whaling work. It would be hours yet before the crews of the *tena* reached land, said Nasu as the Yamaha came up alongside the *Mata Tena*. He thought I might prefer to get back sooner than that and offered me a ride.

Currents and the tide were unfavourable for landing the whale when we reached the shore, as Nasu had foreseen. The three *tena* waited a couple of hundred metres out until conditions changed. The Yamaha ran aground on the rocky side of the beach. Standing up to my waist in water in the dark, I helped to push the Yamaha up over slippery rocks to the boathouse. For the half dozen crew alone it would have been an impossible task. But helpers crowded round and the boat fairly flew up the slope. Hundreds of people had gathered there. They held up flares, rags wrapped around sticks and soaked in blubber oil, to light the passage of the Yamaha into the boathouse.

A festive atmosphere was brewing up on the beach. People stood in groups, talking excitedly. They had brought canisters of *tuak* with them to welcome the *tena* crews when they came ashore. It was only the second sperm whale Lefó had taken that year, both of them by *baléo*. Nasu explained that a *baléo* meant a launching of boats after the whale had been sighted from land. This was a circumstance that usually arose only out of season or on a Sunday. On workdays during the season boats would normally be at sea. But this year, for one reason and another, the season had got off to a slow start and the whalers were caught napping, as Nasu ruefully admitted. He had seen the whale, in fact a number of whales, from a promontory above Animal-around-the-Mountain, where he had gone that afternoon to fetch a pig. There hadn't been enough time to get back for the launching of the boats.

As the day's excitement ebbed I discovered how drained I felt. I was uneasy about the tugging sensations I had in my heart and wondered if I had done myself any damage when helping to push the boat up the beach. After the efforts of rowing, the hours at sea in the mid-afternoon sun, the rush of emotions during the hunt and killing of the whale followed by the numbness after his death, I sat on the sea wall feeling utterly exhausted. The voices of the *tena* crews still waiting out at sea carried across the water. In the dark I could see stabs of light when they lit their cigarettes. I sat watching and listening, too tired even to move.

I heard footsteps behind me. The sound of footsteps was something very rare in Lefó. Insofar as people had shoes at all they wore noiseless rubber sandals. Curious, I turned to look. A white figure loomed out of the dark, scraping its hard-heeled way cautiously up the village street. A man, it seemed, and a rather dapper one at that. From his hat to his shoes he was dressed all in white, or perhaps a light khaki that showed white in the dark. Coming up to me, he stopped to ask for directions to Pak Ani's house in Sitting-in-Palm-Tree. Someone had told him that accommodation was available there for guests, he said, only he wasn't sure he had understood them and he wanted to know if the information was correct. He spoke rather formal English with a slight American accent. I asked him if he was an anthropologist. No, he said with surprise, a little defensively, and wondered why I had asked.

On our way up the hill to the anthropologists' house I explained that institution of Pak's and introduced myself to his new guest. Coming to the steps under the trees, where the darkness thickened to the extent that we could no longer make out anything at all, my companion tripped and fell, banging his shin painfully. We had to stop for a while to accustom our eyes. By the time we reached the top of the steep flight of steps I had learned that the man in white was a retired college teacher from the Philippines, that he had been travelling round the world for the last year or so, was now on his way home and bore the memorable name of Dagáma Espiritu Santu Ponce.

I should just call him Dagáma, he said, that would make things easier. When he submitted himself for inspection at the entrance to Pak's house by the light of the hurricane lamp held up by the housewife who came out to light our way in, I was intrigued to see what kind of person it would reveal. For a man who had been on his way round the world for the last twelve months Mr Dagáma Espiritu Santu Ponce was travelling light. He appeared to have made a trade-off between his name and his luggage, for while he had more than enough of the one he possessed absolutely nothing of the other. He was a little bird of a man whose soft features and gentle eyes were belied by the magnificence of his plumage, an ornamental silk shirt with coloured stitching around the shoulders and ruffs across the chest. A top pocket to accommodate even a toothbrush, the minimum luggage, had no place on such a shirt. In the Philippines such shirts were really nothing out of the ordinary, protested Dagáma to Pak's admiring wife, who was unable to resist tweaking a sleeve to feel its texture. Pak came out too, and fell over him with cries of joy when he learned that his guest was a retired teacher just like himself. Curricula vitae were compared at length during the hour we sat on Pak's porch drinking palm wine while Ema cooked fried noodles for supper.

Pak, to his obvious regret, had promised to accompany his wife to a meeting in the church community hall that evening, leaving the two of us in Fina's erratic care during supper. I had forgotten to warn the new guest about Fina. On first acquaintance she could be a startling personality. When she set eyes on Dagáma she clapped her hand to her mouth and shrieked with laughter. When he put his spectacles on the table to rub his eyes Fina seized them and ran away to try them on. She loved spectacles. Coaxing her to give them back required persist-ence. It seemed selfish, even heartless to take away from Fina some-thing that gave her so much pleasure and the owner so little. In my luggage I had a pair of sunglasses for this purpose. Tonight I had forgotten to put them out, but Dagáma seemed happy to let her play with his all evening.

He was rather more of a schoolteacher than his modest self-introduction had led Pak and me to believe – rather more of everything than I expected.

During our long conversation it emerged that Dagáma had taught geography, not at junior school as a generalist like Pak but as a professor at Manila University; and that he was clearly something of a biologist, and a linguist besides. He spoke Tagalog, Spanish and English and had a working knowledge of the aboriginal language of Hawaii, where he had held a guest professorship for a year. On his journey round the world he had stuck, as he put it, to coastal areas where the continental shelf offered features of particular interest to him. Europe did not possess these features, he said, so he had omitted it entirely. It turned out that while he had been along the sea borders of quite a number of countries he had not gone inland more than a few kilometres in any of them, unless it was to board a plane; the simple reason being, said Dagáma without a trace of irony, that as a whale tourist there was no point in going places where whales didn't live.

I asked him about his luggage.

Dagáma explained that he had been on his way to Lefó by road when the truck broke down. He had walked with his luggage to the village below Standing Person, a few kilometres down a path off the road. From the village there to the village here it was a long way by road but only a twenty-minute boat ride across the bay. People there told him they had seen whales and then boats out in the bay, so it was obvious a whale hunt was in progress. He hired a boat and came over. His luggage was still in the house where he had left it in the village below Standing Person.

That was a remarkable coincidence, I thought, the timing of Dagáma's arrival in Lefó with that of the whale. People could spend months here without ever seeing one. Oh, he said, there was nothing special about that. Wherever he went, Cape Cod, the Caribbean, Ecuador or Patagonia – he had no problem finding the whales. They usually turned up just as he arrived, as had happened today. But the whale hunt he had witnessed here was unlike anything he had seen before, and he had seen hunts of comparable bloodiness off Madagascar and the Azores before whaling there was closed down. I said it had shocked me, too. I had no idea what a gory and protracted business the killing of a whale could be. I had been no less surprised, however, by the whale's inability to make its escape, the passivity of such a powerful and resourceful animal in submitting to its death at the hands of such a puny hunter. I had expected it to put up more of a fight.

A pained expression came over Dagáma's face. Did I then, just because of the size of *Physeter macrocephalus*, assume it to be a fierce and aggressive animal, he asked. I said I suppose I did tend to make that assumption, or once had, probably under the lasting influence of *Moby Dick*, although I now knew better. Of the two writers, Beale and Bennett, whose works on the biology of the sperm whale Melville had studied and incorporated in his own, it was Beale he had largely followed. But not Beale's judgement regarding the sperm whale's timid and inoffensive nature. A timid and inoffensive creature would have made for a poor protagonist in Melville's book. When it came to the temperament of Moby Dick, the writer had adopted Bennett's characterisation of the sperm as the most ferocious of whales.

Which was quite wrong, said Dagáma.

Ahab had projected onto the white whale a ruthlessness that was man's own. That had happened because the only whale behaviour people observed at the time was the behaviour of whales they were killing. Well, animals tended to resist being killed. A display of ferocity might be expected of an animal facing death. In the Indian Ocean and the Pacific, on many occasions he had been in the water at the same time as sperm whales. Not swum with them exactly, but his observations concurred with the judgement of researchers who had. There were reliable accounts of the displays of the remarkable affection sperm whales showed to one another. These were truly gentle giants. Huge males fondled calves by taking them in their jaws. To humans in the water they behaved with tolerance but caution. They were mild animals, easily disturbed. Their response to a threat was not to fight but flee. No, the candidate for most ferocious member of the whale tribe was the sperm whale's greatest natural enemy – man apart – *Orcinus orca*, better known as the killer whale.

During the twenty-five million years since emerging as a species with its own distinctive characteristics, the sperm whale had evolved techniques to counter the attacks of killer whales and not bothered about much else. Probably no other predator in the ocean concerned them. Even these techniques were remarkable for their quietude. The big males, the flagships of the herd, its destroyers in reserve, didn't seem to ram or bite the killer whales as they sometimes did each other when contending for females. No, they adopted a formation resembling the arrangement of petals on a daisy, a circle of animals with tails touching and heads faced out, the calves tucked in under a protective flipper, or the other way round, heads in and tails out, showing the attackers their rear ends. How about that for ferocity? Dagáma laughed.

The point seemed to be that sperm whales really didn't *need* displays of aggression. Who was going to eat them? The animals that travelled alone, the mature males, were protected by their sheer size. Beyond that, evolution had probably not needed to select for advanced weaponry. Females and their young, always moving in groups, were protected by quite elaborate forms of social organisation that had developed among sperm whales – the daisy-petal pattern, the communal care of each other's young when a mother absented herself from the surface on foraging dives. But perhaps their most important line of defence, Dagáma argued, was their diet.

Their diet?

Squid, said Dagáma, giant squid, to be found at depths a couple of thousand metres beneath the surface of the sea. This was the niche in the food chain, which the sperm whale, the supreme diver and forager in the deep sea, had evolved to fill. There were few competitors for giant squid, certainly not at those depths. Not even man fancied it. Considering that the total food consumption of sperm whales was reckoned to be the equivalent of the annual catch of the world's fishing industry, squid was a sound choice. It guaranteed safe conduct through the oceans. Hungry animals left you in peace.

Until the open-boat whalers arrived, I put in.

Dagáma thought not even then. On the face of it, men in little boats weren't a threat to be taken seriously by sperm whales – less of a threat than killer whales. Open-boat whalers had harpoons that were superior to killer-whale teeth, but that was about their only advantage. They couldn't operate underwater. They weren't as fast-moving as the orca, and lacking its sonar technology weren't as effective in tracking down sperm whales. Nor did they have the three-dimensional avenues of attack and retreat available to orcas, only the surface of the sea. Using their diving ability in conjunction with their echolocation equipment, making sure they surfaced well away from the boats, sperm whales should have been able to make their escape from those early hunters easily.

But hadn't, I said.

But hadn't, Dagáma ruefully agreed.

The sperm whale might possess the biggest brain of all animals, I objected, yet relative to body mass man's was still bigger. Was it then a question of a failure to adapt due simply to inferior intelligence? Dagáma wasn't sure about *inferior* intelligence, but he was sure about it being a different *kind* of intelligence. And nothing here was simple. The development of the human brain had taken place in conjunction with the development of the hand and eye. How eyes saw and hands manipulated determined how humans thought and acted, which was on a visual and linear basis. With highly sophisticated acoustic equipment but no hands, eyes that could see only dimly, the sensory evolution of cetaceans had led to a different kind of intelligence, non-manipulative and non-linear, inside a brain of a size and complexity that was nonetheless very similar to our own. The difference appeared to lie in the areas of the brain most developed during evolution. With humans these were the areas responsible for the elaboration of significant motor skills corresponding to the importance of their hands and what they wielded. With cetaceans there appeared to have been greater emphasis on the evolution of social behaviour.

The crucial difference between Ahab's harpoon and the orca's teeth, thought Dagáma, was that while the harpoon could fly out of Ahab's hands the teeth couldn't fly out of the orca's mouth. Ahab took his harpoon from the rack where it had been left by someone else, but the orca couldn't leave its teeth in the corner for its colleagues to use. The manipulative brain of man that invented tools led to a culture independent of its individual representatives, while in non-manipulative cetaceans the use of intelligence remained embodied in the body and behaviour of the individual animal. In the cerebral anatomy of cetaceans, therefore, it was unsurprising if those structures had been most highly developed which favoured social perception, uniting individual efforts into a whole greater than the sum of its parts. It was his belief that twenty or thirty million years ago, when evolution hadn't brought human life beyond the stage of nocturnal insectivores, cetaceans already evinced behaviour he could only describe as moral. They were *kind* to one another.

How did Dagáma know such things, I wondered. How did he always know when the whales were coming? I challenged him, jokingly, to name the sources from which he got all his inside information. From his wife, he said, she knew. I waited for him to smile, for some expression to show he was responding in spirit. But Dagáma seemed to be absolutely serious. If this was a joke it had a long fuse. As it was already late, however, and the guttering flame in the oil lamp on the kitchen table would give us only another few minutes of light, I let the matter rest. It had been a long day. The professor wasn't the youngest of men and must be tired. I wished him good night and went to bed in the next room, passing over his reply without further comment.

Anatomising the Whale

The topographical feature that had attracted Dagáma to Lefó was its location on a gap about a thousand kilometres long between the Sunda and Sahul shelves. This gap provided marine animals with a passage between the Lesser Sunda Islands, making possible a crossover between the Indian and the Pacific Oceans. The whale populations of the world's oceans were partially isolated from each other by the continental land masses, but here, as around Cape Horn, some exchange between the populations took place. These straits were the Panama Canal, so to speak, of the whale world.

Sperm whales were among the most common in the locality, but blue whales and other baleens such as sei and Bryde's whales, killer whales, false killer whales and short-finned pilot whales, not to mention huge herds of dolphins, frequented this passage. The very strong and unstable currents that flowed through the straits, perhaps stirring up nutrients on which marine life fed, were created by the opposing east–west currents of the Flores Sea to the north and the Savu Sea to the south. It was one of the few places on earth where great whales could regularly be observed within a few hundred metres of the shore. As the professor explained to me on an outcrop we climbed up to from Sitting-in-Palm-Tree in order to get a better view of Lefó, the whales came in so close to land because of the steep decline of the seabed here, which attained a depth of a thousand fathoms within a few kilometres of the shore. We were standing on the edge of a sizeable cliff. If you looked down and imagined the sea wasn't there it would be comparable to the view from the top of the Eiger.

It was a Sunday morning and everyone was apparently in church. The village was still. So far as I could tell the beach was deserted. From the mountainside we made out a dark object rolling on the white fringe of the sea five hundred metres below. It was the whale. We went down to take a look.

Other spectators had arrived before us. The three-man crew of Hong Kong TV was on standby. Assorted tourists staying at the *losmen* in Back-of-the-Whale sat in the shade of the boathouses with their cameras at the ready, waiting for the spectacle to begin: three girls from Holland, a couple from Britain, a Swiss Italian. Their presence made it clear to me that Lefó was already on the itinerary of tourists, and that to my regret I must consider myself one of them. But despite the long journey to Lefó and its remoteness at the end of the road, the only way on being the way back, the tourists didn't stay more than a couple of days. That was as much time as they could afford to wait for a whale. They were travelling round the world and had to get on. The news of the catch had already reached Lapang Buhan, the Chinese cameraman told me. More sightseers were expected in the course of the day. The Chinese TV crew had paid in advance for teeth that were still in the mouth of the whale. Whale teeth worked up as scrimshaw souvenirs fetched high prices in Hong Kong.

The object of all this curiosity was a boulder-like mound of dead animal. It was a steely dark grey in colour with a light brownish underlay and flecks of white where the paper-thin layer of its outer skin had torn. The whale stood as high as my shoulder and in the viewfinder of the video camera had a length of twelve and a half metres. About one third of its length was made up of the enormous battering-ram head with its blunt snout and the relatively small underslung jaw so characteristic of the sperm whale. Talk of whales, and this was the shape that most people saw in their mind's eye.

Behind the flat rectangular head, raked with scars probably inflicted by a rival, there was no proper dorsal fin as such but a hump that looked a bit like a low fatty fin. Beyond it was a series of four knuckles or humps, leading to the peduncle, a stalk-like attenuation between the body of the whale and its fearsome flukes, which took up a larger surface area than on any other animal in the sea. Colonies of ship barnacles had established themselves here and around the animal's mouth. The entire surface of the skin was corrugated, giving the animal a shrivelled appearance, patterned with circular scars which might have been sucker marks from the tentacles of the squids it had done battle with. I had read that in the depths to which sperm whales dived there were giant cephalopods up to forty-five metres long. Prey was apparently attracted by the white interior of the sperm whale's mouth, and perhaps by bioluminescent organisms freeloading on their teeth, which glowed in the dark and acted as additional lures. The head of the whale, too, was mottled white on both sides. When these blotches spread, eventually covering the whole body, as sometimes happened with old bulls like Moby Dick, sperm whales could indeed appear completely white.

Perhaps because no face as such was discernible on the sperm whale's enormous head, no trace of a wound apparent other than the trench carved across the spinal column, which had since been washed white by the sea, or perhaps because the bulk of the animal was so impressive, its presence among us still so manifest, a casual onlooker had little way of telling whether the whale was alive or dead. For it still moved. It was unceasingly being washed up the beach and sucked back under by the breakers, as if the waves were undecided whether to give it to the land or reclaim it for the sea. A cable passed through a hole bored between the jaw and the blowhole and secured to a boulder further up the beach made sure, however, that the whale remained on land.

Then the tide receded, leaving the whale high and dry and unmistakably dead. Men came with butchers' knives.

The men flensing the whale reminded me of Lilliputians peeling a giant banana. The cuts were made across the whale rather than lengthways, but otherwise the strips of blubber were peeled off like a banana skin. To do this the men sometimes had to board the banana and bring grappling hooks into position, trailing ropes, which an entire team of helpers took hold of and pulled as if engaged in a tug-of-war. The strips were cut up into smaller but still stupendous portions weighing as much as thirty kilograms a piece. All day the women of Lefó trekked up and down the mountain with piles of blubber and meat on their heads, surrounded by swarms of flies, their faces smeared with the oily blood that trickled out of these bundles and got in their eyes. The drying barns for this harvest from the sea were the racks behind the houses where the blubber was hung and the oil collected in bamboo gutters, later to find its way into frying pans and lamps.

To the corporations that operated the boats a whale presented itself as a block of blubber, meat and bone to be divided according to ancient tradition into a dozen and more sections. Which members of which boat crews received which sections of the whale depended on the nature of the contributions they had made to its capture, in accordance with this long-established system of rights. The division of the spoils represented quite as elaborate a code of values as the laws governing marriage between kinship groups. Without the outline Pak Ani had sketched for me on a piece of paper the previous day the sophistication of this system would have remained invisible to me. I would have had no inkling of the elaborate social arrangements behind the scenes of butchery I saw on the beach. How the whale was carved up and shared, however, may have mattered as much to its butchers as the three or four tons of edible products that had been hung up to dry in their yards by the end of the day. Even I received a share to take back home.

Left to themselves, they would no doubt have divided the whale up just as they had learned from their fathers and grandfathers and gone home content. But in the last couple of years they had to share the division of whales with spectators. Whatever they were doing was transformed into a spectacle. The protagonists became aware of their actions. It seemed a little thing, but they lost a quality of intactness. They ceased to be self-sufficient. Simply in being observed, the people of Lefó forfeited the innocence of actions performed for their own sake without spectators.

There was an invisible threshold here. Once you crossed it you could never go back. Two or three tourists, with an anthropologist thrown in, might not have bothered them. Six or seven apparently did, wielding cameras and sound equipment, or even, perhaps equally unwelcome, just standing around doing nothing. Hong Kong TV had paid the crews of the boats involved in the capture of the whale a fee for their co-operation, not the additional people who came to help dismember it. Voices were raised. There were demands for money from tourists taking photographs. At one point it nearly came to blows. The TV crew agreed to pay a bonus. The tourists withdrew, offended by the idea that they should pay money for taking pictures. The men of the boat corporations, some fifty of them, held a meeting under the *budi* tree to discuss the situation when they had finished their work on the beach.

They left behind them a raw pile of flesh streaked red and white, an abstract sculpture unrecognisable as the foremost block of the whale's head. Beneath the soft outer tissue the skull consisted of a rounded cranium enclosing two treasures: a spherical ten-kilogram brain and a body of yellowish-white spermaceti wax, a honey-like substance which was already known to the old whalers as the spermaceti case. Probably the whalers had been the first to find out that the sperm whale carried not semen in its head but oil. The sperm whale belonged to history's greatly misnamed. It was the whale's oil, not its semen, that had driven the machines of the Industrial Revolution and illuminated workbenches until gaslight was introduced. Because of its special properties sperm whale oil continued to find use as a lubricant for automobiles, in leather tanning and the chemical industry, although substitutes had by now become available for all these purposes. The women of Lefó, still inhabitants of a pre-industrial world, gathered round with whatever receptacles they had to hand – tins, bamboo, coconut shells – and reached an arm into the well of the whale's head, scooping out the oil, which they poured into buckets and carried home on their heads to light their lamps at home.

To a scientifically minded modern observer such as Professor Ponce the spermaceti organ represented not an oil tap but an extraordinary piece of technology, powered by the largest brain on earth. What did it need such a brain for? When the women had gone and the head was fully exposed to view we moved in for a closer look.

The spermaceti organ consisted of a case of muscle and fibre enclosing the waxy substance, now drained, that surrounded the nasal passages. Dagáma showed me where they were located. These tubes filled with water, he said, when the whale dived. As it did so its lungs gradually emptied of air. At a depth of one hundred metres, with a pressure of eleven atmospheres or a hundred and sixty-five pounds per square inch, the lungs were already completely collapsed and contained no air at all. The nitrogen invasion rate was reduced to zero. This made it possible for whales to go to depths far beyond the capacity of mammals like man, whose lungs did not collapse. The remains of deep-dwelling sharks found in the stomachs of sperm whales presented evidence of record dives going maybe as deep as three thousand metres.

Beside the spermaceti organ, which functioned as a buoyancy regulator facilitating deep dives, the head contained a skull that acted as an enormous reflecting dish. The brain calculated a high-density image of the whale's underwater world, based on the volume and time intervals of the signals it received and transmitted, putting together a picture which was probably as complete as, and over distance much superior to, the imaging that sight afforded mammals on land.

I had once read about the means by which sperm whales produced the signals known as clicks. And making clicks was big business. It had been calculated that in the course of a lifetime they might produce around half a billion. The principle of echolocation was simple. A short pulse of high-frequency waves was sent out and reflected from any object solid enough to return them. The high sounds emerging from the sonar system of toothed whales like the sperm whales travelled less far than low ones but provided more detailed images, allowing the animal to distinguish objects as small as a few millimetres across. Clicks were produced by implosive movements of air inside the nasal passages. But it was something else to peer into the mangled head of a whale while listening to Dagáma elaborate on the complex processes taking place there when a click was produced – less aesthetic, more bewildering.

Basically, said Dagáma, this giant contraption of a nose was a telegraph office. It served as a click generator. He distinguished clicks for echolocation, providing the whale with three-dimensional co-ordinates, and clicks for communication, keeping it in touch with far-flung herds across the ocean. A pulse of sound initiated as an implosion of air passed through the spermaceti organ, bounced off an air-filled cushion and was relayed by acoustic lenses inside the oil-saturated mass of tissue of the whale's head to the surrounding ocean. Clicks consisted of a series of pulses. As whales could emit a stream of intense clicks numbering up to a thousand a second it appeared that they must be able to localise sounds to within a couple of degrees, and to distinguish time in units of tens of millionths of a second. Click conversations could continue for days and unfold over large areas. To a sperm whale tuned in to the infrasonic gossip of clan members speaking the same dialect, an ocean basin became a small place.

The sun had gone down behind Animal-around-the-Mountain. In another fifteen minutes it would already be too dark to find our way back without risk of injury. Unfortunately we didn't have echo-location, nor even a flashlight. I suggested we make a move while we could still see where we were going. Dagáma had banged his shin painfully on a rock the previous night. He got up promptly and we set off up the hill. I said I'd never heard of whales being members of clans or speaking dialects.

Well, replied Dagáma, those were anthropomorphic figures of speech, but according to recent analysis of the click patterns known as codas that's what they were interpreted to be. What made a coda was how the clicks were spaced. It depended on the pauses in between. When these codas differed they were termed dialects. Whales using the same coda repertoire were considered to be conversant in the same dialect and to make up a clan. They had clans, cultures, identities, and they had a consciousness of these things. The four or five clans that had so far been identified across the South Pacific appeared to regard a particular area of it as home ground, but these areas overlapped, and sperm whale clans numbering thousands of animals stretched ten thousand kilometres all the way across the South Pacific.

Wow, I said.

Well, replied Dagáma, that was just the beginning.

The Man whose Wife dreamed she was a Whale

Fina had come down to the beach earlier in the day to collect the modest share of the whale I had earned for helping to row the *tena*, so I had been expecting there would be whale on the menu that night. Dagáma went into the kitchen to take a look at the meat and see how it was prepared by Pak's wife, but declined to have anything more to do with it. He remarked on the dark red colour of the meat, which he attributed to a high concentration of myohaemoglobin. He said it combined with oxygen to form an oxygen depot in the muscles of marine mammals accustomed to spending long periods of time under-water. Pak's wife boiled the meat with shoots and papaya leaves picked from the rubbish-strewn hillside around the house and served it with rice. She didn't believe in or perhaps know about flavouring her cooking, leaving her ingredients to fend for themselves. Perhaps it was the myohaemoglobin that pitched in to give the whale meat its strong taste reminding me of venison. It wasn't bad. With cranberry sauce and a bottle of Bordeaux it might have been very good.

Dagáma ate a pancake.

A wind rose and stirred up the night. Waves thundered on the shore with such a roar that they seemed to be breaking just outside the house. Fina came in to clear the plates and fix the latch on the door to prevent it from flying open. Half a dozen candles, glued with their own wax onto the lid of a tin, cast a restlessly flickering light over the walls. Draughts through the cracks in the bamboo slats, patched over with bits of cardboard, flattened the candle flames and chased them, like a glass-blower, into long jets of light. Calendars several years old provided the room with its only decoration; pictures of strawberries I had never seen in Indonesia; volcanoes I had; Sukarno whom I knew only from what seemed to be the same three-quarter-face photograph, branded into the national memory in sunglasses and hat. There was a flower-patterned plastic cover with cigarette burns on the table. We sat there drinking coffee and eating thumb-size bananas. Dagáma smoked.

He asked if I was married. I told him I was. Of course, said Dagáma in a tone of voice that suggested it was as unavoidable for a man to be married as to have arms and legs. He had been married for forty-seven years. Then his wife had died. It was her own fault. She had always eaten too much. She had suffocated in her own obesity. He hadn't loved her the less for that. But whether it was for love or out of habit that he missed her so much he couldn't say.

Did I believe in reincarnation? I said I didn't disbelieve in it. I had no particular views on the subject either way.

Well, said Dagáma, Ronnie – that was his wife's name – Ronnie had believed in it positively, all her life, from the time he had met her when she was eighteen years old and let him in on the secret. She *knew* she had been reincarnated. When he was young and foolish he used to poke fun at her. Ronnie the whale. She was big even then, you know, said Dagáma, opening his arms to give me an idea of the size of his wife. Serene in the privilege of a knowledge she had and he didn't, Ronnie didn't mind.

When she fell asleep at night she used to submerge into her former existence as a whale. She thought as a sei whale, maybe because one used to see them a lot off the southern Philippines where she grew up, or maybe, said Dagáma with a laugh, because she was fat and sei whales were slim. She appeared to have been a whale at a time when there were no humans hunting them at sea, perhaps in a world in which there were no humans at all. At any rate, she reverted to being a whale in dreams in which humans took no part. These were the most serene and pleasant dreams. She said I couldn't begin to imagine what a sensual experience it was to be such a big animal surrounded by water, to be stroked over such a large surface area of body, to cleave water with one's head and feel it flowing along one's flanks. Being a whale wasn't unlike the sensation of flying you had in dreams. That was the only way she could describe to me what it was like.

Dagáma scratched his head. The wind thumped at the door.

It took some getting used to, he said, lying in bed next to a person who dreamed she was a whale, particularly when you were a bad sleeper yourself. Lying on her back, his wife used to make muffled trumpeting calls, which he took for snores. They used to keep him awake. But on a recording of whale sounds he heard something similar. They weren't snores. They were whale calls.

She had no clear visual impression of the sea in which she lived. The sea was something she felt and heard rather than saw. She swam, she said, towards an orchestra that was always tuning up somewhere in the distance. Once – it was after the birth of her third child – she dreamed she was a pregnant whale that calved, without pain or even particular effort, and this experience made her realise what was so special about a whale's existence. It was to be so large and at the same time so light.

This thought played a major part in the consciousness of whales, Ronnie said, because they also knew what it was *not* to be light, when they broke the surface of the water. As they had to rise regularly to the surface in order to breathe, the consciousness of that difference must have been frequent and acute. Of course there was a parallel here to Ronnie's own situation, Dagáma observed in passing, when she broke the surface of her sleep, because she had to rise regularly to the surface in order to wake and return to heaviness. According to his wife, when a whale breached and rose up out of the water, sometimes even leaving the water completely, the animal felt as if it had struck something impermeable and rebounded. It felt crushed by a devastating weight. Male animals, particularly young ones, liked to do this just as human juveniles liked to push motorcycles beyond either machine or human limits. Gravity was the roof of the whale world. They knew one could pass through it to – somewhere else, but they knew almost nothing of that place. And why should they want to? In this other dimension, which they brushed when they breathed, they felt only heaviness, whereas in their own, said Ronnie, they felt only lightness.

I wondered if Dagáma had felt excluded from his wife's experiences as a whale.

Oh no, he said in a reproachful tone of voice, he felt it as a privilege to have been given glimpses into what he understood to be an archetypal dream.

Of being a whale?

Of being in the womb, said Dagáma, of living in the sea. It was really one and the same. Amniotic fluid, the fluid in the wombs of all mammals, was so obviously kin to sea water. Both contained the same salts in roughly the same proportions. Why? Because the source of all life was the sea. The fluids in the womb copied the sea water in which our pre-human ancestors swam. Mammalian mothers created amnion in their own bodies in order to reproduce for their embryos the same conditions as those which had always nourished life. It was this ancestral sea, as the great whale researcher Roger Payne wrote in one of his books, that was lost when a pregnant woman's waters burst before giving birth to her child, and we humans re-enacted the ritual of evolution, the transition from water to land, from lightness to heaviness, from the ancient seas of our mother's amnion to the gravity of our terrestrial existence. He didn't need the hypothesis of reincarnation, Dagáma said. His wife's archetypal dream was the memory in which all beliefs in reincarnation had their origin.

Nasu's Shopping List

By morning the waves had risen so high that they scoured out the boathouses and plucked at the *tena*, threatening to carry them out to sea. Pigs tethered under the sea wall had already been swept away. Their bloated cadavers could be seen bobbing up and down beyond the surf. Lighter boats, the sampan and the smaller Yamahas, had been hauled up the ramp into the village street. Men had been working on the beach all night, putting wedges under the keels of the heavier boats to lever them up, inserting ever bigger logs and finally whole tree trunks, to raise the boats above the waterline on props that wouldn't get washed away. There was no question of putting out in this sea, Pak Ani said. This was a storm wind, and of a storm wind it was said in Lefó that it continued to blow until it had gone to market and bought betel peppers and areca nuts, meaning it might continue for many days.

For Dagáma and myself it meant leaving the village by road. Dagáma wanted to return to Standing Person to pick up his luggage and fly back to Bali. I had to leave because it was Kozue's birthday. Before leaving Europe we had arranged that wherever I was I would call her. The nearest phone was half a day away in Lefó Utara on the north coast of the island. A truck made the journey there two or three times a week. We had been told that it would be leaving at eight in the morning. We sat at the roadside among a group of villagers with produce they were hoping to sell in Lefó Utara. During the year and a half since the road had been built, bringing to an end five hundred years of isolation for the people south of the mountains, they had already come to rely on cash crops like salt and dried fish. The road had revolutionised their traditional barter economy within a matter of months.

At ten o'clock the village headman came by on his motorcycle. He had passed the truck in the mountains, he said, where it had broken down. It wouldn't reach the village until the afternoon.

Dagáma set out on foot along a path that followed the coast. He could walk to the village beneath Standing Person in a couple of hours, he thought, pick up his luggage and wait for the truck at the junction where he had got off it three days before.

I walked down the road to visit Nasu in Back-of-the-Whale. I found him in the yard beside his house where he and Stanis were working on the boat. The bright orange awning tied to the surrounding trees and a corner of the house provided shade for the boatbuilder and his assistant. The scene was unchanged from the first occasion we had met almost two months ago. In the coloured light that filtered through the awning, an orange-tinted haze surrounding them like a tent, Nasu chipped away with an adze at a plank – perhaps the same plank – which was laid on edge and held in place for him by Stanis.

Reo, he called out when he caught sight of me. My dropping in for a chat seemed to provide a welcome opportunity for Nasu and Stanis to take a break for a smoke. Both men reached for tobacco boxes lying nearby on the ground, tore off with their teeth a strip of fibre from the dried palm leaves they used for paper, and rolled themselves giant cigarettes. The strip of fibre was tied round the rolled leaf to keep it together, making the finished product look less like a cigarette than a scrolled parchment, the sort of thing that is handed out at graduation ceremonies.

I asked Nasu what the outcome of yesterday's meeting had been.

Nasu said it had been decided that in future visitors to Lefó would be charged fixed rates. If they wanted to go out in the *tena* it would cost them two dollars a day, three dollars more for taking photographs, and fifteen dollars for making a film. What did I think? I said I thought it was reasonable to charge people a fee, but it might be fairer to ask professional photographers and film-makers to pay a bit more than private tourists. They would be making money with their pictures, after all.

Nasu and Stanis pondered this. Stanis took off his baseball cap and twisted it in his hands. I noticed the logo, which read *Bintang Java*, meaning Star of Java. I had come across that name before. I couldn't remember in what connection.

Benar, said Nasu, ejecting clouds of smoke through the gaps in his teeth. His moustache was a grizzled yellow from all the nicotine it had filtered over the years. He would discuss my suggestion with the other boat owners. And meanwhile, he added slyly, if I was taking the truck to Lefó Utara, perhaps I could get him some things he needed.

The first item on what turned out to be a long shopping list was an article called *murbaut*. As I didn't know what this meant, he did a drawing to scale on the ground where he was sitting. What Nasu wanted were six-inch nuts and bolts, three dozen of them, for the Yamaha he was building. I was surprised by this. The materials used to build the *tena* were all natural products, Pak Ani had told me, available in the forest. Even the sails were made of palm leaves. That was true, said Nasu. But once you put a motor in a *tena* it wasn't a *tena* any more and you treated it differently. Then there was paint to redo the lettering of the name on his *prahu*, red paint, perhaps some black, too, and a few lengths of rope. Nylon was so much lighter and more convenient than the ropes they made themselves in Lefó out of twists of fibre. We scrambled down the sea wall into the back of the boathouse so that Nasu could show me what it was he needed for the *prahu*; harpoon rope, above all, as thick as his wrist, strong enough to hold a sperm whale, twine for fishing off the stern, and perhaps lures for marlin and small shark.

We sat on the gunwale of the raised boat as waves washed in and out beneath. The shopping list grew longer, one thing led on to another, whale rope to marlin lures, the cough mixture for Nasu's wife Tika to vaccines for the village, and the train of thought that had been set in motion by charging tourists for taking photographs arrived with a thump at the sum of the one hundred dollars it was going to cost Nasu and Tika to put their daughter through secondary school in Lapang Buhan for the next couple of years, not to mention the medical bills if Tika were to see a doctor about that trouble in her chest. Nasu wondered if I could help out. He didn't ask me for money in so many words. It was more like he was ruminating out loud.

A long wailing sound came from beyond Back-of-the-Whale. That was the truck's whistle, Nasu said, letting everyone know it had arrived and would soon depart. We climbed back up to his yard. Nasu returned to work. I walked on to catch the truck.

Star of Java

Dagáma was waiting at the side of the road with the two pale green suitcases out of which he had been living for the past year. They weren't particularly big. There was no room for them in the truck, however, not even on the roof, where two live cocks and a pig had been accommodated beside the cardboard boxes that seemed to accompany Indonesians whenever they travelled in rural areas. But the driver of the truck, who was also its owner, seemed delighted when he saw the two cases. Only an enthusiast could have done his job. The road was appalling. Apparently the truck was always breaking down. Loading and unloading passengers with all their animals and utensils required great willingness and patience. But the driver was like a man out of a parable. He enjoyed all these difficulties, because they challenged his ingenuity. Fullness was never full. He kept on re-organising the load on his roof rack until he had somehow found space for the extra cases.

Shortly after our departure we reached the last of Lefó's outlying hamlets. The driver got out and disappeared, apparently to have lunch. The passengers seemed to know the routine. He would be gone for ten minutes, long enough for his passengers to start getting a cramp, not long enough for it to be worth their while to extricate themselves from the truck, stretch their legs and pack themselves in again. The pig on the roof, jolted into silence by the slamming it had been given on the first stretch of the road, came back to life and set up its butcher's-bench shrieking until the driver reappeared and silenced it once more by driving off.

Lurching and bellowing noise and fumes, the truck ground up the hillside. Boys riding shotgun on the rear bumper jumped down from time to time to remove a rock from the road. It was their job to keep the road clear of obstacles too large to be negotiated by the truck, to lift passengers' luggage down from the roof and otherwise to look vaguely menacing by wearing sunglasses and smoking as much as possible.

Squeezed in at the back, Dagáma and I had the job of hanging onto the door to keep it from flying open. Passing through open grassland before disappearing into the mountain jungle, we were rewarded with the last long deep views of the sea we had left behind, the shadow of Timor pale blue on the horizon. I saw to my surprise how close it was. I thought of my grandmother Wanda, who had been born only eighty kilometres away across the straits. I realised how much to-and-fro there must always have been between these islands, and it occurred to me for the first time that I might well be related to the people among whom I had been living for the past months.

Apparently uninhabited dwellings in the gloomy stillness of the forest came to life at the sound of the truck. Dogs and children ran excitedly out into the road. Men and women appeared in doorways, craning their necks. A priest gave the driver a letter to post and asked him to bring him some gasoline when he made the next trip. How did people live here at all, I wondered. They had allotments in the forest where they raised maize, said my neighbour in the back of the truck, they kept poultry, pigs and goats. Having crossed the mountains we made some alarming descents and forded a few streams before the rough track began to even out, producing evidence that it had ambitions of becoming a real road some day. A highway across the island had been under construction for the last ten years, my neighbour told me. Somewhere in the middle it had petered out. Vast pieces of road-building machinery littered the wayside, abandoned to the encroachment of the jungle. Road-menders, it seemed equally forgotten, like lepers in their isolation, shared their fate. Bamboo platforms with palm-leaf roofs provided rest places for them along the wayside, and they started up like sleepers from a bad dream when the truck roared past, perhaps with hopes of a reprieve that would bring them back home.

It was dark by the time we reached the outskirts of Lefó Utara. Dagáma had missed his boat to Lapang Buhan. We would both have to stay in town for the night. Town was something of a misnomer. We drove round and round what we took for the outskirts, dropping off passengers at bungalows in what seemed to be an endless banana plantation, until we realised that outskirts embedded in a banana plantation was all the town had. We asked the driver to let us off at a *losmen*. In the silence after the truck had driven away, and with it the noise that had deafened us for the past few hours, I became conscious of a ringing in my ears. It was the return of my tinnitus. I couldn't remember having heard it at any time in Lefó. Perhaps it was overlaid by the incessant noise of animals.

Lefó Utara's only *losmen* was located at an intersection with the island's only traffic lights, the town centre. It had a lobby with a black and white tiled floor, a TV, sofas and armchairs that looked extremely hot in their dark velvet covers, the familiar portrait of a man in sunglasses and hat, hanging on the wall over a reception desk with keys to no less than fourteen rooms. I was surprised by this sophistication. I was surprised that the *losmen* in Lefó Utara had facilities for so many guests. I was even more surprised that only one room with a double bed was available. It was on account of all the five-legged gentlemen they had passing through, said the receptionist. Five-legged gentlemen? Dagáma and I agreed to share the room with the double bed. I left immediately to get to the Telsat office in the shipping terminal at the harbour before it closed.

Eleven and a half hours after leaving Pak Ani's house that morning I stepped into a phone booth and was connected with Kozue in twenty seconds.

Happy birthday, I said.

Kozue thought it was sweet of me to have called. Was I all right? Only one letter had arrived from me so far. It sounded as if I was living in a rather primitive place. She wondered if it had been difficult to find a phone.

A bit, I said.

After a slightly awkward start we chatted away. The Telsat line was incredibly clear. It was like talking to Kozue in the same room. I asked her if she had any plans for the evening. This evening no, she said. But tomorrow evening, if it suited me, we could have dinner together in Bali.

Bali?

She had happened to walk past a travel agent in Kyoto that afternoon, said Kozue, and seen a stand-by flight to Bali plus a week in Sanur at the Grand Bay View Hotel, all inclusive. From Osaka it was only a few hours. She had missed me. Would I be able to make it at such short notice? Of course, I said, suppressing my immediate doubts regarding the imponderables of Indonesian travel, that was wonderful. I had missed her too. There was a pause. Well, she said,

152

she had so many things she wanted to tell me, but she would prefer to save them up for tomorrow. I love you, I said. I love you too, said Kozue, and we hung up.

I paid a hundred thousand rupees for the phone call. Then I wandered along the harbour wall outside the Telsat office, watching reflections of light in the water as I listened to a replay of the conversation and the tunes that accompanied it in my head.

I was almost too stunned by the suddenness of this reappearance of Kozue in my life to be simply happy about it. I was cautious, and sad that I was cautious, unable to change my own nature and be impulsively happy. I felt estranged, but whether from Kozue or myself or because I hadn't been able to adjust, to accustom myself to her that quickly again, I couldn't say. My heart was a labyrinth in which I couldn't find my way.

CONNECT

Just below me in the deep-water harbour lay a submerged ship. The bows and part of the deck structure stuck up out of the sea. Having surfaced only that morning, in the logo on Pak Stanis's baseball cap, here now was the real thing – a wreck of a ship, true, no longer seaworthy, but still the *Bintang Java* according to the faded name painted on its bows. Whether this was the long-lost ship on which I had been born more than fifty years ago in the Straits of Malacca or just a ship of the same name I had no way of telling, of course, nor did it matter. For it was my own shadow I could see down there in the water.

I had come to believe that, like cetaceans in the ocean, I lived in some kind of conductive medium through which signals were passing all the time. Echolocation was the means by which cetaceans sent messages to themselves. Here was one for me, alerting synapses. Most of the signals I would never register, because I was not attuned to the wavelengths at which they travelled or perhaps because they were not intended for me. You just had to know. This was how Kozue and I had met. To the song of the bereft we owed it that we had been able to make ourselves known to one another, and here my memory was being jogged once again, pointing me up a trail I thought I had lost but knew I was now going to find. There were no coincidences. You just learned to see the connections.

At the Losmen

My third conversation with Dagáma took place in the courtyard of the *losmen* under the open sky. It was attended by about a dozen five-legged gentlemen who happened to be staying at the *losmen* and had nothing better to do with their evening. I had left my dictionary in Lefó, but the lady at the reception could explain to me the meaning of this curious term.

Five-legged gentlemen were travelling salesmen. No less than five legs were needed, it appeared, for all the walking they had to do. Some were Flores men, one came from Java, two others from as far away as Borneo and Sumatra. Most of them were in textiles, but this last gentleman sold Chinese medicines. He travelled exclusively by boat, touring the small islands at the eastern end of the archipelago in order to reach his customers. According to the lady receptionist, from whom I got all this information, five-legged gentlemen often didn't have a home and family. They had more legs than friends. She said they didn't stay anywhere long enough to make friends. For ten, fifteen, twenty years they remained on circuit pretty much all the time.

Perhaps it was on account of this perpetual motion that five-legged gentlemen were disposed, once they sat, to remain sitting for a long time. Outside each room stood a table and chair in the passageway leading round the courtyard on the ground floor of the *losmen*. There the occupant sat with funereal gravity and smoked thoroughly for an hour or two in the evenings before retiring to bed. On the floor upstairs there was the same arrangement, with table and chair so placed that one could look over the balustrade and watch what was going on below.

In my own limited experience, travelling salesmen seemed to be solitary individuals who showed little inclination to talk to one another, confirming what the receptionist had said. Watching some-body else do something – anything – seemed to be all the leisure expectations they had. I had come across them before, without know-ing who they were, at the cheaper *losmen* throughout Indonesia. During the daytime the main watchable activity would be women washing clothes, in the evening men tinkering with motorcycles or children playing.

By the time Dagáma and I came down for our supper all such activities had ceased. The five-legged men had long since eaten and taken up position on the chairs outside their rooms. It was perfectly still in the courtyard. They had been waiting for something to happen and seemed glad of our arrival. Those of them upstairs leaned forward with their arms on the balustrade to get a better view of us having our supper.

The youngest son of the *losmen* owner – he had eleven brothers and sisters, he told us – had just brought *krupuk* and beer to the table. The dining table stood in the middle of the courtyard and could be viewed from all sides. I passed on to Dagáma the informa-tion about five-legged gentlemen which I had been given by the receptionist. A life on tour all the time, with no home to return to – Dagáma thought that might be the thing for him. In a few days he would be back in Manila. He was dreading it, he said. For he *had* no home there, now that his wife was dead. So long as he kept on travelling he had been able to run away from that fact. Once he stopped he would have to face it.

It wasn't easy for me to admit that I would have to face it, too, but I did. Dagáma would never know the effort it cost me to proffer this token of friendship. It wasn't quite the same for me – my wife wasn't dead – but sort of, I said, because if she wasn't home, and she hadn't been for the past year, she was as good as dead and I didn't have a home either. Dagáma asked me if my wife was fat and ugly, and I said no, she was pretty and slim. How come? *His* wife, said Dagáma, was huge – he spread his arms to indicate the size of her – and had a pug face, which had made her look like a Chinese lap-dog. This only went to show how little love had to do with a person's appearance. It had to do with their aura. You felt fondness for their presence. You felt better for it. I watched Dagáma's face soften as he said this. The thought taking place behind his face showed through and made him look rather beautiful.

The youngest son of the *losmen*'s owner brought us two portions of *nasi goreng*. There was a general stirring around us as the spectators tried to get a look at what we had got on our plates. Fried rice was the only item on the menu, but I had noticed that none of the five-legged salesmen ate it. Menus were for tourists. Indonesian guests went round to the kitchen to discuss with the cook what they could have for supper. If they were in luck it might be dog.

We ate in silence while the five-legged men looked on. Dagáma ate only half of his. He pushed it away and lit a cigarette.

The most memorable thing he had experienced on his travels round the world, he said, was a mass stranding of sperm whales in an isolated cove in New Zealand. Dagáma had been hiking on his own along the coast. There were no human habitations within a day's walk. It was just him and the whales. A couple of them had already beached when he arrived. Five more came in the course of the next few hours. They didn't look as if they had lost their way. *They proceeded in all deliberateness*, swimming straight to the point at which the other whales had beached. They seemed to be a family group. Three of them, to judge by the white callouses on the fins, were mature females, the remainder juveniles they had in their care. He exhausted himself trying to shoo them back into the sea. It was futile. When it started to rain Dagáma put up his tent on the beach and sat in the entrance watching the stranded whales all night. There was nothing he could do for them. The next day he walked on and reported what had happened at the first house he came to. Helpers were flown in by helicopters, but there was nothing they could do either. The whales died.

I asked him if his impression had been that the two whales who were already beached at the time of his arrival had called the others, and that they had come in response to those distress signals. Dagáma said he had no doubt about it. Such instances had quite often been observed and were well documented. How could one interpret such behaviour, I wondered. As moral behaviour? An act of altruism? Dagáma shook his head. No, he said, they were probably just on their way home.

Home?

Dagáma thought that home for a whale was wherever it found the other whales to whom it belonged, even in death.

In the silence that followed when Dagáma finished speaking I heard the ringing sound I was familiar with as the theme tune of my tinnitus, a thin whine like a finger rubbing the rim of a glass, but it didn't seem to come from inside my own head, it seemed to rise like a screeching from the five-legged men sitting mutely in the passageway around the courtyard, guarding the doors behind which they kept the secrets of their loneliness.

THREE

Makhluk Istimewa –
The Extraordinary Creature

The Frozen Jug

In three or four metres of water I hung on the surface, looking down through my mask. A swarm of damsel fish drifted through the coral gardens, reversing each other's colours, small black-bodied black-finned *Dascyllus trimaculatus* with the three startling white spots from which they took their name, and the even smaller *aruanus*, their bright white bodies banded by three wide black stripes. When I held out my hands some of the fish rose and suckled my fingertips, just as they had first done in Garrault's aquarium forty years ago. In a hundred-litre tank Garrault had also stocked by the hundred the tiny pygmy rasbora fish that here swarmed around me in their tens of thousands, a veil of minute yellow blobs, undulating in slow gusts with brilliant flashes of red and black.

Over the waving ocean floor and in and out of isolated coral structures that rose like tenements for the myriad reef-dwellers, I followed a gorgeous parade of fish I knew only from aquariums, striped zebra barbs, blue gourami with long flowing fins, silver-scaled harlequin fish with black and red fringes, fish I had never seen anywhere at all, in luminous blue, green, orange and purple attire. The colouring of fish in their natural habitat was more striking than in captivity. For as long as I could hold my breath I went down and floated over a clownfish, broad blue stripes encircling its orange body, nestling between the poisonous tentacles of a large sea anemone where it sang: come hither and take a closer look at me! I had read about the symbiosis of anemone and clownfish but never seen it. For some reason the clownfish was immune to the anemone's poison. Its spectacular colouring lured other fish that weren't. The anemone paralysed them with its stinging cells, and the two of them shared the booty. Nobody seemed to want to keep the clownfish and the anemone company, not while I was around.

I thought of the conversation I had had with Kozue in Sanur as I came back up to the surface.

Nasu and Romualdus, the sampan fisherman, had dwindled to specks on the shore. During the hour I had been snorkelling I had drifted with the current about a kilometre west. The first time I went into the water here I didn't dare to go out of my depth. That was six weeks ago. In the meantime I had returned to this cove with Nasu many times, I to snorkel, he to chat to the fisherman, his cousin, who sat here every Sunday morning mending his nets. Soon I came for a daily swim after the *tena* got back from sea in the afternoon. I paid close attention to the currents and in what direction they took me. I surfaced often to take bearings on some object on shore and check my drift. Gaining confidence, I swam further out. I explored the sea. It felt good to be back in my element. I was swimming strongly again. I put the trauma of my near-drowning behind me. In the sun and salt water my scar healed quickly. It began to fade. I had almost forgotten it was there.

Kozue was shocked when she saw it. She thought I had been in hospital because of an irregular heartbeat. That was what I told her at the time.

My scar was the outward mark, she said, of a change in me. She wondered what had become of me. We began on the outside and worked our way in. A thinner man, for a start. I had lost fifteen kilos. A bearded man – there was no electricity in Lefó and heating water was such a chore. A man who no longer kept time – I had stopped wearing a watch. A man who no longer put number tags on every-thing – I had got out of that habit during the months I lived in Lefó. More of a beachcomber than an insurance agent. Perhaps that was how I had shed my scales, said Kozue.

Scales?

She ran her fingers down my arm, tracing patterns of what was passing through her head. Had I forgotten how much time I spent with the fish in my aquarium? Just you and your fish, sitting down there looking at each other in the basement with its smell of brine shrimp and mould, until you began to turn into one yourself. There used to be something a bit fish-like about you, Daniel, she said.

Once I might even have taken it as a compliment. In an aquarium you had to get light and shade, temperature, pH values, all the sur-roundings of self just right if the inmates were to survive and thrive. This required patience and care, but also imagination; perhaps a fish-like empathy. Kozue didn't understand such things. When I first stepped into an aquarium the size of an ocean it amazed me that so delicate a balance was possible on so enormous a scale. With no one looking after it. It hadn't ceased to amaze me, however often I went into the water.

Slowly I swam back to the shore.

But for Nasu's shopping list, I told myself, I wouldn't have needed to return to Lefó except to pick up my luggage. I would have gone on to Timor and New Zealand to visit my new-found uncle, Arthur Smith, before returning to Singapore where I had arranged to meet Kozue for our wedding anniversary. Whether Kozue would then be flying back to Europe with me was something we had still not managed to clear. First, however, I had a bag full of nuts and bolts to deliver, bought at a Chinese ironmonger in Lapang Buhan, ropes, fish lures, vaccines, assorted medicines and, while I was about it, a frock for Nasu's daughter from a store in Bali. Kozue chose it. Daniel, how *could* you – this when I mentioned the two children we had acquired in Lefó. A nineteen-year-old son who had just finished school and was going on to study – I didn't specify marine biology, marine biology being a sensitive subject – and his elder sister who worked in a bank. They had come up in the conversation, I said, quite spontaneously. Kozue brooded on this for a bit. She asked what the children's names were. I left that for you to choose, I said.

I told myself that I would like to see Nasu finish the *prahu* before I travelled on. Putting the nuts and bolts in, topping the gunwale, fitting the last thwarts and sealing the cracks in the hull with palm resin – these jobs could only take him a week at most. Nasu said we would then take the boat on a maiden voyage round Standing Person to the fishing grounds off the islands to the east, stay there for a few days, sleeping on the beach, and return with the *prahu* laden with *pari* and *belelang*. This was a trip usually undertaken by two or three *tena* in the late summer to lay in reserves in years when the fishing season off Lefó had been slack – and this was such a year. But Nasu stalled and the days passed. It was now a month since I had got back from Bali. The boat was still unfinished. I was still in Lefó.

I wondered why Nasu had stopped working on his boat. That was because Nasu had too many other things on his mind, said his neighbour, Petrus, whom I called the Pirate. His wife Tika was a sick woman. Nasu didn't have enough money to pay for his daughter's secondary school education. He had quarrelled with Ioh over the question of putting motors in boats to hunt whales. Bitter words had been exchanged between father and son. The *leo* was no longer brought to the spirits in the great house every night but left to lie in the boathouse. So long as such matters that were *tidak sehat*, not healthy, remained in Nasu's mind there could be no health in the boat he was building, either. Something would go wrong with it. It would catch no fish. It might drown. An unhappy boat would always come to the grief out of which it had been born.

In Sanur I told Kozue I couldn't take the air-conditioning in our hotel room. She agreed to switch it off. After months adapting to the conditions in Pak Ani's sweltering hut I had come to terms with the heat and was reluctant to dishonour them. In Lefó I thawed out, living in a semi-liquid state, not sweating so much as covered with a fine tunic of moisture. I never took it off except when I bathed, replacing it with another. Heat was an epiphany to senses made cautious by a cold climate. There was nowhere for them to withdraw and hide. It was miraculous. The frozen jug poured. Making love in wet heat was like eels entwining and slithering over each other. Even eels became warm-blooded in a tropical climate, Kozue said.

Technically she may have been wrong, of course, but I understood what she meant.

At House-of-Three-Families

There was no beach under Animal-around-the-Mountain, only a narrow strip of pebbled shore. Sampans could be hauled up here, but not *tena*, because there wasn't enough room. The deep sandy beach, home to the fleet of *tena* at Under-the-Banyan, was the only such beach anywhere on the south coast of the island. Without it there would have been no Lefó. Romualdus was a sampan fisherman. His brother Martinus, known as Marlboro Man on account of his stetson, crewed on the *tena* of which Nasu was the boat master. His other brother Paulus operated a Yamaha. The three brothers and their families, totalling about thirty people, lived in a hamlet they had given its name, House-of-Three-Families, in a banana grove on a turning off the track that passed through Animal-around-the-Mountain.

Gorys, the patriarch of the three families, was the oldest inhabitant of Lefó, a hundred years old by his own account, ninety according to Pak Ani's records. He received visitors after church on Sunday mornings in the great room that was adjoined by the three houses and used by all. Nasu and I regularly dropped in for a jug of *tuak*. A clock that didn't work hung on the wall beside a votive picture of the Virgin Mary and a chocolate advertisement. A few upright chairs around a low table stood at the end of the room by the door through which visitors made their entrance. Otherwise the room was empty. The hens that clucked in and out in search of something to eat found not a grain of maize on the swept concrete floor. There was an air of gleaming austerity about the house. Everywhere in Lefó, but here in particular, I found very restful this lack of objects competing for space.

The spiky-haired gaunt-faced old man couldn't see or hear too well. He possessed an ear-trumpet, a relic of the Portuguese colonial era by the look of it, and a pair of spectacles, which he sometimes managed to wear upside down. These props contributed to the clownish manner he had, or affected to have, I wasn't sure which. Nasu had told him about my *operasi*, the flap made of pig that had been sewn into my heart, the pacemaker run by a battery under my skin. Gorys chuckled gustily when told this cock-and-bull story. They weren't going to fool him. He cringed with laughter in his chair. He wanted to see the evidence, and when seeing turned out to be inconclusive, to touch it. He could feel the outline of something hard and square under my collarbone, even though, like his clock, it disappointingly didn't tick. He asked what happened when the battery ran out. You put in a new one, I said.

It took several visits for the old man to digest this. Every time I came he wanted to see the evidence again. I took off my shirt and stood beside Gorys so that he could get a good look at it through his upside-down spectacles. He had taken quite a shine to me, or perhaps it was to my battery. He touched it like a man who thought it would bring him good luck. Soon the rest of the family and the neighbours wanted to see it too. At first they clustered in the doorway and beheld me from afar. Growing bolder from week to week, they approached and asked if they could touch, too. I was *orang baterai*, the battery man. *Orang baterai!* The children whispered it when I came up the street. Only half jokingly, Gorys began to call me Pak Baterai, Mr Battery. The name stuck.

Old Gorys was reputed to know the whereabouts of a cache of gold buried on the island by Portuguese pirates at a time when the people of Lefó still rode whales. Even in lean years there had always been a degree of unaccountable prosperity in House-of-Three-Families. It was also said that he knew where the ancestors had hidden Beleloko, the last of the sacred stones, the one that got away. All the others had been removed by the missionaries and buried in the foundations of the church. Gorys was the sole inhabitant of the village, they said, who had not converted to Christianity and in secret continued to worship the *pung alep*, the spirits of the place. Even if none of these things were true, the head of the three families encouraged people to believe them. Like the ear-trumpet and the spectacles, they contributed to the part. He might act like a clown, but he was a crafty old fellow.

After Ino's ill-fated Yamaha venture, House-of-Three-Families had been the first in the village to succeed in running a profitable outboard motor business. Nasu told me it was Gorys who recognised the opportunity and masterminded the coup. Where did he get the money from? The Portuguese gold hoard.

Whatever the risks, they were prudently spread. Only the west wing of the House was involved in the Yamaha venture. It turned out to be lucrative, but its dependence on an unknown new quantity called cash, notably to buy gas and spare parts which, unlike everything else in Lefó, couldn't be manufactured from palm trees, made it an unreliable business in Gorys's view. The south wing sailed sampans and caught flying fish. There might not be very many of them in the nets, but at least the sampans would always bring something back home to eat. The east wing contributed *matros* to Lefó's traditional enterprise, the hunting of whales. Seven kinsmen of Gorys crewed on the *tena*, three of them on the *Aro Tena*, of which Nasu was the boat master. These were Marlboro Man, Ben and Romu.

I went to sea with these men every day. I had come to an arrangement with Nasu. I paid him a boat fee of twenty thousand rupees. This was the going rate, agreed on by all the boat masters at the meeting under the *budi* tree two months before. This way I could give Nasu money he had earned rather than received as alms. He shared it with the crew.

He kept his pride. It was less than a pittance, but without it they would have had nothing at all when they returned empty-handed after another day at sea.

Why this ill-favoured *nasib* should continue to afflict the *tena* fishermen for such a long time became the subject they all discussed at House-of-Three-Families on Sunday mornings. Thanks nominally to the Portuguese gold hoard, actually to the catch brought home by the sampans and the Yamaha, the discussion could take place in an atmosphere less strained than it would have been in other households in Lefó.

Paulus, who operated the family-owned Yamaha, believed the straits were being overfished by the fleets coming down from Taiwan and Hong Kong and illegally entering Indonesian waters. They used sophisticated technology, to which many of the houses in Lefó bore witness. The long antennae mounted on drums had been detached from the buoys on which they floated at sea and brought home as booty, serving as flagpoles, totem poles or clothes pegs at the entrance to House-of-Three-Families. Sensors in the drum recorded catch by weight in the nets marked by the buoys, transmitting the data via satellite to the fishing companies' headquarters in Taipeh or Hong

Kong. Their fishing boats would only undertake the long journey down to make their haul at their leisure when the transmitter signalled that the nets were full. Yamahas going beyond the fifteen-kilometre range that was the operational limit for slow-sailing *tena* sometimes encountered these poachers. There had been bloody battles, an official protest from Indonesia, a commission of inquiry when a man was killed.

Marlboro Man, responsible for bringing round the sail on Nasu's boat, and his brother-in-law Ben, a middle-thwart or all-purpose *matros* on the *Aro Tena*, supported the view that volcanic activity in the seabed between Lefó and Timor had driven away the fish. The ocean was heating up and overcooking their food. As for the whales, Ben thought they had been diverted from their usual passage up the straits and now slipped round the south coast of Timor rather than to the north. The column of smoke on the horizon observed from Lefó intermittently over periods of weeks during the past couple of years could only be explained in this way. An article in a magazine they had been shown by one of the American anthropologists lent credence to this view. As the decline in the number of whales visiting Lefó corresponded to the time that had elapsed since the first eruption, Ben and Marlboro Man thought this must also be the cause.

Six wives and twice as many children scattered over the floor also wanted their say. Ben's wife thought there had always been years when the whales stayed away. This was *nasib* and didn't need to be explained. Some day they would return. The village must speak with the missionary and ask him to remember the whales in his prayers. Perhaps a procession with a blessing of all the whalers' houses was needed. What the rest of the womenfolk thought I never found out, because the conversation slipped back into the Lefó language and I was unable to follow what they said.

Romu sat among the children, his arms clasped round one of the younger cousins sitting on his lap, listening with a beatific smile on his moon-calf face to the babble of voices around him. He would have liked to say something but didn't dare. At sixteen he was hardly more than a child himself, much the youngest *matros* in Lefó, the only representative of the next generation who had chosen to become a whaler. Perhaps he had no alternatives. He was given the dishwasher's job on the *Aro Tena*, bailing out bilge water all day in the middle-thwart section next to his uncle Ben, but he was more treasured as the boat's buffoon. Romu had his grandfather's aptitude for clownery without his cunning. He wore a child's blue sun hat. It was too small for his large round head, but he loved it so much he kept it on even indoors. It was tied under his chin and perched high on his head, fringed with tassels like a woman's old-fashioned bonnet. Now and then he risked opening his mouth. Whatever he did or said was greeted with howls of laughter. He once showed up to work wearing his shirt and shorts back to front. He had been known to mistake the fin of a dolphin at two hundred metres for the fin of a shark, a clash of wave crests a kilometre away for the blow of a sperm whale. Such gaffes of Romu's could entertain the crew for weeks. He learned that the only way to avoid them was to keep his mouth shut. Then the crew would try to draw him out and get him to make another. Enjoying the attention, he eventually succumbed to their wiles and did.

The two people whose opinions would have been most highly valued chose not to contribute anything to the debate. They drank *tuak* with the others and joined in the laughter, but whatever Nasu and Gorys thought about the absence of the whales, they kept it to themselves.

The Whale Stone

During *barafai*, the very hot months between the rainy and the dry season, the ebb tides began to go out so far that the coastal sea seemed to be evaporating. At certain times one couldn't bring boats to the shore. One could stand in the Garden of Skulls outside Nasu's house and not even see the ocean, but the smell of it was always in my nostrils when I visited Nasu or, increasingly often, his neighbour Petrus.

For a long time I had misjudged the Pirate because of the ferocity of his appearance, the scowling face under the turban, a voice that seemed able only to roar, the terrific scars on his chest, left unnaturally inflated after he had fallen out of a tree as a boy and broken all of his ribs. They had grown back together, but not in quite the right way. The Pirate resembled a man who had just taken a deep breath and not yet exhaled. He looked as if he was on the verge of an outburst. Yet he was the most gentle and generous person. He was always pressing gifts on me, a yam or an avocado he had raised on his plot on the mountain, an egg, a piece of tortoiseshell or something he had found on the beach.

Petrus shared his small hut with two quarrelsome sisters, a slovenly, overworked, bad-tempered wife, the mother of three unwashed children who ran around in rags. The Pirate needed his bugle of a voice to keep some sort of order in his own back yard. Children, pigs, a goat and a clutch of hens were often to be found tumbling over one another, all clamouring for food at the same time. The Pirate's wife lashed out with the flat of her hand at whatever got in her way. It was left to him to console crying children, taking them on his lap and leaning over them, if necessary all three of them at once, their heads tucked under the protrusion of his chest as if sheltering in an overhang on a cliff. It was Petrus who often fed the family when he got back from the sea. Helpings of sweet potato and snails were gobbled down greedily at four o'clock in the afternoon.

When the family had been fed – I escaped an offer of snails with the excuse that my landlady would be waiting with supper – the wreckage of the day more or less cleared from his yard, the Pirate and I would often sit out there, addressing a jug of *tuak* on the high-legged card table between us. The Pirate had found it washed up on the beach. The folding card table had lost its baize but remained collapsible, sometimes of its own accord. When the moon was full it shone down on us with such brightness that I could read the letters on the Pirate's tobacco tin and watch his garbage disposal unit at work. A sow tethered on a rope passed through its pierced ear grunted contentedly as it buried its snout in the bonus of trash the Pirate's wife tossed out of the window into its corner of the yard.

From the seabed exposed in the afternoons a great heat rose up to lay siege to the land throughout the night. To escape the heat and the stench that rose with it I moved out of the anthropologists' sweltering hut to a dwelling in Does-not-have-Loincloth, some three or four hundred metres above sea level. It was a steep climb up a very roughly cobbled path. In the palpably cooler climate zone you entered on your approach to the village there was a richer vegetation and the crops on the terraced hillside evidently did better. It was a spruce green village, or rather hamlet, with houses half concealed in the trees, the tapestry-like palm-woven walls of the houses decorated with a variety of patterns using the natural variations in the shade of the palm leaves.

The hamlet stood in the domain of Bela Bora, a clan of wizards who had power over mice and rats. Until not so long ago Lefó used to call on them for their services in time of war. Before Lefó sent its troops into battle the king of rats was summoned by the wizards and dispatched with his rat hordes to eat the enemy's eyes. Lefó had won many wars by means of this stratagem. In times of peace the clan was also consulted for other purposes. When a household suffered a plague of mice Bela Bora could get rid of them by calling them and asking them to desist. If the mice continued they fed them morsels of a bitter-tasting wood, and the mice disappeared.

Even after the powers of the clan passed into decline, Master of Mice and Rats remained the official title my landlord had inherited. In civilian life he answered to the name of Gabo and was married to Sinta, a sister of Cor's, a plump, broad-faced woman with Negroid features unusual in Lefó. It was many years since he had seen the king of rats personally, in fact not since he was a small boy. Gabo remembered the king of rats as being the size of a cat. He had a chequered coat, he said, and red eyes. Gabo no longer knew the exact words to be pronounced in order to call the rat king. But the accoutrements that went with his office, a gong for summoning the rats, a set of wooden plates for feeding them and a baton for directing them to their places, still stood on a beam between the kitchen and living-room. In his grandfather's day, before the missionaries came, these utensils had been in daily use to feed the rodents whenever the family also sat down to eat.

As an inmate of the house I did not unduly regret the passing of these rat-feeding customs. I was content to live without scuttling company in my hut adjoining the main house. My room soon accommodated other animal visitors in any case. It had a swept earth floor, a bamboo-frame cot for my own roll-up mattress and two poles to hang up a mosquito net, on top of which the hens liked to come and roost, leaving their eggs behind them as room fee when they departed. Their occasional clucking at night apart, I felt comfortable in this mountain hamlet. I liked its neatness, coolness, the abundance of green, the high-low swooping song like the flight of the long-tailed bird who lived in the tree above my head and regularly woke me with his morning call. Singing birds surrounded the house, filling the shadows and the sunlit greenery with their trills. In cages on his veranda Gabo kept a species of superb singing thrush, probably *mata putih*, or Oriental White Eye, feeding them grasshoppers to improve the quality of their song.

Living in Does-not-have-Loincloth added an hour and a half to my working day. To get to the beach in time for the sailing of the *tena* in the mornings I had to leave when it was still dark. The climb back up the steep rocky path in the full heat of *siang* exhausted me. But I was content. The centre of gravity of my life in Lefó shifted from the sea to the mountain.

Perhaps this was due to the sense of restfulness that emanated from Gabo's wife. Nearly all of the women of Lefó wove cloth, but Sinta wove more than any of them. Her two unmarried daughters Yuli and Etta ran the household, leaving Sinta free to sit at her hand loom all day and weave the motifs of Lefó into her sombre cloths, whales and manta rays, dark seas and forests, a sun in perpetual eclipse. She led a sedentary life, though none the less industrious for that. Weaving was a *cash crop*, Gabo told me, a new word the Master of Mice and Rats had picked up from Pak Ani's transistor and liked to drop into our conversations. Any revenues that might once have accrued from his own hereditary office were non-existent these days. Once a year a five-legged gentleman arrived from Flores. He paid Sinta a few hundred thousand rupees, fifty dollars at most, taking away piles of purple seas and black suns woven into cloths that would decorate tables or be worked up as sarong.

Under a palm-leaf awning in the forest near the house where I lived a group of my acquaintances regularly gathered around a charcoal fire, which they pumped with bellows made of a pig's bladder attached to hollow bamboo poles. Lefó needed a forge, but it didn't need one here. It was no coincidence that the best trees for *tuak* were to be found in this particular spot. This was why the forge was located in a secluded grove of lontar palm trees high up on the mountain, a nice quiet spot for a drink, out of earshot of wives and children, rather than down on the shore where it was most needed.

Lontar palms yielded their wine in great plenty during the season of *barafai*. The term meant literally Drip Plenty in Heat, which was why the hottest months of the year were named after it. Someone had to climb the tree to tap the tips of the fresh palm shoots for their sap. It collected and fermented in a bamboo hanging under the branch. Every so often the tree climber shinned up the trunk with empty bamboo containers and brought down the full ones. It was a demanding exercise. Tree climbers were on a rota system as waiters. They had to remain sober to serve the others. This wasn't always guaranteed. Accidents happened.

Ebony-skinned, fierce-faced Alo was among the regular drinkers at the forge bar, Gabo, Nasu and his cronies, Stanis and Petrus the Pirate, Marlboro Man or one of his many kinsmen from House-of-Three-Families who was good at climbing trees, plus Bapak Cor, who was more of a consumer than a collector of *tuak*. He excused himself on the grounds that he had no head for heights. Often Romu would be roped in for this service. There was always a good reason for a drink because there was always something to be fixed at the forge. The men heated whatever metal they could lay their hands on, a carpenter's file, part of the engine of a car, using it to smith a parang, a *duri* or perhaps a harpoon. Automobile springs were the preferred raw material for the whalers' knives, but they weren't always available. Two men actually worked, one of them smithing, the other operating the bellows. All the others looked on and contributed talk to the proceedings while they sat around drinking *tuak*. Cor provided incidental music with the Jew's harp, percussive effects with hollow coconuts and a stick. Alo and Petrus the Pirate roasted peanuts in the ashes round the fire.

We were sitting here on a Sunday afternoon when the sound of women singing breached the stillness of the forest. Figures became visible on the path that came winding up from Animal-around-the-Mountain. Unlike Sinta, who led a very sedentary life at her loom, the women of Lefó were tall, lean people with muscular bodies and a rhythmic swinging stride developed from fetching and carrying fire-wood and green fodder, fish and pails of water up and down the mountain all day. They were dressed in their Sunday best, white blouses and dark sarong, which they had put on for church in the morning and not taken off since. Some of them also wore their medal for distinction in choir service on a blue band hanging round their necks. This was an indication of the highest priority in the protocol of Lefó. An important ceremony must be in progress. And it was, a Litany sung in procession round the village for the third successive Sunday.

At the head of the procession walked the priest Pater Ybang in cassock and surplice, followed by two incense bearers in what looked like white dressing-gowns. Reaching the first house in Does-not-have-Loincloth, the procession stopped for the priest to bless the house and sprinkle holy water against the walls, just as he had done during the ceremony of consecrating the boats. He moved on through the hamlet, briskly blessing each of the half dozen or so houses, while the incense-swinging acolytes and hymn-singing women traipsed in pursuit. Within a quarter of an hour the entire hamlet had been blessed and the procession turned back down the mountain.

Three Sundays in a row the priest and the procession of singing women moved up and down and round Lefó, asking Bapak to intercede for the fishermen and bring a blessing on their houses.

Sampan fishermen did indeed report a slight improvement of the catch in their nets at this time. Most of the Yamahas pulled in the odd dolphin or killer whale every two or three days, but were having to go out further in search of their prey and were spending more money on gasoline. But the *tena* caught nothing at all. The blessings and the litany sung in procession round the village did nothing to alleviate the dearth of whales.

At the forge under the palm trees the men sat watching the

proceedings in silence, commenting on them here and there with soft, wide-open sounds of what sounded like curiosity and surprise. The efforts of the priest and the women deserved their respect, if not their active participation. Sunday was after all their only day of rest. But as soon as the procession was out of sight there was a call for fresh *tuak*. Alo shinned up the trunk. Not enough time had elapsed since they had last had recourse to the tree, however, and Alo came down again with only one full bamboo.

Cor twanged his harp disconsolately in the twilight. It would be dark in ten minutes. We would have to go home while we could still see the way. Gabo drained his coconut shell and licked his moustache. *Mari*, he said. Alo and Petrus took the path back down to Sitting-in-Palm-Tree. Gabo, Stanis, Cor, Nasu and I followed another path in the direction of Does-not-have-Loincloth. We walked in single file across the terraced hillside. Groves of dusty fruit trees dotted the slope. A smattering of parched corn showed up in patches through the red soil. The path led to a grassy knoll on which a solitary rock stuck up at an angle, conspicuously outlined against the evening sky.

This was the rock named Nose-of-Whale because it resembled the head of a breaching sperm whale. Nasu had shown it to me when I first arrived in Lefó. We passed the rock without stopping. Perhaps I was the only one even to give it a second glance. For the first time I now recognised the rock for what it was, or at least what it signified to me. Long gone and pretty much forgotten since the days in the house on Lake Geneva, the treasured heirloom of my childhood had re-surfaced on a mountain in Lefó. The rock called Nose-of-Whale was indeed a whale stone, and I felt as if it had been waiting here all that time to receive from me the appellation to which it was entitled; waiting for the name to find its way to the one object for which it had been intended, waiting to connect.

The Feeding of the tena

Earlier in the summer, sailing days had come to Lefó like flocking crowds, leaving such teeming sensations behind them that one could easily forget that the *tena* did not go out for the pleasure of sailing, only to catch fish. Lights glanced off the wave crests. The sea sparkled. The moment we had passed through the surf and raised the sail the wind slid in under it, puffing the boat out to sea. On the surface I saw spume, an oily slick of bubbles, left by some animal perhaps, or simply caused by the agitation of the sea. Pieces of driftwood scarred the smooth wakes that had been unravelled by the boats like carpets across the sea. The further we sailed out from the bay onto the open sea the stiffer the breeze became. On a course sometimes south-west, sometimes south-east, depending on the wind and the currents, the *tena* went ever further from the shore in search of prey, the eyes painted on the bows wide open to scour the sea.

All nine or ten *matros*, twelve at most, including myself, took up their allotted positions beside the *Aro Tena* in the boathouse at half past six every morning. I didn't have a watch, nor did I need one. I found I could tell the time, close enough, by the feel of the heat and the shade of the light. Other men gathered in knots along the beach. Often there weren't enough of them to crew a boat and they went home. During the months I stayed in Lefó three-quarters of the *tena* never even left the boathouse. The fleets I had seen in the photographs Mans showed me in Switzerland fifteen years before belonged to the past. Such fleets, as many as two dozen *prahu* crowding the horizon, their rectangular sails balanced on a corner like playing cards, would never set sail from Lefó again.

When we were all standing in the boathouse Nasu removed from the bowsprit a sheath woven from lontar palm, under which the boat slept. He was supposed to bring with him the lead harpoon rope, traditionally kept in the clan's great house when the boat was resting on land. But Nasu no longer had the appetite for the steep climb up to the house twice a day, and so the rope was left overnight in the boat. Once the sheath had been removed and the sleeping *tena* woken, one of the crew said a prayer. The rest of us joined in for the responses. It was the first time I had said a prayer in forty years. Then we pushed the boat over the rollers down to the sea, jumped in and paddled through the surf. We continued paddling for the first hundred metres or so. We hauled up the bipod mast and raised the sail. The harpooner whetted a harpoon. When he had finished we took off our hats. A second prayer was said. Then good morning greetings were exchanged. This procedure was followed without change every time the *tena* went out.

Somewhere out there, at ten or twelve, at most fifteen kilometres from the shore, there was an invisible line where the boats turned once they had reached it. On days when there was a brisk wind giving the boat pace we would turn and head back and then out to sea again any number of times. The *tena* didn't sail directly into the wind. Instead, they might tack off the wind with the sail on the right or the left according to where the wind was coming from. On other days we made just the one passage out, with little tacking on the sail back in. Around noon the wind often dropped, the sail hung slack without a sound, the crew fell asleep.

During the later summer, there were glassy days of a stillness in which the splash of the smallest jumping fish was audible. Once we had left the noise of the surf behind us we became aware of the silence, causing us to turn and look searchingly around the sea. As we paddled out, one of the men began to sing, a singing that managed to be at once harsh and melodious. There were two chants in succession, to which the rest of the crew responded in chorus. Sometimes the response came in on the tail of the lead singer, causing an overlapping effect, like a canon. With this singing they put something in an empty space where there was nothing, no movement in the sea, no sound in the air. The song seemed to challenge this emptiness, to give determination and purpose to a situation that gave cause for neither. The singing rowers rose out of their sitting positions and uttered short sharp yelps as they tugged at the oars, and their urgency conveyed to me that a hunt was already in progress, though there was no quarry to be seen. On a song you could be carried a long way out before the sail was raised, the song died and the routine set in.

Ten *prahu* sailed out on the morning the *Aro Tena* caught the manta ray and the hammerhead shark, more boats than I had seen on any other day.

It seemed that it would be another slow morning when we set out. There was almost no wind, no current. We could do no more than drift out to sea. Sailing east, parallel to the shore, we spotted the shark. Nasu made a big leap for this one. He was back in the boat more quickly than usual. You could never tell with sharks. He made a strike, the harpoon had lodged in the animal, but somehow the nylon line had slipped out of the splice connecting the harpoon lead rope with the rest of the line, which was now uncoiling out of the boat. The shark was swimming off, trailing the loose nylon line behind him. Nasu threw a second harpoon, which missed, and on the throw he again went with it into the sea. Ani, the silent and usually placid man at the tiller, was the first to see what had happened. We would lose the shark. He stood up and shouted in great excitement at the crew, scrambling to the front of the boat, somehow skimming over our laps in that airborne manner which became possible in moments of crisis.

Before I knew what was happening he had plunged overboard, a man swimming in pursuit of a shark, something one wasn't often going to see. He caught hold of the line, which I could see floating in a coil on the surface, gripped it between his teeth and swam back to the boat. The shark hadn't gone far, the line was still slack. The crew made it fast round one of the thwarts. Then they played the animal, letting it come, letting it run. It must have been hurt quite badly, or it would presumably have taken the line much further out. Soon they would be able to haul it in. They stuck a gaffe in the mouth of the shark and tried to pull it over the gunwale. It came up, tail thrashing. It was a big, heavy animal. They had to let it down again with the gaffe still stuck in its throat, the wooden shaft sometimes banging against the side of the boat. This struggle and the dreadful knocking sound continued for several minutes. It seemed to herald some kind of grim admittance to the place where the animal would be done to death. At last they were able to haul it over into the middle section of the boat. It flailed around for a few moments and then suddenly died.

In death it still seemed such a paragon of life, all spurting gleam and gloss, a revelation, bearing witness to an existence that was hidden from us in the sea. It was an impressive animal at such close quarters, a hammerhead shark, about three metres long from tip to tail, and with the oddest shaped head I had ever seen on any animal.

The head was an extraordinary projection, a freakish design, like something that had emerged in the course of an evolution different from the one that had produced the rest of animal life in the sea. If the manta ray had reminded me of a stealth bomber, the shark was a machine designed for space travel. The body was a single muscle. The flat head protruding from this body was shaped like two hammers placed handle to handle, their heads curving round and back in just the way the term *hammerhead* describes, with two eyes set far apart on the outside of the curving hammer heads, mounted there, one might have said, like two searchlights on the twin towers of a craft designed to roam the perpetual night of the deep sea. It remained a taut, vibrant creature even when dead. I had seen it at its most shark-like when it circled the boat, a shadowy presence at a depth of three metres, looking dangerous, as if the boat were its prey and it was moving in to strike. And there it now lay amidships, the victim we had sacrificed, a shark like a Christ, beautiful for us in its death, mysteriously bearing no more visible wound than the small mark of the harpoon that had been thrust in its side.

In seventeen days at sea the shark was only the third catch the *Aro Tena* had made. This momentary improvement in *nasib* still wasn't enough to revive a crew that had become steadily more morose as the summer passed. Things hadn't gone much better for the other boats.

There followed a long and slow drift back to the shore in the course of a windless afternoon. For me this aftermath of the catch was the time that took me beyond my physical limits, the amount of heat and dehydration, the cramps from crouching for hours in a confined space – more, I thought, than I could endure.

The current had carried us far to the west of the village, making it impossible to come in under sail. This meant we would have a long paddle back. The sail was lowered close in to a rocky shore, on which tumultuous waves were crashing. They would have smashed us to pieces if we had been driven ashore. It required all one's strength to keep the *prahu* off those rocks. The boat teetered on the crests and then plunged violently down into the troughs of the waves, almost pitching one out of the boat. But Nasu in his high thin voice began to chant, and soon the others joined in, singing what sounded like a two-line refrain to Nasu's verses, keeping the pace and distracting them from the thought of those rocks and the long haul home. The sight of the sea sucking down from those wave-shattered rocks, opening up chasms, frightened me even after I had seen it many times.

Eh héh héh héh héh!
Méh *éh* méh *éh!*
Hua *heck!* Hua *heck!*
Wailabe wailabe!
Hrr *yá!* Hrr *yá!*

Bo! Bo! Bo! Bo!

A cacophony of animal noises improvised by the crew – yelping, bleating, neighing and barking – added urgency to the chant and the plying of oars until we rounded the point and had passed into the quiet water of the bay. Several *prahu* were lined up outside the surf. The shark was dismembered while we waited our turn.

The little old man in the *Bintang Java* baseball cap, Bapak Stanis, whose menial job on board was to supply the crew with water from the jar beside him, now began to stir and show us what sort of a man he still was. This wizened old fellow with the permanently pinched mouth, as if he was biting into a sour lemon, was the boat's butcher. Whetting his *duri* as slowly as he did everything, he set up a plank between two of the thwarts amidships where the shark lay. Five men heaved it up onto the old man's anatomy table so that Stanis could get to work.

When he was done, the plank passed to Nasu at the bows. With equal skill, or so it seemed to me, he dissected the manta ray, although here lay a cause of many of the *Aro Tena*'s later troubles. By the time we reached the shore the manta, too, had been divided up among us. Everyone had his share strung up and knotted on a strip of palm fibre for carrying home. Marlboro Man washed the plank by dipping it a few times over the side of the boat. Bits of gristle, dark red clots of blood swam past me in the transparent green sea like underwater shooting stars, flashing brilliant crimson colours as they emerged from the shadow of the sail and were caught in the sunlight before disappearing in the sea behind us.

Sometimes there weren't many men on the beach to help bring the boats up out of the water. Despite repeated efforts we were sometimes unable to move a boat up any further than it had already been carried by the wave. But the old men who hung around on the beach to help bring in the heavy *tena* knew that nothing would be accomplished with force. However young and strong you were you had to wait until the boat was ready to go. They leaned back and chatted and showed no sign of wanting to do anything for a while, until one of them gave the cue with *satu, dua, tiga!* as if to make up for the lack of strength in their limbs by giving voice to the urgency of the task. Boats that had refused to budge a minute before now seemed to glide up the beach of their own accord.

After we had brought the *Aro Tena* in I gave Petrus the Pirate some money for *tuak* to celebrate the catch. We lounged in the shade of the boathouse, recovering from our exertions. It had been a good day in the end. *Nasib!* Fate! It was always the same word I learned to give in answer to people's questions when I walked back up the village street, acceptance of what was given, however well or poorly we had done, because – and this was the mystery of *nasib* – it wasn't we who had done it. After the crew had gone home Nasu remained lying alone on the beach, staring silently out to sea as he was doing more and more these days, as if trying to fathom the ocean's secret.

It was on the following morning, having waited in vain for a crew to assemble on the beach, that Nasu took me to the great house, or what was regarded as the guardian house in which the soul of the *Aro Tena* found safekeeping. This was where the *leo*, the harpoon lead rope used on board the boat, had traditionally been kept whenever the boat was not at sea. It was still kept there for the six months of the off season when the *tena* remained in the boathouse. The old custom, however, of taking it there at the end of every day at sea and picking it up again the next morning had fallen into disuse, at least in Nasu's clan. I guessed one reason might have been the extremely steep climb up to the house, which was situated high on the mountain directly above the village. In more conveniently located great houses, I was told, the *leo* was still returned to its place every night.

My imagination had led me to expect that a *great house* would be something along the lines these words suggested, a thatched, timbered barn of a house full of shadows and heirlooms of the clan, perhaps with a skull or two lurking on a shelf at the back. I was disillusioned when the path emerged beside a spruce little brick dwelling with a tin roof topped by a television aerial, well-kept and gardened, with a magnificent view of the sea. An old man who was blind, an uncle of Nasu's, lived here with his wife, daughter and son-in-law. Nasu showed me around the house. There was a surprisingly well-appointed sitting-room with a sofa and a TV (it was the first house to have installed a diesel generator providing it with electricity), and it was on a table by the TV that the *leo* had its place. I had thought there would be some kind of shrine. Nasu pointed to a space on the table. I could more easily have imagined a programme guide or TV-dinner tray resting there than a hallowed piece of rope from a whaling boat. This was where the *leo* was kept when the *Aro Tena* was not at sea? Well, yes, said Nasu, and he began to qualify the yes. It wasn't here at the moment. It was in the boathouse.

Before walking back up the mountain I stopped off at the village shop. It had only recently opened and was run out of a shed for fishing gear in Back-of-the-Whale. No barter was accepted here. It was cash only. Soap, detergents, clove cigarettes you could buy one at a time for a few rupees, instant noodles, biscuits – the bottled water excepted, all the products on sale here came with a smell of fish. Anything with even a suggestion of sweetness was welcome, simply to get a taste in my mouth of something other than crusted salt. I tried whatever the truck happened to bring on its sporadic deliveries, Roma Quality Biscuits, Malkist Crackers, something called Mengandung Malt *untuk tenaga baru*, to renew your energy, as the ad on the package promised. These, plus the occasional Coke or beer when in stock, which I would share with Gabo and his wife, had to be transported back to Does-not-have-Loincloth inside a rucksack. I did not feel comfortable about this deviousness. But anything I held visibly in my hands would have to be shared by the people who met me on my way, hailed me, in-spected my purchases and helped me to consume them as we walked along. Before I had even reached Sitting-in-Palm-Tree it would have all gone.

On coming out of the shop I saw that a meeting was being held in Clearing-under-the-Banyan. Chairs had been put out in facing lines with the geometrical exactness favoured in Lefó when any kind of official community business was afoot. I noticed that most of the crew of the *Aro Tena* were there. Romualdus, the sampan fisherman from Animal-around-the-Mountain and *sekretaris* to the headman of Lefó's two western hamlets, attended the meeting with a big book under his arm, suggesting he was there to take minutes.

Bapak Cor emerged from a house in Back-of-the-Whale and fell into step with me as we made our way up the mountain. I asked him what the meeting was about. Cor said there was an argument between the crews of the *tena* and the Yamahas because recently the Yamahas were felt to be cutting in unfairly on prey being pursued by the much slower sailing boats.

This argument had long been brewing. At the root of it was the modest success of the Yamahas and the resounding failure of the *tena* throughout the season. How often had we idled along under a slack sail, waiting for a breeze, and watched with envy as a Yamaha sped past, the crew standing on a smoothly boarded deck with streamlined hair and their hands behind their backs, like some team of inspectors of the sea, not bestowing even a glance in our direction. How bitter to row back an empty boat in the afternoon heat and find dolphins laid out in a glistening line on the beach, white-bellied sharks and killer whales harpooned by Yamaha crews who sat smoking at their leisure in the shade of the boathouse as we came scrambling through the surf.

I was sitting drinking coffee with Gabo and Sinta on their veranda after supper when Cor materialised out of the dark. Usually so laid back in his manner, an ironic tone never far from the thoughts to which he gave expression, Cor was serious for once. He spoke for some minutes in a low, urgent tone. Gabo listened without interruption. Then his wife got up and disappeared. A frantic clucking of hens was audible from behind the house. A few minutes later Sinta reappeared with a burning torch in one hand, a mute hen in the other, hanging upside down on a strip of fibre she had tied round its claws. In this position, it seemed, rowdy chickens could be instantly silenced.

There was a problem with the *tena*, Cor said to me in Indonesian, followed by something else I didn't understand. Cor rephrased it. The *tena* was sick, he explained. It needed medicine to make it better. My presence at the sick bed of the boat was required. Hadn't it carried me on its back across the sea all these weeks? I must go down the mountain with him to visit the boat now. For the time being that was all Cor would tell me. Only later did I learn the background to this affair.

It seemed that certain crew members of the *Aro Tena* had been dissatisfied with their share of the manta ray and the shark we had caught the previous day. This came out at the meeting held under the *budi* tree that night. The complaint had nothing to do with the meeting. It had been washed up among the general grumbling. But until a ceremony had been carried out to remove the fault the boat would catch no fish.

The responsibility for this lay with the boat master Nasu. Probably there were quite a number on the *Aro Tena* who wondered, as I did, whether Nasu at his age was still up to the demands of a harpooner's job. He was slowing down. His judgement was no longer reliable. He had missed a few certain targets earlier in the season when there had been more targets around. Perhaps it might be better for Nasu to step down and let Ioh take over, but these were thoughts to occupy the boat master, not his crew. Each man must look into himself and, if he found a fault, root it out. Ani the helmsman, discontented with his share of the ray, would know what that was, as would Nasu who had divided the ray and continually neglected to bring the *leo* to the great house, as would the anonymous offenders who had been urinating on the fishing nets in the boathouses of other clans, just as I myself came to realise it was unacceptable to take food on board that was not shared by the others or to hide my purchases at the village shop in a rucksack and smuggle them up to Does-not-have-Loincloth. All these actions were lapses in the caring behaviour it was necessary to show the *tena*. Improper conduct towards the boat, or towards others, which did not accord with behaviour regarded by the community as fitting, would have fatal consequences for the boats and their crews.

To amend the fault it would be necessary to make an offering to the spirit of the boat before it next went out to sea, namely tomorrow. Cor came up that night to fetch a chicken from Does-not-have-Loincloth because the person or persons who had done the complaining – in fact it was Ani the helmsman – were bound to provide from their own hamlet the live animal traditionally prescribed for the boat-appeasement ritual. All crew members had to attend the ceremony, so my presence was also required.

It was a very dark night. Despite the flare carried by Cor to give us some light, I stumbled and slithered a good part of my way down the steep mountain path. The warm air breezing over my skin felt like velvet, then like the wings of moths. The light must have attracted them. I didn't see any but I could feel them brushing my face and crawling in my hair. Not a single light was burning when we passed through Sitting-in-Palm-Tree. By nine o'clock most of Lefó was in bed. A pounding and sucking and clamouring began to fill the darkness as we came down the mountain. By the sound of the waves breaking on the shore, more and more clearly audible the further we descended, a big sea was rising, flooding the night.

We ducked down one of the narrow alleys between the boathouses and came out onto the beach, it seemed as if to huge applause, beneath a breathtakingly star-crowded sky. Grains of sand absorbed and reflected grains of starlight and lit up the ground under my feet. It was like stepping out onto an illuminated stage between the dark land to the rear and the dark jostling mass of the sea to the fore, tumultuously applauding in the auditorium.

Cor planted the torch in the sand in front of the boathouse of the *Aro Tena*. Other lights were already burning on the beach. A small fire had been lit in a hollow in the sand. A hurricane lamp hanging from a roof beam illuminated the prow of the boat. A knot of men entangled round the fire dissolved as we approached. Nasu came up and Cor handed him the chicken. Nasu slid the stretched neck of the chicken along the blade of the *duri* Cor held out for him and cut off its head so deftly that I didn't even see it happen. I saw blood leaping out of Nasu's hands, spattering his chest and shoulders. Muttering a few words, he held up the headless chicken and smeared its blood over the gunwale, the planks around the bows and along the sides, or what were also called the boat's chest, shoulders and flanks, for *tena* had a body like men, and a soul no less. Everyone came forward and touched the boat on the places where Nasu had smeared blood. Cor nudged me to do the same.

A murmur passed through the onlookers standing round the entrance to the boathouse. Nasu held out the chicken for Marlboro Man to impale it on a metal rod. His brother-in-law Ben strung the head of the chicken on a separate wire. Marlboro Man balanced the spit on forked sticks stuck in the ground on either side of the fire. The head was slung over the spit to roast alongside the body. Sparks flew into the boathouse. Several of the crew gathered round the fire to shield it from the wind.

There we all sat while the chicken roasted and the men talked among themselves in the language of Lefó, huddled in their sarong, their voices sliding into the softly crooning sing-song mode I sometimes heard at sea, which sounded like a lullaby. The burned chicken that came off the spit looked even scrawnier than the raw bird that had been impaled on it. Shared out among nine men, it hardly made a mouthful for each of us. The head, the liver and the heart were given to the *tena* to eat. The head was placed in the boat's mouth at the top of the bowsprit, the innards on the strakes in its bowels, and when I came down to the beach the next morning it had all gone.

Signs and Portents

Pater Ybang was the first Indonesian incumbent to run the mission in Lefó. At the time of my visit he had been in residence there for seven years. Now in his forties, he was born and had grown up in the mountains of Standing Person at a time when European missionaries were already established in Lefó. He was kin to the people here. He knew their language and customs as well as any of them. He must have known what was going on in the village.

Practices associated with the spirit worship of the island's pre-Christian past had been suppressed by his predecessors in the parish but never entirely stamped out. Here and there they survived in secret, and where they did they flourished with the vigour of a forbidden cult. The pater must have known that the whalers of Lefó still believed their boats were living beings and had souls. He might also have observed that the strength of these beliefs faded from one generation to the next. Spirits distinctly defined in the consciousness of Nasu were no more than vague presences at the back of his son Ioh's mind, while for his grandsons they no longer existed. Doubtless the pastor recognised all these things but chose to say nothing, knowing that time was on his side.

How Sinta knew of the goings-on in the village, house-bound as she was with her bad leg, remained a mystery to me. Apart from her visits to church on Sunday, the wife of the Master of Mice and Rats never went down the mountain. Even within the confines of Does-not-have-Loincloth she seldom left the house. She sat all day at her loom, weaving her dark seas and suns. But she had the gift of listening. People were always dropping in for a chat. She put them under her listening spell, continuing her weaving while they talked. The words that left their mouths passed ceaselessly through her fingers and entered the cloths she wove, reconstituted as signs and symbols, a trail of circles, pyramids and rhomboid shapes, arrowheads, fish bones, skulls and bird-claw marks, left as clues scattered across her sombre landscapes. Almost incidentally, reassuring in its ordinariness, I recognised in Sinta the paradox I had thought was an impossibility, the weaver who did not weave, a doer so much at one with what she did that she no more wove than was herself woven at the loom through which her life passed.

From Sinta I heard rumours of increased activities that went on at night, the feeding of certain ancient trees, certain rocks regarded as sacred and favoured with yams and morsels of fish, but where the trees and rocks were, or who fed them, she couldn't say. Sampan fishermen took to washing their nets and removing them from the beach at night for fear that someone, men or demons, it was not clear which, had been urinating on them in order to prevent them from catching fish. At this time there were strange signs coming out of the sea, too, a herd of dolphins, in numbers unknown before in the living memory of Lefó, not a single one of which the fishermen were able to harpoon, and a baleen whale they were forbidden to, though it accompanied the boats during the long days of the sea's emptiness and sometimes came so close we could have touched it with an outstretched oar.

From a distance of about two kilometres the passage of the dolphins looked like an endlessly breaking wave, a mysterious channel of rough water pouring across the surface of the sea. They were Risso's dolphins as far as I could tell. The bodies of the dark bluish-grey dolphins weaving in and out of the sea, hardly distinguishable in colour from the metallic water out of which they rose, resembled a disturbance in the surface such as might have been caused by a strong upstream or current. It was a herd of a couple of thousand animals, dipping and rising head to tail, head to tail in a dense stream of plied needles, flowing liquidly, river-like, over the plain of the sea. They would pass directly across the *Aro Tena*'s bows. I thought that if we had all paddled to give extra speed to our slow sailing pace we might have reached them in time. But no one stirred, not even Nasu crouching motionless on his platform. The crew sat as if paralysed, leaving the boat to the sluggish progress provided by the faint breeze. By the time we reached the herd it had passed out of reach. Nasu laid the harpoon back on the outrigger rack and didn't reach for it again.

All day the boat crept over the sea under an overcast sky. The great expanse of water retained a metallic colour between blue and grey. It ran in a soft rippling swell that reminded me of wind passing over a field, flattening the grass. With no warning the whale came up like an emerging island only thirty metres from the boat, taking everyone by surprise.

Woh!

It was a big animal, about fifteen metres long, whether a sei or a Bryde's whale I couldn't tell. It seemed to me as if the exclamations of *kelaru* and the faces of the men exclaiming were tinged with regret, for *kelaru* referred to a baleen whale, and the hunting of whales with the comb-like plates known as baleen, hanging from the upper jaw in place of teeth, was taboo in Lefó. It was on the back of a baleen whale that their ancestors had been rescued from the great flood and crossed the sea to the place where they had founded the village. They averted their faces, unwilling even to look at the whale. It spouted a few times and came riding up high out of the water, displaying its buoyancy, showing us its whole head and back, as if confident of its immunity. I was hoping it would dive, and we would see the flukes plunging down as it went. But the whale just sank away out of sight.

I came to believe that there were such things as closed and open seas. Sometimes I was sure the sea was closed and I knew it would show us nothing. Then it suddenly came alive. A shoal of flying fish often heralded the emergence of a predator in their wake. The standing men went into a glaze as they scanned the sea, but these were the signs they registered and which caused a surge of attention, of hope. *Something might happen at any time.* This was the fishermen's mantra. On days of wind and waves I could persuade myself that the ocean was open, about to show us something at any moment. But as the winds dropped during the long heat of *barafai* and the sea turned white, day followed day when no one on the *tena* seemed to have even the expectation of making a catch. Sometimes I wondered about a symbiosis of the catcher and the caught, of the fisherman who did not fish and the prey he did not catch. I wondered if the resignation of the fishermen was an intuition of an absence of fish in the sea, and conversely, when the will was there, if the will of the catcher had any influence on the likelihood of fish being caught.

An overcast morning that began with a breeze, the sea scudding away in short, sharp waves, much choppier than usual during the weeks of *barafai* when the sea lay there as if poured on like a glaze, might alone be sufficient reason to raise the crew's hopes. Hope made one superstitious, willing to believe all kinds of omens. The unusually dark day, which might have been called a whale-coloured day, the relatively sail-crowded sea when I looked east, where a line of seven playing-card sails standing on one corner were sliding across the horizon, the oily olive-coloured swell, all these signs seemed to be auspicious.

Sperm whales, even pods of them, were alleged to have been variously sighted from land and at sea in the last few days. So we rode out in a concentrated mood, and soon the breeze picked up and blew us far out. A monologue delivered by Cor in one of his wailing moods accompanied us all the way. Somehow, in the course of this monologue, the crew lost their feeling for whales. They should have been thinking about the quarry, instead they were distracted by Cor droning on. There had been a sense of anticipation on setting out, but then, after the sky cleared and the wind dropped, and Cor had helped to talk the sea back into its customary state of listlessness, the anticipation was dissipated and came to nothing. It would be another empty day, like most of the sixty-seven preceding ones on which the *Aro Tena* had put out to sea.

All morning the sea was at tilt. The swell rode slowly, every so often with one big wave, or rather a kind of exhalation, sending a great sigh through the sea. Fishing was perhaps no longer the reason why a few remaining crews took the *tena* out. We took the boats to sea because if we didn't they would die. Usually there were four or five of them, never more than ten, far too few to comb such a vast expanse of sea. With motor-powered Yamahas it might not matter. But the slow-sailing *tena* had no chance of making a big catch unless they went out in significant numbers. They just didn't cover enough of the ocean. Watching the tilted sea I sometimes had the impression that I was looking up an incline, an endless hillside of water it would be impossible for the boat ever to climb.

Throughout the day we were accompanied by the sacred animal the people of Lefó called *kelaru*, the whale that had given their ancestors life and to whom their descendants gave life in return. For the most part I didn't see it, but we could hear the whale. An eerie sound of breathing followed the boat, audible from half a kilometre away. Sometimes the breathing presence became visible to us as a spout. The baleen lay hidden behind the hill, swimming in the long deep trough on the far side of the swell. The breathing of the whale seemed to me like the ocean's swell become audible, rise and fall given voice as a kind of muted, hollow groan, as an utterance followed by silence. It wasn't until the middle of the day that I got a closer view of the whale.

When we passed it some fifty metres away, rising slowly out of the water and sinking back into it, the embodiment of the deep-breathing ocean, it seemed to me as if it was not the whale but the sea I heard groaning.

The Testament of Gorys

It was years since Gorys had left Animal-around-the-Mountain or even taken a step outside the banana grove where the three families lived. The old man wasn't able to walk too well. On his own he couldn't have made it as far as the village. How he had managed to get himself there while no one was looking remained a mystery. Gorys encouraged it. He believed in the old magic and had no objection to being regarded as something of a magician himself. He didn't mind making use of the advantage people gave him by considering him weak in the head. In reply to their questions he smiled and did a pantomime with his hands, suggesting that he might have levitated from House-of-Three-Families to the chair under the *budi* tree where they found him sitting one Sunday morning when they came out of church.

Most of the morning passed in the shade of the tree where the old man held court. Individuals came and went, but there was always a large crowd of people surrounding Gorys, listening to what he had to say. He didn't mind repeating it for the newcomers. Thus many of Lefó's inhabitants learned not by hearsay what Gorys had dreamed the previous night but got it several times straight from the horse's mouth, his dream of the mountain being gobbled up by a fire-breathing creature that was half snake, half dragon.

Pak Ani was familiar with this creature from the Hoard of Stories that was the repository of Lefó's past, and of which he was the curator. He didn't question the right of Gorys to see images of the dragon-snake in his sleep. He did question Gorys's claim on behalf of his own dream as the begetter of the serpent. The volcanic creator-destroyer from whose fiery turmoils the giant mountain Sack of Snakes had arisen out of the Endless Water existed, independently of the old man's sleep, in the myths describing Lefó's origins at the bottom of

the sea. Pak Ani knew of no stories, however, in which the once re-
gurgitated mountain had reversed the process and consumed itself.
The old man's dream was a new and disquieting version of these long-
established events. To dream that the dragon-snake had gobbled up
the mountain was to dream the death of Lefó.

From the *budi* tree he proceeded on a tour of the houses in Back-of-
the-Whale, not out of courtesy, as some of the inmates thought, but
from a desire to verify that everything was in place. There were a few
surprises in store for him. He inquired after householders who had
long since been dead. He confused grandsons with their grandfathers.
He was troubled on meeting people he had never even heard of. One
house seemed to have got lost, until it was relocated in the building
that now served the village as a store. Gorys was unfamiliar with the
notion of buying goods for money and seemed puzzled by it, just as he
had been puzzled by the absence of the stone seats where the heads of
the clans used to sit in the village square before they were identified
as objects of pagan worship and removed by the missionaries, half a
century ago.

With what feelings he toured the boathouses on the beach could
only be inferred from the stillness of his otherwise always mobile face.
Whatever else he might have forgotten, Gorys knew all the *tena* by
heart, their names and the flags they flew, the upsets and injuries they
had sustained during a lifetime at sea, the memorable whales they had
encountered and fought, the exact order in which they lived in the row
of thatched houses along the beach. A small crowd followed him. He
went into each of the houses, ran his hands along the bleached sides of
the boats, sniffed at them, patted and talked to them just as if they had
been sea horses in their stables. All but one of the first dozen boats he
inquired about had not been taken to sea that season, most of them
not during the preceding season either. For two, three or perhaps even
four years – never too strong on numbers, no one in Lefó could say for
sure how long a particular boat had been laid up. Even the boat
masters seemed to have lost count.

Nasu came out of one of the alleys leading between the boathouses
onto the beach just as Gorys was passing. Sitting down together under
the bows of the *Aro Tena*, the old man asked Nasu about the health of
his boat and seemed extremely pleased to hear it was well. The two
of them remained sitting there all afternoon, long after the crowd
attracted by the sudden appearance of Gorys earlier that day had lost

interest in him and dispersed. Later they were joined by Ioh and Cor and a number of Gorys's sons or sons-in-law. When Romualdus helped his father to climb into a sampan and paddled him home, back round the point to the little beach below Animal-around-the-Mountain, darkness had long since fallen.

Sinta at her loom in Does-not-have-Loincloth had foreseen the pattern of these events and woven them fast in her cloth landscape before they had time to happen. The mountain had disappeared. In its place lay the coils of the dragon-snake that had devoured it, its jaws open now to drink up the sea. What was left of the water in the sea had turned into diamonds. All the other diamonds had flown out to the edges, like pieces shifted in a kaleidoscope, regrouping in a pattern bordering the cloth.

When I went down to the boathouse of the *Aro Tena* in the morning there was no sign of any crew. It was only just light. Smoke from the fires in kitchens hung in grey strands over the village like an early-morning mist. A few sampan had gone out in the night and were now on their way back in. At the far end of the shore a Yamaha had been hauled halfway down the beach in the shadow cast by Standing Person to the east. It was surrounded by a group of people too far away for me to make out. The boat would shortly put to sea, probably across the bay to the village below Standing Person where there was a market and a *kantor* regularly visited by people with official business. I watched a figure come walking towards me. It was Paulus, the skipper of the Yamaha operated by the three families. *Woh*, he greeted me, *Pak Baterai apa kabar. Woh*, I replied, Mr Battery was fine. Paulus plonked down on the sand beside me, took out his tobacco tin and rolled himself a smoke.

Paulus wondered how much longer I would be living in Lefó. He had heard from Nasu that I would soon be returning to Swis. Returning, I said. Two, three weeks from now. Paulus made sounds of dismay and surprise. And never coming back to Lefó, he asked, as if seeking confirmation but not eager to receive it. Coming, I replied, though possibly not for a long time. Taking my battery with me? Taking. *Wah!* exclaimed Paulus and fell silent. We lay on the beach looking at the sea while Paulus screwed up his mind to speaking point. *Mari*, he said at length, and got to his feet. He was inviting me to join him, as usual without saying what for, assuming as people always did in Lefó that at any particular present moment there was only one particular thing to do.

Gorys was already sitting in the Yamaha waiting to go out at the far end of the beach. Paulus, Romualdus, Marlboro Man, Marsellinus, Nasu, Cor and myself, the seven of us pushed the boat into the water and jumped aboard. Paulus started the outboard. The bows of the boat lifted out of the water and it purred away.

I stood at the stern watching the land recede. Bit by bit, as we pulled away, the mountain grew on the shore. Behind the promontory on which Sitting-in-Palm-Tree perched, dominating the beach, hamlets higher up the mountain that were not visible from the beach because they lay behind the promontory gradually came into view. Stack by stack the mountain unfolded, rising higher and higher, as if it was being built before one's eyes. Only at a distance of several kilometres from the shore was the building complete, visible in its entirety. Gorys sat on the little triangle of deck at the bows, facing the stern and watching this spectacle of the mountain unfolding. When it had done so to his satisfaction he called out something to Paulus. His son cut the motor. The bows sank back into the water. The momentum of the boat carried it a little further before it was left to drift on the silence of the sea.

From this vantage point we could see a dark green wooded hill and hollow on the mountain. It was a striking feature of the landscape known to the villagers as the Conch, so named for its irregular triangular shape, bulging at the base and wearing two spiralling horn-like tips, marked by two white rocks. When the volcano brought forth the mountain above the village it cloned itself in miniature. The lopsided hill called the Conch had the same shape, colouring and contours as the mountain of which it was a part, a replica of the Sack of Snakes on a much reduced scale. It was an hour or two's walk from Does-not-have-Loincloth, but I had never been there. The villagers regarded it as a sacred place and fearsome, perhaps on account of the wild boars and poisonous snakes one was likely to encounter on one's way. They avoided going there. Gabo had done so as a boy. He told me that if you stood in the hollow between the tips and whispered, the echoes of the whisper sounded like the hiss of murmurs you heard when you held a shell to your ear. Sinta believed this shell was the womb out of which the mountain had been born, the selfsame sack out of which the snakes had crawled.

Marlboro Man squeezed past me and squatted on the horn-like projection at the stern, which the tiller man hung onto when steadying a *prahu* bucking in the surf. It served also as the crew's toilet when there was a serious call of nature, requiring a man to throw big water, as the Indonesian phrase had it, off the back of the boat. Normally the crew would be facing in the other direction, to the bows, but since it seemed we had come out for the sole purpose of viewing the mountain everyone was now looking back past the stern. Squeezing past the tiller man, pulling one's shorts down and squatting on the narrow edge of wood, if necessary in a rough sea, had become so much a second nature to all *matros* that they did so unthinkingly. Marlboro Man had already taken up position on what was jocularly called the Big Water Board when he realised he would be doing his business there in full view.

Wah!

The others hooted and screeched, but tactfully turned away to take an interest in the horizon for as long as Marlboro Man needed in order to move his bowels.

A 10-gallon canister of *tuak* was produced and a variety of receptacles were being passed round as cups when Marlboro Man stepped back into the belly of the boat to receive his. A sly suggestion from his nephew Marsellinus that it might do for throwing small water but not big was greeted with howls of laughter by the crew, sheepishly by Marlboro Man. The man with the broad-planked face under the big black hat was the butt of stock jokes on this subject owing to his frequent need, almost a symbiotic compulsion, to throw big water when surrounded by sea. This mischievous nephew of his, at thirty still something of a scamp, who endeared himself to me as much for his self-made pranks as for the flower-pot woollen headgear crocheted for him by his wife, went into paroxysms of laughter, piling jibe on jibe and sweeping the rest of the company along with him on the crest of his glee until they all sank down exhausted, threshing their legs in the bottom of the boat. Marlboro Man, reluctantly amused, took off his hat and scratched his head.

Slowly the lidded eye of the day opened. Climbing to mid-morning heat south of the shoulder of Standing Person, the sun blinked once behind a passing cloud and stared searchingly down, wide awake now, on the solitary boat adrift on the sea. The men aboard laughed, drank, talked and snoozed the morning away, their speech shedding consonants as if melted down by the noonday heat, making room for long stretched vowels that thinned out like yawns, rocking the boat on lullabies of sounds.

timu todaro moro hau
hau dua dori tena

fara bafaro moro haka
haka lide dori ele

kive rae lua lodo
nutu ike lau tai
fate weli poun pai
nutu tebe weli ojo . . .

The old man stood in the boat and tremulously keened his *lie*, his song, scraped it off in the thin space between the top of his voice and the ceiling of silence overhead. He called on the east wind to bring the whales, on the west wind, too. He called by their names the smaller Fishes-near-the-Stones to come up out of the sea and swim to the *tena* so that the fishermen could catch them. Facing Standing Person, he called on him to bend over so that the people in the mountains could climb more easily down his back and bring their crops to market, for lo! the fishermen of Lefó would soon have fish again to give in exchange for them. He called on the winds from all twelve directions to breeze the boats and ease the rowers' labours, on the currents to give them good landfall, on the limbs of the boats to remain sturdy and stand by them, not to flinch from the buffets of the waves or the scraping on the rocks.

Turning from the land to the ocean, the old man called last on the larger Fishes-in-the-Endless-Water. He named by name the great blue whale and all fellow baleens, whom the people of Lefó remained indebted to for bringing them to this place and would never harm, pursuing, in accordance with an ancient covenant, only the toothed whales that once swam here in great numbers, but had now gone. Perhaps they had already departed to feed in the cold waters to the south.

Bring them back with you, the old man sang out, when you return next year. Why else did your ancestors save our ancestors from the flood and put us down in this place? Was it was not meant for us to feed on the toothed whales that swam here in great numbers, in return for which we would do no harm to the baleens that swam benignly with them, honouring them according to the ancient covenant? Oh, listen! Listen all you baleen whales in the deeps of the sea! We ask you to remember it before it passes beyond recall, for otherwise the people of Lefó must die.

That was a lot of work for one song to do, a long way to carry to the allied whales, who might not have been within hearing, let alone listening, in the deeps of the sea. Trembling with exhaustion, Gorys sat down when he had finished. Not that I had understood what he was singing; only, from his turning body and outstretched arms, that it must be some kind of invocation addressed to the sea. But Bapak Cor later wrote down for me the words of the *lie* and translated them into Indonesian, when it became meaningful to me as a song of the bereft. From my own experience I knew how far such a song could carry on wavelengths of mutual sympathy, in a deep sound channel even across the ocean no less than it could across the ages, and the speech that followed, all of it – delivered in the archaic language of Lefó – a kind of liturgy, words sacred for being remembered un-changed from ancestors who had been chanting them for hundreds of years.

The sea stirred as if in response to Gorys singing. Flying fish flashed over the water in silver ripples near the boat. A baleen, perhaps the sei whale that had been visiting in these waters during the last week, came up to blow in the middle of the bay. Another large animal was porpoising further out. Having shown itself, the sea closed up again and made no further sound. The drip from a paddle resting on the gunwale was the only thing audible in the silence until Gorys began to speak.

This was his will. We must go to the Conch and speak with Beleloko. This was his will. He could not go himself. We must ask Beleloko to help us. The stone of Beleloko stood in the hollow between the horn-like tips marked by the two white rocks, facing the sea just as they had left it there when they hid it from the missionaries. The lord of the land should take gifts, one made of woven palm, one made of rice, one of water. He should blow his conch so that it was heard by the whales. The lord boat master from Back-of-the-Whale should take one offering of salt and one of blood. Pak Baterai should take his battery for Beleloko to touch, imparting to Beleloko the secret of Baterai's renewable life and so making him immortal. The secret that had been entrusted to Gorys passed herewith out of his keeping into the keeping of his sons, who must fold it up in their hearts and take it wherever they went.

Gorys asked for his rocking-chair to be taken to the terrace behind the house that evening and set up facing the mountain. He wanted nothing but to be left alone. He could hear the three families in the

197

great room just behind and they could hear his chair rocking, back and forth, back and forth far into the night, and when it stopped rocking they heard the silence.

In the Conch

Gorys was buried in the graveyard beside the chapel on the track that led through Animal-around-the-Mountain, an annexe, so to speak, of the great church and cemetery where most of Lefó's dead lay buried. The annexe was only a stone's throw from House-of-Three-Families. Although consecrated, it was the site of a pre-Christian burial ground, nowadays reserved for marginal cases in the sense that some outlying hamlets did not really belong to Lefó or were ambivalent with regard to their belonging to its new faith. Father Ybang was probably relieved to see his oldest parishioner fielded out to the annexe. Gorys would certainly have been.

At dawn the morning after the funeral the seven of us who had been to sea with the old man met at the chapel and followed the track up the mountain. Although I had smeared mosquito repellant on my arms and legs I was plagued by them for as long as we continued to climb up in the early morning shadow. Once the sun came round the mountain the mosquitoes disappeared. Instead I began to sweat, attracting flies. The men walked fast and I had difficulty keeping up. Soon I dropped behind. But Cor and Nasu, seeing what had happened to me, waited for me to catch up. Cor carried a cloth bundle, Nasu a sack over his shoulder that continued to wriggle and swing even when he stood still. Together the three of us brought up the rear while the others went on ahead.

We took a path leading off the track into a primeval mahogany forest. Once in the forest we moved back into a silent clammy twilight. There was more moisture in the air. A faint roar gradually became audible. Tall ferns and grasses crowded in on the path. Here and there it was necessary for Paulus to clear a way with his *parang*. The path led down into the cleft of a valley where a waterfall dropped clear from an overhang into a rocky basin at our feet. The spray drenched us as we passed. Veils of spume hung in the trees around the basin and on our walk up the far side of the valley we were surrounded by a mist that stayed with us for as long as the waterfall remained audible.

For about an hour we traversed the forest before emerging on a bare slope. A short but steep climb up this slope led to a plateau. Standing on the edge, we could see above us the two white rocks marking the tips of the Conch. The grassy cleft at the base of the Conch was smooth and extraordinarily verdant, as if fed by its own spring. It wasn't necessary to search for Beleloko. One saw the stone, an unmistakable landmark, as soon as one came out onto the plateau.

Butterflies flew up from under my feet as I walked over the grass. They settled on my clothing and hair, large blue, white and yellow butterflies, some of them with a wing span as wide as the spread of my hand. I wondered what attracted them in such extraordinary numbers. No flowers seemed to grow in this place. But the ground was littered with small dark brown pellets, apparently the excrement of animals that lived here. The butterflies came to feed on their dung.

Even had one not known that Beleloko was a stone with a name and a history, attributes given to it by men, one would have guessed that it was not a natural artefact. There was no mistaking that it was a seat of some kind. The L-shaped monolith, a smooth greyish-brown chunk of lava like all the stones that had once been poured down this mountain, stood upright on its short end, reaching about one and a half metres above the ground and leaning slightly forward. The tools of men had given the stone its chair-like shape. It faced the ocean. To view the ocean must have been why it had been erected in this place; perhaps not for a man to sit here and do so but for the stone itself.

House-of-Three-Families, Nasu and Cor, all of them walked round the stone, crooning in their softest sing-song mode, giving voice to their wonder. Had I been able to, I would have done so, too. For how had the Elders brought such a stone from the sea to the mountain?

Such a stone from the stone from the sea to such a sea from the stone to the mountain sea such a mountain stone . . .

Immediately we were surrounded by ghostly sounds, sibilance of sing-song, overlaying itself with encircling layers of echo that only very gradually faded, continuing long after the question had first been voiced in this enchanted place. We looked up in astonishment. For a moment one might have thought that the wing beats of the cloud of butterflies surrounding us had mysteriously been invested with sound.

Here was that marvel of which Gabo had spoken, the coil of echoes we had stirred up inside the Conch. It seemed an admonition to leave sleeping things in peace.

Thereupon Cor, who had stepped forward and been about to speak, chose to keep his words to himself. Silently the lord of the land laid his offering on the seat of the stone, a sheath woven from lontar palm such as was kept on the bowsprit of a *tena*, under which the boat slept when it was at sea, and two coconut shells, one of them containing water, the other a sprinkling of rice. He was followed by Nasu, who took a new-born suckling pig out of his sack. He cut off its head with the *parang* Paulus gave him and walked round the stone, pumping blood from the animal's neck and marking a circle with it on the ground. Then he took a vessel, which he had made of bamboo in the shape of a *prahu*, filled it with salt from a pouch, and placed it on the headstone of the seat.

Cor and Nasu now looked at me in case I had forgotten my promise to Gorys. Now it was Baterai's turn. Pak Baterai should take his battery for Beleloko to touch, Gorys had said, imparting to Beleloko the secret of Baterai's renewable life, thus preserving him for future generations. So I came up behind Beleloko and quickly put my arms round him, pressing up against his cold back in order for the spirit who inhabited the stone to feel the secret of my renewable life.

I wondered if that brief, half-hearted embrace had been sufficient. Gorys, who had shown us he could talk the fish out of the sea, would have managed this business for us much better. Perhaps the others were thinking the same thing, wondering about their inadequacies, their ignorance, the littleness of their faith, whether to speak to Beleloko, to ask for his intercession, and if so with what words. But Cor was already turning away from the stone to face the ocean. He put the conch to his lips and blew a blast. It was immediately swallowed up in the ding-dong of gigantic echoes which sprang out of it, each of them impossibly louder than the last, a storm of sounds that broke over our heads and tumbled helter-skelter down the mountain to the bay where an enormous whale breached once, standing on the water, it seemed, like a column in the sunlight, his great gleaming body hauled fully clear of the surface before he toppled back into the sea and sank from view with a soundless splash.

The Extraordinary Creature

Had we been the only ones to witness the great sperm whale standing on his tail – from a viewpoint far up on the mountain in the spiral of the Conch, one must remember, belaboured by the echoes of Cor's terrific blast and perhaps disposed by the events which had preceded the whale's appearance to behold something extraordinary – we might reasonably have doubted what we thought we had seen. At least I for my part, with uncertain memories of *Ambulocetus natans*, the walking whale, might have felt more comfortable explaining it as one of the tricks sometimes played by light and shadow, creating the kind of illusion that was apparently not uncommon when seen at a distance at sea.

But people down in the village saw the whale, too. Romualdus, the sampan fishermen at House-of-Three-Families who was out that morning pulling in his nets, told his kin what he had seen from a boat no more than half a kilometre away from the spot where the whale breached. Rising clear of the water, it had indeed seemed for a moment as if the huge sperm were standing upended on its flukes, shuffling over the water in the kind of extraordinary display he had otherwise only seen spinner dolphins perform.

In the village, however, even among next of kin at House-of-Three-Families, no one knew what had happened on the mountain. It was known we had been up on the mountain, in connection with the last wishes of Gorys, but not what we had done there. In time the story would leak out perhaps. But the secrecy to which we had been sworn by Gorys, the nature of the secret, the powerful taboo with which it was invested and the circumstances under which the patriarch had entrusted it to us, would rule out its betrayal to anyone outside our circle for some time to come.

To the village, the spectacle of such a large whale so close to the shore was something extremely unusual, perhaps unprecedented. The seven men who had been on the mountain, however, were naturally taken not so much with the striking appearance of the whale as with the striking coincidence that it appeared when it did, with an obscure connection between our visit to Beleloko and the whale's arrival.

Were they shocked to see the whale come when called? *Because* it had been called? Because their expectations of an old covenant, in which they had ceased to believe, had been fulfilled despite their doubts? Was it their own doubts they had seen surface with the whale? Was it *that* shock which the whale embodied and had presented for them to see, a reminder of what they had forgotten, of what separated them from their ancestors and had long been lying in dereliction at the bottom of the sea?

All day the crews of the *tena* crouched in excited huddles on the beach, like a band of petitioners kept waiting too long and now aghast at the prospect of their petition being heard after all.

With the cool of the evening they wrapped themselves in their sarong. None of them thought of going back to their houses. The beach was the front porch where the villagers gathered for an hour or two between a late homecoming from work and retiring early to bed. On the rare days when the sea had opened to disclose something particularly spectacular they seemed more than usually reluctant to turn their backs on it. Wives and mothers brought food in palm-leaf bundles to the beach, supplies of *tuak* and tobacco, so that their men folk could stay and keep an eye on the sea. Children and mangy puppies, eternal players with nothing but their own games in mind, ran laughing and barking up and down the twilight strand.

Rumours of the sighting of a *makhluk istimewa*, an extraordinary creature, had also lured the local dignitaries to the beach. The village headman and his committee were there. So was Pater Ybang. Even Sinta had managed to hobble down the mountain in the dark. Trampling noises, an occasional clang of tin when curiosity got the better of caution, betrayed the presence of free-ranging bands of piglets behind the boathouses, rooting around in the trash for something to eat. A full moon shone down on this scene, so bright that Pak Ani could read by its light the address on the envelope handed him by Pater Ybang.

It was a letter from an old mutual acquaintance, Father 't Maart, writing from the mission hospital at Lapang Buhan with news of an extended stay in Jakarta, from which he had apparently only just returned. Pater Ybang told me that many years ago his Belgian colleague had done a brief term of service in the parish of Lefó Selamat. In those days, he said, there had been parishioners living in such remote places along the southern shore of the island that the only way for a priest to reach them was by horse. I was about to tell him about the role played by Father 't Maart in the remote places of my own early life when I was interrupted by the return of the whale, breaching not five hundred metres from the shore.

He rose at a steep angle out of the sea, perhaps twenty degrees wide of the perpendicular, piercing the surface with such speed and force that the sound of breaking water was audible to people in the village beneath Standing Person on the far side of the bay. The whale twisted as he soared through half an arc, barely bringing his flukes to the surface, before dropping down flat with a terrific splash. That it was a male was beyond doubt. In no species of cetacean was sexual dimorphism so great as between male and female sperm whales. No female ever came this big. Probably no female would have ever felt disposed to give such a display of power as the solitary animal out in the bay gave the villagers of Lefó that night. If there were other whales he was signalling with his series of gunshot breaches, rolls and lobtails, huge smackings of the water creating explosive sounds which must have carried far out into the ocean, there was no sign of them on that or any of the following days. It was difficult to imagine what else he could have been doing if he was not signalling. More than that. It was as if the whale were giving this demonstration of power play for the particular benefit of the spectators assembled on the shore.

That wide bay, which on breathless afternoons I had paddled across often enough to wish it much smaller, seemed to shrink in the presence of such a huge creature to the dimensions of a pond, an aquatic forum for the solo performance by the *makhluk istimewa*. In the full moonlight one could see the silvery spume of his spray trailing over the sea two or three kilometres out. Minutes later his great head loomed up out of the water only a couple of hundred metres from the shore. Everyone knew how a *tena* appeared when viewed at that distance. This animal appeared almost twice as large, perhaps eighteen metres long and weighing up to a hundred tons. Probably no whale approaching that size had ever come in so close to the village, and in that breathing proximity, where the warm spume of the whale's blow even drifted up onto land in fine droplets that could be felt by the people sitting on the shore – stained as it was, and as the whale seemed to know it was, with the blood of so many murdered animals, scattered with their smells, dried blubber and bleached bones, the trophies of innumerable hunts at sea – the village had never appeared so vulnerable or its inhabitants experienced such awe as was inspired in them by this whale who brought his wet living presence right up to them on dry land.

Sometimes he just upended quietly and showed his flukes, the rest of his bulk invisible, hanging down underwater for long periods of time, impressing on us the silence he could bring equally to the ocean when he chose to remain inert. Diving suddenly, he carved out chunks of the sea with a great sucking noise of his flukes and hurled them up into the air. Swimming back and forth he ploughed up the still sea, unravelling long furrows of turmoil that slowly subsided into quiet water again, leaving smooth whale ways behind him, bales of flung brightness criss-crossing the bay for freeloading moonbeams to slide up and down. As abruptly as he came he disappeared. The tide drained from the shore. Far off, the last white smear of sea crawled along the horizon where the moon was setting, until the light went out with the tide, plunging us into a darkness that saw no difference between land and sea.

The Strike

Came the morning, and five *prahu* put out to sea.

These were the *Horo Sapa*, the *Mata Tena, Boko Lolo, Teti Heri* and *Aro Tena*, Ioh and his father Nasu being the harpooners on these last two *tena*, with a total crew complement of fifty-one men on board all five boats. The bows of the *Horo Sapa* had been patched up and fitted with a new harpooner's platform after they had been demolished by the whale killed earlier in the year. It now swam with a lame leg on the side of its heart, as they said in Lefó, meaning the boat listed on the port side.

Only five boats mustered for a *baléo* – I found this a disappointing turn-out for such an occasion, perhaps our last putting to sea at all that year. But for the appearance of the *makhluk istimewa* we might not have ventured out again. Not enough *matros* showed up to crew the five or six other *prahu*, which had sometimes helped to make it a still respectable fleet that could still be seen setting sail from Lefó. These *tena* were left to sleep under the sheath in their boathouses, as they had been doing for so much of the season. Nasu told me there was always a natural falling-off at the end of the summer. The men lost interest in going to sea. It was a seasonal change in men, just like the changes at sea and on land. Harvesting crops, digging ditches, mending roofs that had been neglected since the end of the previous rainy season or repairing leaks in the pipes that brought drinking water down the mountain to the village, all such chores began to seem a more attractive alternative to spending long unprofitable days at sea.

But this time the whale was out there. No one had any doubt about that. He was not spoken of in so many words, because Lefó's whale hunters believed to do so would bring them bad luck. All the crews were unusually taciturn. It was an overcast morning, matched by the subdued mood of the men, left to pursue their own thoughts in silence. There was none of the banter exchanged between boats as they came through the surf and raised their sails, no jokes volunteered in anticipation of Marlboro Man's visit to the big-water board, only the perfunctory removal of hats and muttering of prayers.

Nowhere in the world was there a greater proximity than that of a dozen men crammed into a small floating space on the sea, nowhere a place where one could be more alone. Cor might sit and play his Jew's harp by the hour on land, but his thoughts remained land-bound. Passers-by hailed him. The sight of work still left undone intruded. All the familiarity of his world enclosed him. Left to his own thoughts in the long periods of silence out at sea, however, a man could have an intense experience of being alone. The expanse of sea around him was able to disperse that sense of human proximity it was impossible to escape on land.

Currents and a fitful wind carried the five *prahu* towards Standing Person. They were strung out in a line, about one kilometre apart. At a distance the planked body of a boat was soon lost to sight, with only the tall rectangular sails showing up on the horizon. The *Horo Sapa* led the line, identifiable by the black patch in the middle of the sail, followed by the *Boko Lolo*, flying a striped pennant from the top of the mast. These two veered off to the east on a course that would take them round Standing Person into the adjacent bay, while the three other boats tacked back in a south-westerly direction, heading out to sea.

Critically, the crew of the *Aro Sapa* followed the manoeuvres of the two boats that had remained closer to the shore. We wondered why they had chosen this course. It was assumed that they had sighted prey and had taken up pursuit. Sure enough, the sail of the *Horo Sapa* came down, a sign that the *tena* was about to engage with a larger animal. The *Boko Lolo* soon followed suit. Nasu conferred with his crew as to whether they should turn and stand by in case the two boats needed help. The wind picked up as we moved out from the shore and had already carried us several kilometres away from the *Boko Lolo* and the *Horo Sapa*. Even at that distance the men could still tell it was not a whale they had engaged but a *belelang*, a giant manta ray. The two boats could deal with that on their own. The men quickly lost interest and turned back to their scrutiny of the sea ahead. At the same moment the man at the tiller gave a shout. Ani was the first to sight the blow of the sperm whale, who had surfaced about a kilometre to the south-east on our port side.

The single blowhole of the sperm whale, situated well to the left of the midline down its great nose, produced a spout with a bias unlike any other. Even from considerable distances the sperm whale's signature blow was unmistakable. Seen from the side, the blast shot up five metres at least, leaning forward at an angle of about forty-five degrees, saturated with moisture, the warm breath of the whale that had condensed on mingling with the air. Before I saw the blow I heard it. The first exhalation after what had presumably been a deep dive – there had been no sign of the whale during the previous hour – sounded like an explosion. It was clearly audible to us two kilometres away.

That was the first breath. Each of the following breaths I counted lasted about three seconds on the exhalation and a second for the next intake of air. I knew that sperm whales usually spent about ten minutes at the surface, breathing deeply every ten to fifteen seconds before diving again. I also knew the old whalers' rule of thumb that for every foot of the whale's length it would breathe once at the surface and spend one minute submerged during the subsequent dive. Because we had to tack back to where the whale had surfaced, a couple of minutes more or less might well decide whether we reached it in time to harpoon it.

Ani brought the boat round and the boom swung over as soon as the blow had been sighted. But before engaging the whale the sail would have to be lowered. The wind had meanwhile dropped in any case. There was no motion for the boat except what we gave it ourselves by paddling. I counted forty, fifty, sixty-three breaths before the broad tail flukes were thrown up into the air and the whale went down on a vertical dive when we had come within eighty metres of him – a very big animal, judging by his breath count between dives, as much as nineteen or twenty metres long.

No one among us can have doubted that it was the *makhluk istimewa* in the sea beneath us. No one would say so, for to speak the whale's name might bring us bad luck. I had been warned many times not to do this. After living in Lefó for months I had acquired some of its habits of mind and come to share such beliefs myself. For those of us who had been up on the mountain there can have been no longer any doubt that this was the creature who had been invoked by Gorys and who with his own great blow had now just answered the blast that Cor had trumpeted on his conch from the mountain, that this was the echo come back from the sea.

On board the *Aro Tena* we sat panting over our oars, drifting towards the spot where the whale had gone down. For us he wasn't there, all I had in the flatness of the surface we inhabited was an eerie sense of him underneath us, the depth in which he lived. We were in his room, and to him, lurking beneath us on the floor, we must have seemed like turtles swimming on the ceiling of his three-dimensional space. The *Mata Tena* came level with us on the starboard side, the *Teti Heri* on our left, the crews on both boats bent over their oars just like us, catching their breath. Men at the tiller and harpooners shouted back and forth. There seemed to be agreement that after a big dive the whale would probably come up close to where he had gone down. After a short discussion the two other boats pulled away leaving us in the middle. We formed a line with a gap of about fifty metres between each boat.

For an hour we sat there and waited, simmering in the sea-skillet of the midday heat. The only shade I had I wore on my body, a seigneurial white Tilley hat with a broad rim, a long-sleeved T-shirt and knee-long jeans so that arms and thighs were protected from the sun. In the small rucksack I always kept on my back to prevent it from landing in the bilge water at the bottom of the boat there was a litre-and-a-half bottle of drinking water, a camera, sun block with the highest factor I had been able to buy. I still burned. All the crew wore shirts. Most of them had on some kind of headgear, too. The sarong which the Pirate wound up into a turban, Romu's bonnet fringed with tassels, the blue and white woollen hat crocheted for Marsellinus by his wife, Marlboro Man's black Stetson, were among the more memorable sun-hat items on board the *Aro Tena*. With a deep, un-quenchable longing, Nasu coveted my white hat and the breeches I had bought in Mataitu. I had promised to bequeath them to him when I left.

Perhaps it was the dullness induced by the noonday heat that accounted for the laid-back atmosphere on board. It might have been just another fishing expedition. Prospects of the imminent struggle with the enormous creature that would presently be coming up out of the sea did not seem to concern anybody but the two sentries posted on every boat, the harpooner and the man at the tiller. Nasu at one end of the boat and Ani at the other never stopped turning their heads, keeping their ears tuned for breaking sounds, scanning the sea with watchful eyes. Cor tapped a rhythm on his teeth. Paulus cleaned his ears. The others lolled in the bottom of the boat with their feet up on the thwarts, a lazy eye on the outcome of the encounter between the giant manta and the two distant boats, their sails still down, hovering on the sea just off the point of Standing Person.

The quiet was disturbed when the whale made a three-quarter breach about five hundred metres further out to sea, falling back with a tremendous splash. The crew was immediately galvanised by the sight of the surfacing sperm, as if tapping into the energy that had surfaced with it, accelerating within seconds from indolence to frenzy, Paulus and Marlboro Man seemed to be snatched up by the strings of an invisible puppeteer to the thwart where they sat facing us, oars already in rowlocks, rising and tugging with short pulls, shouts that sounded like explosive popping – *bo! bo! bo!* – offset by the grinding *wailabe-wailabe* chant of the crew every time they drove their paddles through the water.

The *Teti Heri*, with a younger and stronger crew, Ioh on the platform flapping his arms as if about to fly off it, was the first to come into the whale's water. In Lefó this was how they called the smell that surrounded a whale at the surface, the briny odour of his great wet body encrusted with barnacles and parasites, the island of microflora and fauna which he heaved up with him out of the sea. At the range where you could smell the whale's scent you were within his water. The *Teti Heri* came into this whale's water, sliding up alongside his great body, and Ioh flew.

The harpooner struck the whale with his shoulder and skidded off into the sea between the animal and the boat. The boat rubbed up against the flank of the whale, Ioh went under between the two. His harpoon had stuck deep and fast in the blubber quite far down the head, gripping it like a claw. Other than a momentary surge out of the water, the whale showed no reaction. The *Aro Tena* approached from the other side, cutting across the whale's path. Nasu harpooned it from directly overhead, twisting in the air and landing in the sea beside its head without his body touching the animal. With one hand Nasu was already reaching for the stern of the *Aro Tena* and hanging onto the curved horn there as it passed him. He had aimed his harpoon at the blowhole. But at the last minute the animal rolled away and the harpoon entered his body lower down. The whale pulled steadily forward, ignoring the *Teti Heri* and the *Aro Tena* bobbing behind him in his wake. He swam in a straight line, as if he had already set his course south and would be moved by nothing to change it, paying no attention to harpoons, harpooners or the boats from which they came, appendages he had apparently taken in tow but which otherwise did not concern him.

Throughout the afternoon we watched the *Mata Tena* gradually falling back until it had disappeared behind us in the dusk. Steadily, never slackening or changing its pace, the extraordinary creature headed out to sea.

The Tow

In deep darkness the sea felt like a small place. The range of my observations was confined to what I could see, my immediate vicinity in the boat. Stanis, beside me, dispensed water from the earthenware pot between us. The bamboo cup was passed forward into the dark. Paulus and Romu, two rows ahead of me on the thwart amidships, could be seen lifting the cup and drinking. But Marlboro Man at the mast was no longer visible to me other than as a shape somewhat more dense than the night surrounding him. Lefó words which I could not understand went back and forth with the cup. Ani squatting behind me at the stern sometimes gave me the gist in Indonesian. What we had to eat. What we had to drink. What the *makhluk istimewa* had in mind to do. Now that we had been taken in tow by the whale our man at the tiller no longer had the boat in his charge. He had stowed the paddle he used as a rudder and taken out reels of fishing twine. We should put out lines, he said. He and Stanis began unreeling twine, baiting hooks and laying out lines off the back of the boat in the pitch dark. Twenty metres behind us the night already seemed to come to an end.

But when the moon came up over the horizon the sea rolled back and I discovered the immensity of a place I had never seen before. The horizon itself was swallowed up in the bright expanse now spread out before us. Behind us, the bluff mountain that dominated the daytime sea I was familiar with had disappeared into an unrecognisable shore-line of smoothly undulating hills. Between the dark hills behind us and the limitless stretch of bright water that lay spilled out before us the boats seemed to be stationary, pitched like tents on the vast plain of the sea.

This was the whale's country, his home, not ours. It had upwellings and currents, the drift of tides and winds, the contours of distant coasts, shelves and deep seabeds, a whole submarine topography, of which we knew nothing, but which had been imprinted on the whale. On the course he was headed he would pass the west coast of Timor and go down into the Indian Ocean. I wondered how much he already knew of what lay ahead. Close to him, grappled in his outer skin, was the barbed irritant, or worse, the pain caused by our harpoons, perhaps not unlike the barbed thoughts of thirst and hunger we carried in our bodies, but this wound would have no effect on the workings of the echolocation system by which the whale navigated. He appeared to know where he was going. He appeared to be following a plan.

Had he taken bearings on invisible islands in the landless mass of ocean that lay to the south-west? On deep-sea features unknown to us? Would the coast of north-west Australia, still hundreds of kilometres away, soon begin to take shape on the whale's ultrasonic map? Did he already have inklings of Africa, thousands of miles away on the far side of the Indian Ocean? Did it belong to his vicinity as my neighbour in the boat belonged to mine? And how did he calculate such distances with no knowledge of numbers? Still growing at the age of fifty, a relative youngster when my great-grandfather's ship went down in these waters, had he memorised the world's oceans in the perhaps two hundred years he had lived? Could the whale's sea feel contained and mapped to him, as close and familiar to him in his wide-reaching age as to us it seemed boundless?

But he was flesh and blood. The whale would tire. Let him tow! Eventually he would tire and in the morning we would finish him off. Shouts were exchanged between the two *tena*, the *Teti Heri* in front, trailing the whale by three or four boat lengths, the *Aro Tena* two boat lengths behind again. But the whale did not tire. The moon rose and we rode on his whale's way, the path his great body smoothed on the wrinkled sea. Sometimes he raised his head. Sometimes we saw just the gleaming knuckles along his back. The moon set and we lost sight of him altogether. But he did not tire, kept his distance, never allowing the rope that bound us to him to slacken. All night he pulled us further and further out to sea. A wind came up, making waves for the whale to plough through. He ploughed. We could hear him breaking the waves. He did not tire. When day broke there was no sign of land anywhere on the horizon.

We saw a sail. *Woh!* A sail! Making the best of the east wind that had come up during the night, the *Mata Tena* rode straight before the wind, approaching fast on our starboard side. Soon it would catch up. Let the whale raise his sail! Come on! Let him try! Undeterred by our shouts or the commotion as the crews got ready on the three boats, the whale swam slowly, steadily onwards on his south-west course. On the *Mata Tena* the crew had thought up a strategy to ambush the whale. Ambush the whale! They lowered the sail and waited, a couple of hundred metres ahead of him, on the path along which they expected the *makhluk istimewa* to pass.

But such a cunning animal had no intention of being ambushed. He veered off to the west. The crew of the *Mata Tena* paddled in frantic pursuit. For an hour or so they could keep up with him but never come close enough for a strike. Soon they had dropped behind. Towards the middle of the morning, before the noon lull when the eye of the day stared fiercely down and not a breath more would stir on the face of the water, the *Mata Tena* again caught enough of a breeze to make up the sea it had lost earlier in the day. This time there was no attempt to ambush the whale. All they wanted was a lift. It was crucial for the boats to stick together. Ani caught the rope thrown him by the harpooner, hitching it to the stern of the *Aro Sapa*, and we took them in tow.

We! Our benefactor, the whale, took them in tow. Our tugboat seemed to be slowing down. Yes, he was tiring! Pile on the load he had to drag until it brought him to a standstill! If only the *Boko Lolo* and *Horo Sapa* had been there to help us! Five boats would have been too much, even for this prodigy of an animal. The crews in the three boats he now had in tow fretted and jabbered. The harpooners reached for the poles on the outrigger racks and took up positions on their platforms. Definitely the whale was slowing down. Soon he would stop, exhausted. Then we would come alongside and board him, bleed him to death with harpoons, lances, the long-bladed *duri* which the crew were already whetting. The whale was slowing down, but still he did not stop.

During the long, aching noonday heat, when not a breath stirred on the water, the full realisation of the extremity of our situation began to sink in on me. This was not a normal animal. This whale still swam. He showed no signs of tiring. He was not going to do us the favour of stopping and allowing us to kill him. And what if he did? Where would we go? Earlier in the day, when the morning haze lifted, we had seen the mountains of Timor to the east. But after the inter-vention of the *Mata Tena* the whale had veered west, changing course, and the outline of Timor had once again receded. Ahead of us lay landless sea where we would drown or die of thirst.

The boat's water supply in the earthenware pot had run out that morning. Lefó's whalers didn't reckon on spending days at sea. Boats either went home or – very rarely – were sunk within twenty-four hours of putting out. The bottle in my rucksack was also empty. The constriction in my throat was painful, making it difficult to speak. As the grip of the claw in one's throat became tighter even those members of the crews who were naturally talkative, like Cor, became chary with words. The boats rose and fell in silence on a monotonous deep-sea swell, inhalation and exhalation spaced out over a long interval, as if they had been placed on the diaphragm of the deep-breathing ocean as marker buoys, registering the crests and troughs of a gigantic respiration. All through the day and night we continued to rise and fall on this systolic-diastolic rhythm of the sea as if we had no other business than its measurement to mind. It encompassed Kozue, too, the child stirring in her belly, the boy who had hurried to get out so that he could stand under the tinsel star on the landing, whom we had once seen in our combined imagination. I saw through his image as I looked up at the unknown constellations of the southern hemisphere, dense nebulae flaring like breath frozen across the bowl of the sky.

Sometimes the sea was no less bright than this unfamiliar star-strewn sky. During the night the ocean flowed like a river, its breezes sweet and soft, cooling my burning skin. They stirred up waves that came charged with a phosphorescent glow, perhaps attributable to luminous plankton living in the surface of the water. As the waves broke against the sides of the boats they opened into rivulets of light. We seemed sometimes to be moving on a surface of muted flame, leaving a wake we watched burning behind us before it snuffed out in the night. The sea-river was the mirror of the heavenly river, down which the stars floated like candles in jars. I could feel the heartbeat of the world in the shape of the whale, heard his breathing in the eerie dark as the respiration of the sea, of the tides rising and falling on its shores, of terrestrial rivers flowing down from mountains into estuaries, all the earth's breathing through the great watery diaphragm of the ocean and the flowing firmament above, the inhalations and exhalations of a universe in unceasing motion, rocking me up and down until, exhausted, I fell asleep.

The Tip

When I awoke it was getting light. My head felt as if it was about to split. All my bones ached. I had knots in my stomach, cramps in my legs, a sore backside. My tongue was so swollen it felt as if something hard and dry, an old shoe perhaps, had been stuffed into my mouth.

During the night they had pulled *kemanu* in on the lines off the back of the boat. The men around me were sucking out the eyes of the fish and told me to do the same. They bit the raw flesh off the bones and tossed the remainders into the sea. But nothing would fit into my mouth, even if I had the stomach for it. Nothing would have passed down my throat. Towards noon on our third day at sea the whale came to a halt. He sank into the water, rose and submerged again, spouting a few times before he swam towards the *Teti Heri*, raised his flukes and dived.

Plunging down on the port side of the *tena*, the whale yanked the rope hard over the gunwale and tipped the boat over broadside, pitching the crew into the water before he staved in the hull with a blow of his flukes as he descended. It was all over within seconds.

For a moment the *Teti Heri* disappeared from the surface, completely submerged in the sea. The force of the pull on the bows of the *Aro Tena*, trailing thirty metres behind, was so great that the stern jumped clear out of the water. Then the capsized boat burst foaming out of the sea ahead of us, bottom up, and beyond it the whale, displaying his flukes before submerging again and swimming powerfully away from us on a long shallow descent.

Somehow we had lost the third boat in the convoy – later I would learn that the ever watchful Ani had had the presence of mind to cast off the rope by which we had taken the *Mata Tena* in tow – and shortly we would lose the first, the wreckage of the *Teti Heri*, which we watched slammed across the surface of the water, bouncing and cartwheeling, bits and pieces flying off until it had completely broken up, all but a section of the bows with the rope still miraculously fastened to the whale.

Like a float on a fishing line it bobbed in and out of the surface a couple of times before it went under for good. We could clearly see our own rope, by which the *Aro Tena* was separately attached to the harpoon in the whale, becoming shorter, the angle alarmingly steeper, as the whale took it down.

The boat groaned. One of the gunwale thwarts burst. An immense force crushed the hull down into the water. Clots of resin that had been stuffed into the cracks to prevent leakage shot up into the air and the sea poured in. The bows sank lower and lower. The harpooner's platform, usually riding high and clear of the sea, began scooping water.

Marlboro Man was the first to react. Hat and all he flew over the side. Romu, Paulus, Cor followed him, leaving the middle section of the boat empty. But as fast as it emptied it seemed to be filling up again. Something incomprehensible was taking place there. A tasselled blue hat danced on a fountain spurting out of the bottom of the boat. Nasu standing ankle-deep in water on his platform disappeared. A sheet of water separated the bows from the stern. It came up to my waist. Something pulled me from behind, but as hard as it pulled I instinctively clung to the thwart I was sitting on. I still hadn't let go of it when the *Aro Tena* went under. The rushing in my ears instantly shut off. I wondered how Stanis beside me was able to float upwards and dangle his legs in my face. Then I floated off myself. I had an impression of groping through a silent bluish-green light in which I had lost all sense of direction. I felt momentary terror. Something grabbed me by the arm and plucked me away. It was the helmsman Ani, who had stayed with me and pulled me back up to the surface after the *Aro Tena* went down.

Adrift

The walker did not walk, nor did the weaver weave, no, and the swimmer did not swim. No doer was distinct from what he did, for it was not he who did it. There was doing and the doer was contained within it, inseparable from the ground on which he walked, the loom at which he wove, the water in which he swam.

In the reduced gravity of the sea it became more easy to discard that heavy sense of self which weighed one down on land. Swimming, I was carried only in small part by my own effort. I was contained in-the-swimming, sustained as a floating part of the sea-washed wholeness, like the plankton, the brine, the light breaking the surface. One must merge with it. If the walker tried to detach himself and walk against the road or the swimmer to swim against the sea he would soon be exhausted. This was the truth of all doing, and by it we would survive – myself, the helmsman Ani, his sea-soaked blue and white bonnet still plastered on his head, and our water provider old Stanis, whom I saw for the first time without his *Bintang Java* cap on, his dented blue skull shockingly uncovered, bobbing on either side of me.

Some way beyond I saw my hat floating, and quite a bit further again a dim cluster on the surface, like a flock of birds, resting on the waves. I reckoned this must be the main body of the crew, Marlboro Man, Paulus, Nasu and the rest, who had jumped into the sea before the boat went down. I noted with surprise how distant they seemed to be. Could we have travelled so far in such a short time? How much further away was the *Mata Tena*? Gone adrift, or something to that effect, according to Ani treading water beside me, before the whale had turned and given fight.

One boat must have survived, then. I looked around but I could see no sign of it. Dagáma, the retired professor from Manila, swam into my mind. I remembered looking down with him from the Sack of

Snakes and Dagáma saying that without the sea below it would be like looking down from the top of the Eiger. Submerged mountain peaks might be all around in the sea beneath me. There I hung, suspended over an abyss the sea had filled. I imagined someone far below looking up at the paraglider soaring overhead, which in fact was me floating on the surface of the sea.

From the surface of the sea I looked up at the midday sun. In fact I hung there in the middle of the day and could already feel my head beginning to burn. I sank under, gliding through the sea in the direction of my hat. I had just reached it when I heard a splash.

About halfway between us and the rest of the crew our boat came bursting back up to the surface. Ani immediately began swimming towards it. I could make out others swimming from the opposite direction. There was no sign of the whale. The old man and I swam after him. Ani told us to stay where we were. He would salvage the boat – what was left of it – with the others before the whale took it down. At least we would have something to hang onto until the *Mata Tena* came. But then we saw the blows – we counted several of them – and before the swimmers were able to reach the *tena* it had again gone under with the whale.

This chasing after the boat was repeated several times, only to be thwarted by the whale diving at the last minute. The swimmers tried to swim against the sea. How slow and feeble they were, how quickly they tired! The whale seemed to be having a game with them. He let them come close. He disappeared, taking the *tena* with him. Five or ten minutes later he surfaced somewhere else, bringing the elusive boat back into play. This continued for about an hour, with the crew swimming around aimlessly and some of us worried – I for my part was – that the whale might come up right under them. Perhaps the repeated diving was the whale's strategy to get rid of the appendage that tormented him. Someone, I couldn't see who, Stanis thought Paulus, swam in under the upturned hull. Apparently he was able to locate and retrieve a *duri* from the place where it was wedged behind a rib of the gunwale. With the knife he cut the rope that tied the wreck of the *tena* to the whale. The whale threw up his flukes and went down, this time leaving the boat on the surface and a straggle of men floating in the water around it.

The front section of the *tena* had gone. The middle section and the stern floated bottom up. Swimmers hauled themselves out of the water onto the island this wreckage provided. Nasu, Paulus,

Marsellinus, Cor, Romu, Marlboro Man, Ani, myself, Petrus and Stanis, one by one the crew of the *Aro Tena* arrived to take refuge on what was left of it.

From this elevation it was possible to make out men in the water at quite some distance from us. They appeared to be moving not towards but away from us, in the direction of the *Mata Tena*, visible on the horizon at last, some five or six kilometres to the north-east. Why had it fallen so far behind? What was holding it up now?

A stillness settled after the whale had gone. Only with his departure did I become aware of the solitude in which he had left us. He had accompanied us for so long that it was difficult to accept he was no longer there. His presence remained, magnified by the silence of the surrounding sea. It was almost more palpable than when the whale had actually been there. I thought: the whale is strong, but the idea of him is stronger still.

I slid off the hull and came up inside the dark enclosure underneath where there was enough air to breathe. Eventually, I supposed, the oxygen supply in this bubble would run out, but I didn't care. I was so tired, that I just I wanted to lie down in my water hole and be left to sleep. But Ani wouldn't let me. He and Nasu pulled me out. During the time I had spent in the sea since the *Aro Tena* sank I had inadvertently swallowed quite a lot of water. At first it soothed. Now my throat was parched and swollen, clotted with crusted salt that tasted foul. I was unable to speak. None of us spoke. The men lying on the hull dozed off. They burned, but unlike me they feared the sun less than the sea and they didn't seem to mind it.

In the shade of my hat, in the cool of the water, a hand hanging onto the ripped keel of the boat, my feet resting on a submerged plank still attached to the boat, I remained immersed in the sea throughout *siang*, the hottest hours of what seemed an interminable afternoon. The third day was the longest. It seemed it would never pass. The sun stood still in the sky, a blazing dial on which time never moved, reminding me of the clock with the motionless hands on the wall of the hospital where I had waited just as desperately six months before. And yet it had moved in the end.

As the eye of the day began to close and the sun moved a few degrees down the sky a tiny shadow grew at one corner of the wreck, an illusion of shade, a handkerchief to which I swam, covering myself with it in the expectation that it would bring me relief. And it did. There were insights into the nature of ordinary life to be had only in extremities. It was not so much the thing itself as the idea of it that inhabited the imagination and infused it with reality, not so much the whale as the sense of his presence, not time passing but the belief that it passed, not shade but the idea of it that cooled.

Creaking through the twilight, low in the water because so heavily laden, the *Mata Tena* rowed towards us over the purplish sunset sea. There were twenty-one men on board, the full complement of the *tena*'s own crew plus all the survivors of the *Teti Heri*, picked out of the water hours after it had gone down. Martinus, the boat master and harpooner, stood somewhat nonchalantly on one leg on his platform, answering the barrage of questions hurled at him from our float. Relief expressed itself as anger.

What had happened to the boat's mast and sail? Where had the *Mata Tena* been all this time? Half full of water, apparently. Cracks had opened up that wouldn't be stopped with the usual resin treatment. They bailed and bailed. They were still at it. The leaks had been more or less stanched with T-shirts. And what about his father's boat, the *Aro Tena*, Ioh wanted to know. We were sitting on what was left of it, all ten of us, Nasu answered. Of the thirty-one *matros* making up the crews of the three *tena* not a single man had been lost.

When all were aboard the *Mata Tena* we joined in a prayer of thanksgiving. The boat was put round and headed back east. We watched the hull of the *Aro Tena* recede and vanish in the enclosing dark.

As soon as the thanksgiving had been said the previous unfinished argument was resumed. Before picking up the crew of the *Teti Heri* the boat master had jettisoned mast and sail to make room for more men in the middle of the boat where these bulky articles were stowed when it was not under sail. Why then hadn't he just raised the mast and proceeded under sail? With an additional twenty men in the boat conditions became not only extremely cramped, Martinus said, but the *tena* would be impossible to manoeuvre under sail. It was too heavy, it lay too low in the water. In even a moderate breeze it would ship water faster than we could bail it out. There was a long argument about the wisdom of this, although there was now nothing we could do to change it.

Despite Martinus's drastic measure, four men still had to take turns sitting out on the harpooner's platform to provide space for the other twenty-seven in the body of the boat. Someone or other was always dozing off and at risk of falling into the sea. This did indeed happen several times during the night. We bailed and paddled in shifts, so there were always crew awake to watch for men going overboard and to fish them out. The men paddling and bailing prayed out loud, and whoever else was awake prayed with them in unison. They prayed in Indonesian, the established language of the church, their cracked voices losing half the words in the gaps between. They prayed generally but urgently to the Virgin Mary for help in their need, more specifically to God the Father for food and water and their return to Lefó. But the urge to sleep was so strong that it overcame even the agony of thirst. As the night wore on there were fewer and fewer men awake to pray. The moment a rower was relieved he succumbed to sleep.

In the surface of the sea the phosphorescent plankton was so bright that every dip of the paddle left a streak of blue-green light in the water. Liquid light ran off the tips of the paddles each time they were raised out of the water, as if invisible jugglers were rotating chains of illuminated droplets in endless cycles through the night. A hand net towed off the stern of the *Mata Tena* was brought aboard with a couple of fish so full of plankton that they shone as they lay at the bottom of the boat, their stomachs bulging bodily with phosphorescent light. When we bit into a fish it left luminous smears around our mouths. The glowing limbs of men who had gone overboard and got the plankton all over their bodies showed up like hands on a human clock, their slightest movement registered meticulously, as if they were signalling in the dark. What is this wealth, I wondered, the richness of all these minute organisms, this infinite variety of the sea? What is it for?

Somewhere far away in the night we heard thunder. Clouds massed. The stars went out.

The sea lay flat out in a dead calm. Under the ceiling of low cloud it became oppressive. On the boat it was sweltering. Among the dank stench of fish, human filth and sweat, so many men huddled in the heat with all their bodily and spiritual sores rubbing up close together, the rowers paddled without pause and prayed unceasingly for rain. *Bapak membantu selalu, Maria membantu selalu, Bapak membantu selalu.* Repeated in canon, the litany was mumbled so long until it had lost the sound of recognisable words and rose as a collective groan, a ragged pennant the *Mata Tena* trailed behind it through the night.

One could feel the rain hanging in the low cloud just above the boat. Some of the men stood up at the oars and shouted their prayer, the better to be heard.

Bapak membantu selalu!

It sounded more like a tongue-lashing than a prayer. Perhaps if you shouted long enough at the sky you might dislodge the rain, and it would come down.

It descended in such a flurry that we were unprepared for it. A torrent fell straight and hard on our upturned faces, into cupped hands and open mouths. We tore off our shirts and held them up for the rain to soak the fabric through and through, wringing them out into our mouths. In panic we grabbed at the rain – so much of it falling everywhere except on us, drips wasted in the bottom of the boat, huge quantities of it poured futilely into the sea! – to obtain what amounted to no more than a few mouthfuls of water in the end.

In mid-downpour it stopped all at once. It had lasted about a minute. There was no gentle drizzle trailing off. Point blank the rain stopped and not a drop more came down.

The air cleared. The cloud passed over. We took off whatever garments we still had on and squeezed them for the last beads of moisture they would yield. A shiver passed through my body. I was alternately hot and cold. A dull ache like a clamp or a vice seemed to be screwed more and more tightly round my head. Briefly the stars came back out before fading away again in the early morning sky. We licked our arms and hands.

It was a good rain Bapak had sent us. Why didn't he send us a little more?

Perhaps the crew thought it would be ungrateful to ask for more so soon after they had received. Perhaps they were disappointed by what they regarded as Bapak's half measures, the chariness of his bestowing hand. And that it was Bapak's hand that had given them the rain they didn't doubt. For whatever reason, when the rain left off the praying stopped, too.

As they paddled they talked softly among themselves in Lefó. Everyone was awake now, reanimated by the rain. Marsellinus even laughed again when Marlboro Man headed for the big water board. It was as well that there was such a calm sea and no one missed the sail, which Martinus had perhaps rashly jettisoned. For although we had paddled unremittingly all night there was still no sign of land when day broke. Directly ahead of us we had been expecting to see Timor on the horizon to the north-east. The rowers rested their oars. An argument broke out. There seemed no point in going on paddling until we were certain of our direction. But we were certain. There was no mistaking where the sun had risen.

Not far behind us a storm of flying fish broke the calm surface of the sea, followed by a dolphin, soaring extraordinarily high out of the water and turning a complete somersault. A killer whale pursuing the dolphin rammed it in mid-air, tossed it again and caught it in its jaws. We could hear the smack of the two animals colliding. A furious turbulence erupted briefly in the water. When it subsided we could see something floating on the surface. We brought the boat round and paddled over. The tail end of the dolphin drifted in a slick of blood. The orca had ripped it clean in two and taken the upper half.

Contemplating this windfall that had landed in the sea right beside them, all the men began to croon sounds in the Lefó language that were expressive of wonder and astonishment.

Duri in hand, Stanis leaned over the gunwale and cut up the dolphin lying just as it was in the water while someone else held it by the tail. Slices of raw meat were passed round. The flesh was tough. I found it very difficult to swallow. Like everyone else, I realised that given this windfall of food, coming shortly after the freak rainfall had provided us with even more essential water to drink, our chances of survival had much improved. But I hadn't prayed for Bapak's help myself, nor was I able to believe that Bapak had provided the dolphin and the rain in answer to those prayers. I regretted that I was unable to.

Would it have rained if they hadn't prayed? Once I became the beneficiary of the situation that had subsequently arisen I found it hard to resist the idea of it not just having done so coincidentally but of having been caused to arise. Once it had arisen, this point of view carried more conviction. To be an unbeliever and at the same time a beneficiary of belief put me in a quandary. It also seemed mean-spirited. Feverish, unpleasant thoughts turned and turned in my mind.

The whale must have towed us much further down into the Indian Ocean than we had realised. We paddled all morning and saw no sign of land. This was our fourth day at sea. It had only just begun, and it already seemed longer than the third, incomparably more extended than the second. I peered through the magnifying glass of seconds that made things happen much more slowly, the smallest distances appear enormous. We were adrift on an infinite moment. It seemed to be the entirety of life. Everything preceding the present belonged to a remote past, everything following it to a future that was unimaginable.

The uplift provided by the events earlier in the morning faded away. No one spoke. No one even prayed. Nothing we did had a connection with anything else. In the heat of the day we allowed ourselves a break from rowing and never resumed.

FOUR

The SUSUS Principle

Ghosts

You can look at something for a long time without seeing it. When you do see it, it may seem to be a revelation, although perhaps all you have done is to catch at the right moment what has been staring you in the face. The night that Kozue arrived in Singapore she dreamed of the little fair-haired boy. Ever since she had first seen him in the image I had shared with her at her apartment in Geneva he had continued to appear to her in a recurrent dream. Sometimes there were intervals of years during which he remained absent. She never saw him really distinctly in her dream. It showed the unchanging scene on the landing, where the boy stood at the top of the stairs under a star hanging on a thread from the ceiling. But over the years, as the camera in her mind blurred out the background and moved in to focus on the boy's face, it became more distinct. Now he came right up to Kozue, until his face completely filled out her dream. In the Singapore dream she saw the resemblance for the first time. It was more than a resemblance. Astonishing! The boy was indistinguishable from photographs of myself at his age. Where are you going, he asked. I'm not going anywhere, said Kozue – and felt such remorse that she woke up.

There was no point in her waiting any longer at the hotel where we had arranged to meet, because she knew that something must have happened to me and that I wasn't going to come. She flew to Bali the same morning. There she had to wait another three days for a flight to Flores. It took her almost a week to reach Lefó. She arrived on the day the village held a memorial service for the thirty-one men lost at sea. For the past week all the Yamahas had gone out daily and searched the coastal waters. They found nothing. They stopped searching. At last the families gave up hope. This was the worst disaster in the island's history. Twenty-two women had been widowed, more than fifty children were fatherless. Three of the half dozen boats on which the village depended for whaling had been lost, and with them a third of the whaling crews that were still in active service.

The village had frozen in a state of such shock that no tears were shed at the memorial service. Even the orphaned children, not yet comprehending their new status, kept quiet in the church. Kozue checked in at the *losmen* off Back-of-the-Whale, overlooking the square where the villagers assembled under the *budi* tree. The villagers stayed together all day and night. But they wouldn't go down to the beach. Even the sampan fishermen didn't put out. The sea was too painful a reminder. If they could have moved the village far inland at that moment they would readily have done so. Instead they walked in a mourning procession to Animal-around-the-Mountain and all the other outlying hamlets. They attended meetings in the church community hall. They congregated under the *budi* tree and sang hymns. They even chose to sleep out there rather than return to their own homes. They couldn't speak to Kozue in a language she understood, but they took her into their togetherness, surrounding her day and night so that she would never be alone.

A couple of days after the memorial service the old cargo boat that brought rice to Lefó once a month anchored out in the bay. Sampans put out through the surf to unload the rice sacks and bring them to the shore. Their arrival went unnoticed. No one else was on the beach at this time. The village still shunned the sea. No one else saw what the old cargo boat had brought until they came ashore.

From the steps where she was sitting in front of the *losmen* Kozue watched a group of men walk up the road towards the *budi* tree. Even by Lefó's standards they were very poorly dressed, literally in rags. There were children playing in the road. The men called to the children, but the children shrieked and ran away. A commotion started up in the surrounding houses. Women appeared in the doorways of houses, hollering and banging tins. When the men called out to them and tried to enter the houses the women screamed. Go away, they shouted at the men, go away! Hardly less frightened than the women, the men sat down under the *budi* tree, waiting until things had calmed down. This was the reception given to the survivors of the three *tena* when they returned to Lefó and were taken by their own families for ghosts.

Physically, at least, there seemed to be nothing wrong with any of them. Kozue gathered that they had survived their odyssey at sea without ill effects and were discharged from the mission hospital in

Timor only hours after having been taken there. But language problems made it impossible for her to find out how they had got there and why I wasn't with them. The only thing she established with certainty was that it had taken the personal intervention of God to save them and that I was still alive, or at least had been when the men left the mission hospital two days previously and were put on a boat back to Lapang Buhan.

The constitution of these men was extraordinary, but one should keep in mind that the ordinary course of their daily lives had prepared them to survive such a disaster. Evolution had selected for resilience to long periods of deprivation and made Lefó's inhabitants fit for their environment. That they were still suffering, and for some time would continue to suffer, from a sort of spiritual fatigue in the aftermath of their ordeal might may not have been apparent to the survivors themselves. This only emerged in the course of my later correspondence with Pak Ani. All that Kozue saw before she left Lefó for Lapang Buhan were thirty men in what seemed to her perfect health, and all that concerned her was that I was not one of them.

On the Boat to Kupang

From my description of the Nusa Tenggara shipping company terminal, about which I had written to Kozue in one of my letters to Japan, she recognised the building the moment she walked into it. There were the ticket booths sunk into the wall under the clock embedded in the cross, booths so low that you had to stoop to talk to the teller, as if peering at someone in a cave. There were the vendors selling banana fritters in plastic sacks, the benches in the middle of the hall on which prostrate figures reclined, miraculously asleep, if need be for hours, despite the noisy bustle all around them. She noted this ability of people to make themselves so at home in a public place that they fell fast asleep as something you would be likely to come across only in Asia. It didn't belong in the west. It was a peculiar feeling to be new in a place and then find it so familiar. Kozue was reassured. She felt secretly connected with me in this anonymous forwarding space where she spent six hours waiting for the boat to Kupang. Among the invisible coil of tracks left by all the passengers who had walked up and down and used up their energy in this hall she knew I had also left traces of mine.

This notion accompanied her onto the boat and never left her throughout the long journey to Timor. Perhaps because she was travelling alone in a country she didn't know among people whose language she didn't speak Kozue was especially susceptible to a sense of her solitariness, her anonymity in the tide of life on which she was being swept along. Had I not been in Kupang she wouldn't have been going there. This reflection was so obvious she hadn't given it any further thought, but under the circumstances of her journey it struck her as something remarkable.

You can hear something for a long time without listening to it. Insights come only when one is ready for them. Perhaps there is a greater likelihood of this happening under the circumstances of a journey. At the centre of a journey is a place of stillness. There may be a greater likelihood of the walker who does not walk coming to you in this place than of your ever finding him. On the voyage to Kupang, which was actually a very roundabout trip via Kyoto, São Paulo, Paris and New York with Lefó as the final way station, Kozue was also beginning to see that on her own she lacked any sense of belonging. Left to herself, there was nowhere in the world where she had any particular reason to go. This came to her at a time when *left to herself* was a prospect she knew she might soon be having to face. It was possible I was no longer alive. It also came at the end of a disappointing year in Japan, although it wasn't until she found herself en route for Kupang that Kozue was ready to admit this disappointment to herself, and to accept the reason for it. Nationality offered only an illusion of belonging. The ties that people formed were mostly a matter of habit. She lacked the ties because she had never formed the habits. She didn't belong in Japan. She didn't belong anywhere. For a person like herself there could only be another person like herself with whom she shared a sense of mutual belonging, and that happened to be me.

Why it should be me still puzzled her. She could see the likelihood of orphans sharing a song of the bereft. She could see there was a kind of belonging in the deprivation we had as a common background. But at least until my mysterious grandmother Wanda had surfaced, passing on to me via my dark-skinned father the Mongolian Spots that betrayed my true origins, my life appeared to Kozue to be such a straight and solidly built highway, like the insurance company for which I worked – a predictable, securely Swiss kind of life, as she had sometimes remarked with scorn.

During the journey to Timor Kozue appears to have experienced a particular *moment* at which she realised she was no longer young. Although she was already in her late forties, this realisation came to her as a shock. Perhaps it had been delayed too long. Now it overwhelmed her in a rush. She understood that certain things for which she had vaguely been waiting were never going to come about. She was not going to begin a new life in Japan, or anywhere else for that matter. There wasn't a better life waiting for her to step into. She would have to accept her life as it had turned out.

Perhaps she felt sorry for herself, and why not? She was having to part company with the sustaining idea of youth – the idea that there was still so much more to expect from life. Was that all there was to life? Surely there must have been more to it than that?

More likely she felt sorry for both of us – for herself whom she was having to give up, for me because in the event that I died she wouldn't have given me my due. A true appraisal of one's circumstances is the mark of the maturing of a person, something that is only possible given a willingness to step over one's own vanity and pride. To accept her circumstances as actually quite all right didn't mean that Kozue must become resigned to them. It meant only that she must renounce the fantastic claims of youth to be in some way destiny's privileged child, the demand that youth so confidently asserted to lead the charmed, fascinating, memorable life to which it felt entitled, in the end to exemption from the necessity of death. Kozue had been listening to the voices murmuring such things deep down inside her for quite some time, but it was only on the boat to Kupang that she paid attention to them.

Edward and Louise

The old mission hospital in Kupang at the southern tip of Timor was housed in a colonial building, formerly some governor's residence, at the end of a cul-de-sac about fifteen minutes' walk from the harbour. The Spiritus Dei mission had taken over the building at the time of the First World War and turned it into a hospital. On the property behind it, formerly the governor's park, there was a chapel surrounded by a graveyard. During the next weeks Kozue had ample time to explore the premises. A few of the large old trees still stood their ground. The walks that had doubtless been laid out to lead the visitor from one enchanting prospect to another now led her nowhere. After the trees had been cut down, and the ornamental lake filled in, all prospects other than of rubbish-strewn scrub dotted with occasional palm trees had been effaced from the park.

Kozue found me asleep in a room upstairs on the first floor. After she had been there all day, and I still showed no signs of waking up, she began to get anxious. The nurse in the corridor could speak no English, but she fetched a young doctor who could. He assured her I was not unconscious but just asleep. I had been intermittently delirious and running a dangerously high temperature when I was brought in, he said. At first he had thought my condition might be the effects of sunstroke and dehydration after the long time I had spent on an open boat at sea. To be on the safe side, however, they tested for malaria, with positive results. Perhaps thanks to the anti-malarials I had been taking the full force of the illness might have been blunted. I had responded quickly to treatment. The fever had been reduced and I had come out of the crisis within a few days. I still appeared to be so exhausted, however, that I needed to sleep all the time. And while that was not unnatural, the doctor said, he was concerned about further complications that might have arisen or would yet arise given my recent history of heart illness.

Malaria put a considerable strain on the body's resilience. It was impossible to say how a heart-valve prosthesis only recently installed would cope with the extra load. Unfortunately they had no means of establishing that here, because they lacked the equipment to do so. The nearest such facilities were in Bali, a couple of hours' flight away. Kozue asked the young doctor what was the best thing to do under the circumstances. Just waiting-waiting, he said, with a twinkle in his eye behind his glasses. For the time being it wouldn't be advisable to move the patient. To Kozue he looked like a boy who had only just left school. She was disconcerted that he was so young and managed to have a twinkle in his eye when discussing such a matter.

Kozue settled into my room, as was the custom for relatives visiting their kin in hospitals in Indonesia. They slept in the patient's room or in the glass-fronted ante-chamber separating it from the corridor, many of them on the floor, children and grandparents, entire families. To keep down expenses they brought their food and kitchen utensils with them and cooked on balconies or in the corridors of the hospital. Kozue ate and whenever possible fed me food that was cooked in the hospital. She slept on a leather couch beside an old air-conditioner built into the wall under the window. No longer in proper working order, it sent an ice-cold blast into the room and had an infuriating rattle that wouldn't let her get to sleep, so she turned it off altogether.

She spent an upsetting first week in the hospital. She could hardly get me to talk about anything beyond my immediate bodily needs. I was too weak to go to the toilet on my own, sometimes even to eat or drink. She fanned me when I became too hot and took the blanket off the bed. When I began to shake with cold she put it back on and gave me warm tea to drink. Had Kozue not been there to help me with all these things and to sustain my interest in life there wouldn't have been anyone else to take her place. Every night she had to get up half a dozen times to change my clothes, hospital shirts that were so soaked through with sweat that she could wring the water out of them into a bucket. Often I was too exhausted to give her any help with this. She had to pull me up, take off the drenched shirt, dry me with a towel and put on the new shirt all by her own efforts. Once or twice a night the sheets became so wet that all the bedding had to be changed, too. The night sister came and gave her a hand with this. Before the nurse went off duty at dawn she carried out a huge pile of laundry and dumped it in the corridor for the washerwomen to collect.

My illness had a sort of choreography it required us both to follow.

It demanded of me that I let go, and, on the assumption that Kozue would be there to catch me, I did. It drew us both into an intimacy that was unconditional, without reserve or safeguards. There was no holding back at all. She had to be completely there for me – and I had to let her be. Sometimes I thought: perhaps this is why it was necessary for me to become ill, so that Kozue could become my fellow conspirator, an accessory to my illness, and through my illness to me. During these embattled nights Kozue and I became closer than we had ever been. The notion first crossed my mind: my illness could be about something, it could be seeking to express something it had not been possible to express in any other way. In fact, this was the continuation of a fixed idea I had already held for quite some time – that the events of one's life constituted an allegory, perhaps with a meaning to be referred to something somewhere else that was not itself a part of life. When I began to feel stronger I told Kozue about the extraordinary creature and the no less extraordinary conclusion to which it had led us.

On the fifth day at sea, a day after the whale had left us, a cruise ship came over the horizon. It was a big ship with eight hundred passengers on board. It had departed from Perth and was bound for Singapore, via Flores, Bali and Java. The appearance of the ship on the horizon had naturally raised our hopes, but we were drifting too far south-west of their course to have any reason to expect that we would be spotted. On that vast expanse of ocean it seemed most unlikely that anyone on board would notice such a tiny speck – a boat lying that low in the water, hardly ten metres long. Yet this was what happened. A couple of passengers, nature enthusiasts on the lookout for whales, made us out in the binoculars with which they were always scouring the sea. The ship changed course to pick us up. They took us on board, all thirty-one of us. They even had the *Mata Tena* winched up, stowed it on one of the cargo decks and put it down in the sea again when the ship reached Timor a few hours later. They stood some way off Kupang harbour and let us down, boat and all, and we paddled ashore.

Reconstructing the events at sea as we sought to synchronise our lives again, knitting together the last year we had spent apart, we incidentally established that I had thought of the boy at the top of the stairs on what must have been the second night I had spent on the boat, the same night Kozue had dreamed of him in Singapore. What were we now doing in this place, I wondered, why the complex interlocking of all the foregone events in such a roundabout way as to bring a shipwrecked tangle of lives to this particular outcome, given so many likelier alternatives it would have been easier for fate to arrange?

Kozue said things were as they were, you could look at them any way you liked but it wouldn't change the way they were.

Regarding the way they were, I still had a lot in store for me. I was beginning to see how abstract, elaborate and artificially wrought the so-called raw material of life in fact was.

After two weeks in hospital I had put the big wave of malaria behind me – but I had an inkling of something even bigger looming up behind it. Something seemed to have burst in slow motion inside my heart. It wasn't a heart attack, according to the electrocardiogram, but it was a bit like one. What was it, then? A scanning machine would have told us but the hospital didn't have one. I described it to the doctor as an implosion, a kind of cardiac meltdown. The way I read the twinkle in the youthful doctor's eye – Kozue was right, he looked like a high-school kid – he had an inkling of it, too. Tacitly we agreed to say nothing about it to Kozue. I was convalescent, and gave the impression that I was getting better, despite daily shivering fits so violent that they made the whole bed shake. They passed off in an hour or two and appeared to leave no ill effects. The doctor told Kozue they would cease altogether when I was back in my own climate. She was pleased with my progress. Soon she had me up and about. We took walks round the hospital cloisters where mangy emaciated cats prowled and scavenged, tipping over the trash cans, howling and snarling horribly over scraps of food in the corridors where a peculiarly familiar smell of vinegar always lingered. Once I could manage the stairs up to the third floor we made our way to the end of the passage leading out onto the roof. For hours we sat watching hundreds of fluttering kites in the shape of birds, fishes and dragons, day in day out, as if tied up in the sky.

In another few days I would be fit enough to travel. I would have liked to have paid a last visit to Lefó, but the doctors thought another journey to the remote island too much of a risk. We would be flying straight back to Geneva via Bali and Singapore at the beginning of November. The superiors of the youthful doctor had even been in favour of my checking into a hospital in Singapore, but once I had given up the idea of making a detour to Lefó I wanted to return home as soon as possible. Making the arrangements at a travel agency in Kupang took Kozue several hours a day for the best past of a week. I sat up on the roof, missing her, and watched the kites on my own.

At the entrance to the chapel in the park there was an assortment of concrete benches and tables where children from the adjacent mission school came to eat their lunch. We used to go there in the evening after taking a stroll through the park. It was a peaceful place at that hour. We sat and watched the night come down over the kite-swarming sky.

You can look at something for a long time without seeing it. When you do see it, it may seem to be a revelation, although perhaps all you have done is to catch at the right moment what has been staring you in the face. I had been sitting on the concrete bench every evening for a week before I saw the stone plaque mounted into the masonry of the church wall right beside me and read the valediction inscribed on it.

To the memory of
Edward and Louise Smith
who died here of dengue fever
on June 10th 1947

The SUSUS Principle

I went into hospital the day we arrived back in Geneva and was immediately operated on. The lining membrane of the heart had become infected, and the valve replacement, attacked by bacteria, had become partially detached from its anchorage in the aorta. Everything was infected – valve, pacemaker, it all had to come out. The surgery done only the previous year had to be done again, this time with an extremely slim chance of success. Many patients with this kind of heart infection died on the operating table. That I had been able to undertake such a long journey in this critical condition and at the end of it walk off the plane alive was something the heart specialists could not satisfactorily explain. The success of the operation confirmed their expertise and at the same time challenged it, for my recovery, my survival at all, appeared to owe hardly more to their contribution than it did to other factors as crucial as they were elusive, such as the will to live, about which nothing was known to medical science and over which it had no control.

Within a year I was back at Assurances Helvétiques. D'Agostini, my former boss at the Lost Property Office, had gone into retirement a few years earlier and we lost all trace of him. He was replaced by my friend Roche. I was assigned a sedentary, wholly undemanding job in the rejected claims section. The company gave me to understand that they were doing me a kindness in consideration of my health, although I was overdue for promotion to a more responsible position. From Roche I learned that my superiors didn't regard me as suitable for promotion and were wondering what to do with me, which may have been why a few years after my return from Indonesia they offered me early retirement.

Father 't Maart died in the mission hospital outside Lapang Buhan at the age of ninety. Although we never managed to meet, we kept up a regular correspondence during the last years of his life. It brought a number of intriguing details to light. Sent out to the Far East as a young man in his early twenties, the padre had once been stationed in Kupang. Occasionally he was dispatched from there to assist the missionary on the other side of the straits in Lefó, a mountainous island parish whose scattered flocks, very recently Christianised, were only accessible to a shepherd travelling on horseback. It was on one of these journeys that he came across a group of men in an isolated spot in the mountains. They fled at the sight of him, leaving behind them the tools with which they had been shaping a monolith at the edge of a clearing overlooking the ocean. The stone appeared to be a cult object having to do with religious rites, although he never found out what it signified. But for me this information solved the riddle of Beleloko. That immense stone seat had not been moved up the mountain from Under-the-Banyan. The Elders had found it there and shaped it on site.

The padre was working at the mission hospital in Kupang when my parents arrived there with me in 1947. It appeared that they had come to Timor to look up relatives of my father's who still lived on the island. They both contracted dengue fever and died on the same day within a week of arriving in hospital. I was looked after by local women at the mission for about a year, he told me, before he accompanied me back to Europe and delivered me to an address in Switzerland, from which my mother had received letters found among her possessions after her death. I was two and a half at the time and would hardly have any memories of it, he thought. But when I described to him the smell of vinegar I had come across in the corridors of the mission hospital, and how it struck me as familiar, Father 't Maart expressed surprise, confirming that a kind of vinegar had locally been used as a disinfectant in those days and indeed still was.

I wrote a long letter back to Father 't Maart, telling him about the deep sound channels used by whales to communicate over long distances. At a certain depth and frequency, I explained, sound waves could be conserved and transmitted without significant loss from one side of an ocean to the other. I wondered if by analogy memories could be encoded on sights or smells and preserved intact over long periods to emerge, perhaps decades later and on the surface long forgotten, from the subterranean corridors of time into which they had disappeared.

One of the most closely kept secrets to have emerged from the Cold

War was the system known by its acronym SUSUS. It was developed by the US Navy to track Soviet submarines. I wrote at some length about it in my letter to Father 't Maart. The system linked underwater microphones, known as hydrophones, from all over the North Atlantic and the North Pacific to central analysis facilities where the incoming signals were monitored. It could tell where all the submarines were in relation to one another all of the time. Once Soviet submarines no longer posed a security threat, SUSUS was due to be dismantled. Marine biologists intervened. They pointed out what a pity it would be to jettison a system that could most usefully serve to locate and track whales over the range of an entire ocean basin. Advances in the power and miniaturisation of electronics would soon make it possible to put sophisticated digital acoustic recording tags directly onto marine mammals, and thus greatly refine this tracking system. Human observers would be able to follow not just the submarine path of individual animals, whose lives were for the most part spent hidden from us in the depths of the sea, but the interaction of groups of animals over great distances and sustained periods of time.

I was glad to have found Louise and Edward. Had their bodies been lost at sea, as Emily had led me to believe, presumably because she knew no better herself, there would have been no grave and no certainty. It set my mind at rest. But even had there been nothing more than the smell of vinegar in the hospital in Kupang, it would still have seemed to me to have been worth the journey there. Unremarkable in itself, it disclosed a secret, supplying evidence of a marvellous hidden design of which it was a humble part. I wrote to Father 't Maart about SUSUS because of the idea it had sparked in my mind. I had come to think there was a SUSUS already in nature, a worldwide membrane, some kind of conductive tissue. Like flying insects impacting a spider's web, all events impinged on it. Because the tissue was a conductive medium, their impingement could be felt in all its parts. For every ear there was the sound, for every eye the image. Each had mutually shaped the other and could only exist in this symbiosis. I conjectured that there was a law of affinity, which would dispose one to register certain persons and events that were relevant to one's life's design and to ignore others that were not. It provided guidance in what would otherwise have been an unmanageable complexity of choice. In the world I inhabited there had ceased to be coincidences. One might even come to believe that one's path through it was predetermined. Father 't Maart wrote back a very short letter in response to this long, rather obscure rambling of mine. The SUSUS principle I had described to him was what he knew as God. Perhaps it was a similar idea under a different name. This was the last letter I received from Father 't Maart, who died soon after.

Postscript

In retirement I would have liked to travel with Kozue, and to a limited extent we did. My health made travel to remote places without medical aid a hazardous undertaking, however, so that I was never able to return to Lefó. We toyed with the idea of arranging a meeting in Bali with Mans Gerardus and a group of villagers, but a further deterioration in my condition made long-distance air travel anywhere inadvisable, and the idea had to be abandoned. Even keeping up a correspondence with Pak Ani presented problems that could only be surmounted with the help of the mission in Lapang Buhan. At that time there was still no postal service to or from Lefó. Letters I sent care of the mission to Pak Ani were handed to certain trustworthy persons as and when they happened to be passing through on their way back to the island. It was sometimes months before the letters reached the addressee.

It took the village several years to get over the shock that had been administered to it by the Extraordinary Creature. Two boats had been lost irrecoverably. A third, the *Mata Tena*, was still lying hauled up somewhere on a beach in Timor. But the boat master kept putting off the journey to Kupang for so long that in the end everyone knew it had become impossible to make the *tena* seaworthy for such a long voyage and to sail it back safely to Lefó, so in effect it was three boats the village had lost. In effect, the village did not recover and never reverted to itself. That village disappeared for ever. Lefó became something else.

Until this date, boats lost at sea had always been rebuilt, or, as they said in Lefó: boats that died were brought back to life. The spirit of the ancestor after whom the boat was named might be resurrected any number of times within the new body built to house it. But if no new body was given to it the spirit would be extinguished for ever. This would happen to the spirit of Nasu's ancestor Aro, as Pak Ani predicted to me in one of his letters. Of course Nasu told everyone he would some day get round to rebuilding the *Aro Tena*. But Nasu had enough to do to complete the Yamaha that had been under construction in his yard for the past couple of years. Once it was finished, Nasu fitted it with an outboard motor and took it out to sea, adding to the growing fleet of Yamahas patrolling to the south of the island and overfishing its coastal waters much more quickly than one would have thought possible. Only baleen whales were still left untouched in accordance with the ancient taboo.

When a sperm whale was sighted from the land the *tena* still occasionally put out to sea, Pak Ani said. There were still half a dozen seaworthy boats drowsing in the sheds on the beach, enough *matros* who knew how to kill such a large animal and get it back to the shore. But a few years after the extraordinary creature had towed the three *tena* half the way to Timor a whale harpooned within a kilometre of the shore broke up a boat with a blow of its tail, killing two men. This incident was a particular shock to me because I knew the two individuals concerned. One of them was Martinus, boat master and harpooner on the *Mata Tena*, which had picked us up out of the sea after the other two boats had gone down. The other was Iohanes, or Ani, the quiet, dependable man who steered the *Aro Tena*, the friend who sat immediately behind me and kept an eye on me during the many voyages we had made together on Nasu's boat. It was Ani who had pulled me out at the last moment when the Extraordinary Creature finally took the *tena* down with it into the sea.

Martinus and Ani were among the most experienced whalers in Lefó. Their death tore a hole in the fabric of the village's whaling traditions that was never closed, for there were no longer enough young men willing to take over the positions left vacant by older men retiring from the business. For two years after their death no *tena* put out at all, even when sperm whales were sighted close to the shore. As for regular whaling, which began every year with the arrival of the south-east monsoon in May and ended when the prevailing winds faded away in October, it was discontinued until such time as the three dead boats had been brought back to life, a circumstance often discussed but postponed for so long that it gradually ceased to be a declaration of future intent and became an expression of the village's commitment to its past.

Marlboro Man married a Lebanese woman ten years older than

himself and of independent means who came to live in the village after getting divorced in her own country. After the death of his wife Tika Nasu became a confirmed alcoholic. Triplets, the first in the history of Lefó, were born to the barren wife of the *sekretaris* at the age of forty after hormone treatment in a Denpasar clinic. The first helicopter ever seen in Lefó landed on the football pitch with a presidential candidate who gave an address in the community hall. Alo fell out of a palm tree and broke his neck. In his long and painstaking letters, omitting nothing that he thought might be of interest to me, Pak Ani expressed astonishment above all at the speed with which Lefó changed.

What powered the speed of change was money. Within a couple of years the island's prehistoric barter system had been completely swept away and replaced by a cash economy. It poured over the landscape like a flood, a beneficial irrigation in the main, Pak Ani said, filling out every nook and cranny of the village's traditional life. During the last decade of his life he watched Lefó transformed from an aboriginal whaling community into a modern Indonesian town of five thousand inhabitants.

Within this decade the road across the island was finally completed. It opened the village up to the outside world. Electricity, cellular phones, TV, running water and even garbage disposal facilities reached households in the remotest outlying hamlet. It was no longer necessary to collect one's garbage in a sack and dump it in the sea as the people of Lefó had always done. Even Does-not-have-Loincloth became accessible for cars with four-wheel drive. Sinta's impediment was no longer a reason for her to remain house-bound. Once motorised, five-legged salesmen became prone to swift evolutionary mutation. Lured back by all these modern conveniences, many people who had left to look for jobs and make their lives outside Lefó returned to the island when they reached retirement.

Taking advantage of the only beach on the south side of the island large enough to haul up boats larger than sampans, a fleet of three or four dozen Yamahas operated an extremely successful commercial fishery. The fish came straight off the boats into refrigerated trucks parked along Back-of-the-Whale and were driven to the new airport on the north side of the island, reaching markets in Hong Kong, Taipeh and Japan on the same day they had been taken out of the ocean. Increasingly rare delicacies like manta rays, giant turtles, some of the smaller species of whales and even hammerhead sharks, headed for extinction somewhat less quickly in the waters off

Lefó than in the South China Sea, fetched exorbitant prices on these markets.

The success of the fishery was short-lived. The once abundant fish stocks in the twenty- to thirty-kilometre zone within range of the horde of small-engine Yamahas were so depleted within a few years as to put most of the corporations out of business. But the people of Lefó, anticipating this decline, had invested the money they made during the boom into infrastructures that would open up other markets. One of these was tourism.

A limitation on developing the island's tourism had been its remoteness. Visitors from Europe, Australia and America made up to ninety per cent of the tourist trade. But just getting to Lefó took up more holiday time than these tourists usually had available. That changed with the construction of the airport and the road. A journey that used to take a week from Bali now took a day. Within an hour and a half of arrival at the airport on the north side of the island tourists could be brought to the new hotel built on the site of the former *losmen* overlooking the square still known as Under-the-Banyan, although the *budi* tree, not to mention the banyan that had preceded it and after which the square was named, had long since disappeared to make room for a bus terminal with a Telsat office and public latrines.

Another limitation had been the smell of the village. So long as whaling was carried out from Lefó, there was nothing to be done about that. The moment whaling ceased, of course, the smell problem was solved. With the suspension of whaling activities, however, there was no reason for tourists to want to make the still very long trip to Lefó. The swimming was dangerous, there was no beach to speak of, no surf, no coral, no entertainments, no restaurants, nothing to do but to go deep-sea fishing, climb the volcano, have a bout of high-risk malaria, or do a package deal of all three. Apart from the unusually high standard of education and the above average intelligence of the indigenous population, which visiting scientists like to attribute to their high-protein diet, all Lefó had to offer was its reputation as a historic whaling settlement.

The inquiring mind of Lefó's inhabitants, whose natural alertness did not appear to have suffered from exposure to so much anthropological study, soon established that in those places where the whaling industry had closed down it had been shown that there was more money to be made from watching whales than from killing them. Fitted with sun canopies, cushions and cold drinks, the old *tena* that had remained beached for the last ten years and the Yamahas made redundant by the decline of the fishing industry were soon generating a higher profit than they had ever done in their working lives. The tourists were booked in by the travel agencies for adventure holidays during the May–October season when the whales were running through the straits. They were encouraged to muck in as crew, tending to the sail, bailing and helping to paddle. From a vantage point so low in the water they got a much closer look at the animals than was possible on a conventional whale-watching craft.

Perhaps the biggest draw were the dummy runs offered during the off-season or when no whales showed up to be watched. Three or four original *prahu*, bleached and bare of any ornament, re-enacted an aboriginal whaling hunt in the bay of Lefó. The quarry was a life-size sperm whale made of styrofoam. It had weights attached underneath to keep it low in the water and was towed by a Yamaha. Pak Ani sent me a video of one of these dummy runs. The very young harpooners I watched flying off the platform from which they hurled themselves and their lances at the styrofoam whale were the grandsons of Nasu, Martinus and Bapak Cor. Among the elder *matros* I could identify a few faces of men I had known, Paulus, Romu, Marsellinus, all of them clearly much better dressed and better nourished, one might actually say *gemuk*, plump, than they had been a decade previously.

Lefó became the top tourist attraction east of Bali, one of the most prosperous places in the still backward and largely undiscovered Nusa Tenggara province. All the dwellings on the beach side of Under-the-Banyan, directly overlooking the boathouses, were eventually demolished to make room for a souvenir shop where *tuak* was sold in bottles, a bar where Bapak Cor played a Yamaha harmonium in the evenings wearing one of Sinta's whale-pattern sarong, a museum with original whaling artefacts where visitors could watch a video showing footage of actual sperm whale hunts that had been filmed as long ago as the 1970s and 1980s. The inmates of the old fishermen's cottages were allocated more attractive modern housing up on the mountain. They could afford sanitation, air-conditioning and proper medical facilities. Sick people like Nasu's wife Tika no longer needed to die at the age of forty-eight because they couldn't pay to see a doctor in Lapang Buhan.

Pak Ani was proud of the transformation to his village, although he did not conceal from me the price they had to pay for this affluence.

He missed, he said, the mornings and evenings the villagers used to spend together on the beach, just talking and keeping an eye on the sea. These days the sea took care of itself and didn't need much watching. Winds, tides and currents, which made up a lore inscribed in Lefó's collective memory were no longer relevant to the village and the knowledge of them was gradually lost. It was years, he said, since he had last heard the cry of *baléo* when a sperm whale was sighted out at sea. Once *tena* no longer put out to sea people on the lookout for whales stopped calling *baléo*. In time they stopped looking out for whales at all.

A more sentimental man than I had given him credit for, Pak Ani missed the rows of chairs that used to be put out for meetings under the *budi* tree and the markets that used to be held there. It was not just that the *budi* tree and the square it held together in its shade had disappeared to make way for the bus terminal. Scattered across the mountain in their new houses, the old inhabitants of Under-the-Banyan and Back-of-the-Whale had disappeared too, leaving the heart of the village empty. He still called it a village, although it had become a town. In their new houses up on the mountain, people began to lead lives that were separate from the old life of the village. As their common enterprise crumbled they became aware of something called privacy. They began to make a difference between time devoted to the common enterprise and time they had just for themselves. Something called private enterprise fragmented the village, which might have been why it was no longer a village but a town. These days it was no longer necessary for people even to come down to the waterfront. You could spend a month in Lefó without once setting a foot on the beach.

Byroads linked the mountain hamlets directly with the trunk road across the island and the drive-in supermarket located there. There were not often boats needing the presence of several dozen men on the beach to haul them out of the water into the boathouses. There were no whales requiring columns of workers to carry the meat away. There was no more of that never-ending trekking up and down the mountain to forage for firewood, to fetch drinking water or sea water to be boiled to obtain salt that could be bartered for the fresh fruit and vegetables brought to market by the women from the mountain villages of Standing Person. Life was a lot easier these days. You could buy what you wanted in the store down the road, even if you didn't need it. There was now a shop in Does-not-have-Loincloth where Pak Ani's wife bought deodorants and paper napkins, though he had little use for such things himself, he confided. Life in Lefó was a lot easier these days, but strange to say, there was something missing from it. Pak couldn't determine exactly what. It was difficult to put one's finger on it.

He even missed the anthropologists, who had stopped coming to Lefó. They must have missed something there, too. If they had stopped coming to Lefó, Pak wondered what other places in the world could still be left for them to visit, and what the world was coming to when anthropologists were no longer left with anywhere to go.

Twice a year his great-grandchildren arrived to spend their school holidays with Pak Ani and his wife. With their father, his grandson, who had moved with his parents to the north side of the island when he was a little boy, Pak had always conducted conversations in the language of Lefó. Quite naturally, he thought. But it seemed nothing was natural, in the sense that it was just given and could be taken for granted. His grandchildren, for example, often didn't understand when he spoke to them in Lefó. Pak wouldn't have thought it possible. It was all right for Indonesian to be the accepted language in school and church. As a teacher, Pak had spent his life doing much to propagate the use of Indonesian himself. But within ten years of the arrival of television it was fast becoming the language of preference inside the home, too, at least for his great-grandchildren's generation. Pak cut out and sent to me a newspaper article entitled 'Endangered species'. It was about the decline of regional languages in the Indonesian archipelago, and quoted the scarcely credible findings of a UNESCO report that one of the world's languages became extinct every two weeks.

'Lefó will soon be one of them. Where are *our* conservationists?' Pak had scrawled across the bottom of the page.

What he missed, in the end, was the sea. It was still there, visible from his house in Sitting-in-Palm-Tree. He could see it, he could hear it down there. But did it still hear him, the dry whispers of the cracked and broken down sea horses asleep in the boathouses, whose keels it could no longer feel? The descendants of the old whale people of Lefó had fallen from grace with the sea. Somehow they were no longer of it, or it of them, for the sea had withdrawn its favours, retreating behind an unpassable barrier that divided the ocean from the land.